Gipp at Notre Dame — The Untold Story

Other books by Emil Klosinski

*Pro Football in the Days of Rockne*

*Notre Dame, Chicago Bears and "Hunk"*

# GIPP AT NOTRE DAME
## THE UNTOLD STORY

### BY
## EMIL KLOSINSKI

FLORIDA SUN-GATOR PUBLISHING CO.
ORLANDO, FLORIDA

## DEDICATION

In memory of fellow authors Donald Chet Grant and James Caleb Beach, both of whom were going to write a book such as this but ran out of time on earth to do it.

Second Printing

For information contact:
FLSunGatorPublish@yahoo.com

ISBN:
9798404095784

Published by
FLORIDA SUN-GATOR PUBLISHING CO.
ORLANDO, FLORIDA
Printed in the U.S.A.

# CONTENTS

# PREFACE

In recent years, some books and newspaper articles that have been written about Notre Dame not only cast aspersions on the University's integrity regarding athletics but also deal iconoclastically with Notre Dame's greatest heroes, Knute Rockne and George Gipp. This book covers primarily what has been written about Gipp. What is true will not be denied; what isn't true has been noted and the researched and/or corroborated truth is presented.

Who was George Gipp and what did he do? Notre Dame's George Gipp was the best all-around football player in the era of the triple threat back who could do or had to do everything on offense on the gridiron. In Gipp's day — just prior to and after World War I — a player had to play defense as well as offense and Gipp was among the best on both sides of the ball. George was a sure tackler and an extraordinary pass defender who never had a pass completed in his territory during his entire career at Notre Dame.

Although Notre Dame had All Americans before Gipp,

he was the first Notre Dame man to make the most prestigious mythical All America team of its time, the Walter Camp All America. Despite the fact that the Camp selections were biased toward Eastern college football and Gipp played for a "Western" school, Gipp was nonetheless selected as Camp's 1920 fullback, a highly desirable honor in football at that time.

Was Gipp better than the great Jim Thorpe? You bet he was! His coach, Knute Rockne, gave Gipp the nod based on first hand experience. Notre Dame's then assistant coach Rockne played against Thorpe in a post season, inter-city, home and home championship pro series in 1916 between Massillon and Canton, two northern Ohio rivals. Rockne indicated that Gipp was the better player when he picked an All-Time All America team for a magazine, having placed both Gipp and Thorpe on his mythical team.

Backing Rockne was the opinion of Heartley "Hunk" Anderson. (It should be noted here that there were three Andersons in the Gipp saga. Hunk was from Gipp's home town, and was his best friend and teammate. Eddie Anderson was a starting end on Gipp's team and Eddie "Goat" Anderson was Jimmie Welch's partner in the Jimmie and Goat's Cigar Store in South Bend.)

Sometimes during practice at Notre Dame Rockne would have the regular backfield scrimmage behind the second string line with the first string line playing defense, instead of the freshmen team that prepped the varsity for upcoming games. Hunk told me that you couldn't be sure of tackling Gipp because he had so many quick moves with variable speeds. "Gipp would give you the hip and then take it away," said Hunk. "Sometimes he would run over you, but most of the time he evaded a would-be tackle with a side step and a straight arm...or he'd generate a sudden burst of speed after a pivot. A head feint in one direction and then a take-off in another was also used by Gipp with great success. Yep, he was a better runner than Thorpe in my book. Both were excellent runners, though, and very hard to bring down."

When Hunk Anderson played for George Halas and the Chicago Bears, he played against Thorpe and sampled Jim's running ability. Thorpe played for several teams against the Bears in the young NFL, including the Canton Bulldogs, the Oorang Indians, a team Thorpe organized and coached, and the Rock Island Independents. "Thorpe had speed, but he tried to run over a tackler," said Anderson. "He'd lower his head and shoulder and with his powerful leg drive he would try to ram you out of his way. I had no problem hitting Thorpe. Jim ran out of the single wing and I watched his knee. As he began his cut for the spot where the hole was to be, I hit him low. There was a rumor around the league that Thorpe had iron sewn into his shoulder pads, so I always tried to hit him low."

Hunk also thought that Gipp was a far better passer than Thorpe, but Thorpe mostly ran the ball so he wasn't called upon to pass too often to display that skill. Pete Bahan, also a Gipp teammate at Notre Dame, played for the Cleveland Indians pro team in 1923 and he agreed with Anderson that Gipp was a better runner and passer than Thorpe.

Perhaps the International News Service account of Gipp's performance in the 1920 Army game adds more concrete impact on the greatness of Gipp. INS rated Gipp's talents as being superior with a terse and emphatic statement: "Gipp against Army gave the rooters thrills galore; critics pronounced him the greatest halfback ever seen on an Eastern gridiron...and they had seen the likes of Carlisle's Jim Thorpe, Yale's Ted Coy and Harvard's Charlie Brickley."

Scholastically, Gipp's indifference to attending class and doing his classwork brought him to the brink of expulsion on two or three occasions. His spring of 1920 ordeal, when he was expelled and subsequently reinstated, is dealt with fully in this book. In recent books on Notre Dame and/or Gipp, much misinformation has been generated on this topic because some facts were unknown or unavailable. This book presents first-hand information which will attempt to clear up prior errors regarding Gipp's scholastic career at Notre Dame.Besides being lax in regard to his school priorities, Gipp also had vices, but there have been exaggerations about them as well. As the saying goes, "There are two sides to every story" and this book will try to set the record straight regarding the other versions of Gipp and his escapades. Our version has more substance than mere hearsay from unknown sources with a derogatory "spin" or an author's speculation or invention that demonizes Gipp. Modern day writers have called Gipp a "bum," "the Gypper" instead of Gipper and a womanizer, among many demeaning names. If Gipp was a womanizer, then it seems that every young man in his twenties who is unattached and therefore "playing the field" before commitment, can also be labeled a womanizer.

One writer failed to research South Bend in Gipp's era, then spun off a yarn that Gipp's forte was picking up bar girls. Bar girls in South Bend at that time? They didn't exist.

Even a wife looking for a boozing husband could not go any farther than the door and had to wait for him to come out or to be tossed out. Bars were off-limits to women — all women. Only Carrie Nation, the Prohibition crusader, had guts enough to go into a bar full of men while wielding an axe to chop the bar up.

A book on Gipp containing much fresh information and not too much rehash of old material was to have been written in the 1980s by Donald "Chet" Grant, who was Gipp's quarterback and teammate at Notre Dame. Chet and his other teammates weren't as close to Gipp as George's Laurium, Michigan friends, Hunk Anderson and Fred "Ojay" Larson. But Chet managed to see a lot of Gipp in downtown South Bend in 1919. Grant, upon his discharge from the Army after World War I, did not go back to school at Notre Dame in 1919; he returned to his old pre-Notre Dame job of a reporter covering the city beat for the South Bend Tribune. Chet called himself "the perpetual undergraduate." He did return for the 1920 and 1921 football seasons and at the age of 29 and weighing only 138 pounds, quarterbacked the 1921 team to a 10 and 1 record. Chris Weinke, Florida State's quarterback and the year 2000's Heisman Trophy winner was a year short — at least for quarterbacks — of Chet Grant's age record.

In his job for the Tribune, Chet would check for news at the county courthouse on the corner of Washington and Main Streets, which was directly across the street from the main entrance to the Oliver Hotel on Washington Street. Many times Grant would bump into Gipp, whose residence in 1919 was the Oliver Hotel, and they would chat awhile or if Chet had some time to spare, the two would go to Jimmy and Goat's place for a sandwich and a coffee or a beer depending on the time of day. Chet told me that he learned a lot about Gipp from these short encounters.

Sometimes Gipp would have to leave to make it to an afternoon class and practice afterwards. Gipp usually hailed a cab for his return to campus rather than taking the street car.Gipp's class attendance in the early part of the 1919-1920 school year was sporadic from October to February and that got him in trouble. Gipper was being treated by a doctor — a fact unknown to Rockne or Gipp's professors at that time — and he took advantage of that by absenting himself from class too many times. In previous years, Gipp was reasonably faithful in his class attendance even though residing off campus put a burden on his punctuality.

In 1980, Chet Grant told me that he was going to write a book on Gipp after he had finished writing the biography of Jess Harper, Notre Dame's head coach just before Rockne. Harper's son, Jim, persuaded Chet to attempt the time-consuming project when Grant was assisting Herb Juliano, who took over after Chet retired in 1975 as the curator of the International Sports and Games Research Collection at the Notre Dame Library. (Since that stint by Chet, the Collection has been renamed the Joyce Collection and the library is now the Hesburgh Library.)

Grant had a lot of information on Gipp but was reluctant to share it until his Gipp book was finished. After I indicated that I was through writing books and would give him all my notes on Gipp that I had jotted down during my interviews with Hunk Anderson (I compiled much unused material on Gipp while preparing Hunk's biography), Pete Bahan, my father, John Klosinski, and other relatives who knew Gipp, as well as interviews with South Benders for a book on the pioneer days of pro football, Chet then would loosen up a bit with his information.

Chet Grant died July 24, 1985 at the age of 93. With him went a large amount of unwritten Notre Dame history. He never began writing his Gipp book and as far as can be determined, he never finished Jess Harper's biography. Chet's "working file,"as he called it, was four storage boxes full of folders that were nestled in the dining room corner of his widowed sister's, Madge Reeder's, house at 122 East Pokagon Street, South Bend. Chet used the dining room table as his office desk.The "working file" he had contained many personal documents as well as material pertaining to Notre Dame history. Chet indicated this "treasure" would be given to Notre Dame upon his demise. When Chet passed away, his sister tried via phone calls to get someone at Notre Dame to pick up those boxes. When she asked for a pickup on several occasions (during a four year period after Chet died) she was promised that it would be done in due time. It wasn't.

I kept checking with Herb Juliano who still had liaison with his former colleagues at the Hesburgh Library although he was no longer employed by Notre Dame, if Grant's cartons were in Notre Dame custody. I always received a negative reply from Herb after he made inquiries. In 1989, I managed to finally reach Madge Reeder after several days of phone calls. She told me she had just returned home from a long hospital stay, that she was 94 years old and she wasn't going to bother herself any longer with calls to Notre Dame.

She said that she was going to have those boxes dumped with the trash. Then she excused herself saying she was going to bed and hung up. If she did have the trash man pick up and dump Chet's files, a lot of valuable history has been lost. I feel fortunate that Chet leaked some of his material on Gipp to me, which is presented within this book.

I had also been in contact with Jim Beach who had written several books about Notre Dame. He was a sportswriter, a TV and radio commentator and a politician, having been on the 1956 Adlai Stevenson speech writing staff when Adlai ran for president.

Beach, too, had material on Gipp which he said had not been published but he wasn't sure what to do with it, because he too was through writing books. He said he was in total retirement and would try to enjoy it with his wife to the fullest.Beach traveled from Tarrytown, New York, to Florida almost annually during baseball's spring practice season. Jim phoned me saying that he would be in Vero Beach (I live near Orlando) while the Los Angeles Dodgers were in camp there and he and I could get together. He said he would call me when he got to Vero Beach.

Spring practice for baseball came and went and I did not hear from Beach, so I assumed he either was too busy if he did arrive there or perhaps something happened, requiring the cancellation of his trip. I had written a letter shortly thereafter but received no reply. About nine months later, I received a phone call from Jim in which he told me the sad news. First of all, his wife had died of cancer. One month later, Jim suffered a severe stroke which left him immobile...in fact, he said that the woman attending him at home dialed and was holding the receiver to his ear so he could talk with me. On top of that, he said his eyesight had gotten worse.

That was indeed an awkward phone call for me to handle. I told him that his brain was still operating and perhaps it might be a good time for him to put his unused Gipp material to work by writing a book about Gipp. I suggested that he could get a taping system set up. He said that was exactly what his daughter and some close friends had urged him to do. I offered to give him all of my of material on Gipp and said I would help him in any way he thought I could. I believe that offer swung Beach over because he said he probably would do it.

About 1996, Beach decided to get going with the Gipp book. I sent Jim my material, promising that it would be exclusive — that I would not give the information to anyone. I asked him in return that if he couldn't finish the book and dropped the project, I would like to have my material returned. I didn't want it to fall into the hands of a "sensation" writer who might dilute, pollute or "spin" the facts to suit an agenda of derogation.

Beach's daughter Martha felt Jim should be undergoing continuous therapy, and after he moved in with her in Carrboro, North Carolina, she saw to it that Jim did undergo therapy. It did help and he recovered some use of his hands whereby he could punch enlarged numbers on the telephone dial. So Jim did his research via the telephone. Beach also had some Duke University students helping him with the book.

Unfortunately, Jim had many other ailments that interfered with his writing. He passed away November 16, 2000 without finishing his book. Jim's room was thoroughly searched and no manuscript or tapes were found at that time.

The story on Gipp that was in the hands of Chet Grant and Jim Beach cannot be left unreported. Because of urging by friends and a sense of historical duty that keeps telling me that there is never-before-released information on Gipp that must be put on the record, I will assume the task in an attempt to give football historians, Notre Dame followers as well as critics, and sports fans in general, a new perspective on Gipp, based on how his close friends and acquaintances saw him.

This one is for the Gipper.

# GIPP
# AND THE RECORD BOOK

For many decades, despite the steady parade of outstanding backs who followed him, Gipp held six Notre Dame running records that also included punt and kickoff returns.

Gipp amassed a total of 2341 yards in 27 games, some of which he played only a half whenever Notre Dame was comfortably ahead. Gipp gained those yards on 369 rushes. Although Gipp's records were from 1917 through 1920, he missed two and a half games in 1917 after his leg was broken in the Morningside game; the war year 1918 was abbreviated to six games because of the flu epidemic. This career rushing record lasted almost 60 seasons. It was broken by Vagas Ferguson during the 1979 season. Ferguson's total career yardage gained, from 1976 to 1979, became a new record, the total being 3472 yards in 41 games with 673 carries. Since Ferguson's achievement the Notre Dame career record has been broken a few more times and at this writing it belongs to Autry Denson whose career spanned from 1995 through 1998. Denson rushed for 4318 yards on 854 carries in 48 games, bowl games included.

After 82 years, Gipp still holds some Notre Dame records in spite of a changing game. During the course of those 82 years, rules that helped the defense in Gipp's day have evolved into rules that now help the offense. Gipp still holds the average yards per carry, per season, established in 1920. His record is 8.11, followed closely by Reggie Brooks' 1992 effort of 8.04. Gipp also holds the all-purpose yards (rushing, punt and kickoff returns) per game record of 357 which he gained against Army in 1920. Gipp also held a career all-purpose yards running per game record with a total of 113.5 yards, but that category has been dropped because it included running with interceptions and in modern football players do not play both ways, so the defense now has its own records categories.

That isn't all. Gipp's total offense yards per attempt, per season, of 9.37 yards, is a record that still stands. While Heisman Trophy winner John Huarte is second in this record, Gipp is second to Huarte in the total offense yards in a career category.

Gipp is also first in total kickoff returns at eight (157 yards) against Army in 1920 and also total kickoff and punt returns combined, 10 for 207 yards in that same game, in which his overall performance prompted critics to say that Gipp was the best football player they had ever seen.

# 1

# GIPP: SAINT
# OR SINNER?

ather John W. Cavanaugh, who became Notre
Dame's president in 1905, delivered the University
from the image of a religious "hick" school, to one of
national prominence during his tour of duty that ended in
July of 1919, when Father James Burns replaced him. While
always in need of money, he raised it with help from Notre
Dame's "Religious Society" and the spirited youngsters who
filled the rosters of Notre Dame's athletic teams. As Father
Burns would one day write to the Superintendent of Public
Instruction in the State of Indiana in reply to a questionnaire
concerning Notre Dame's endowments: "Notre Dame had a
'Living Endowment.'"

Father Burns elaborated further that while Notre
Dame did not possess an endowment in the financial meaning of the term, it had a valuable productive endowment in
the life service of the faculty of Priests, Brothers and Sisters

of Notre Dame's Religious Society, who gave their services gratuitously and were a more reliable asset than any financial endowment. These excerpts were taken from "Notre Dame - One Hundred Years," written by Rev. Arthur J. Hope, C.S.C. Father Burns also could have mentioned the sacrifice of the lay professors, who were grossly underpaid, but remained a dedicated and loyal asset. When Burns finally put his hands on collected funds, the first item of expenditure was raising the professors' salaries by 25%.

The Hope book further reveals why fund raising was such a tough sell. Father Burns' attempt to get contributions from executives of companies who received volumes of business from Notre Dame almost hit a dead end. They weren't interested in Notre Dame's problems; they didn't believe that college prepared men for life and as one executive put it, "I have a thousand people working for me and I'm proud to say not one of them is a college graduate, nor ever went to college." Nevertheless, these executives were so impressed with Father Burns' presentation that they sent him fairly sizeable checks — considering their reluctance and the value of a dollar for that era — with a note saying that it was Father Burns' salesmanship that influenced them, hence the contribution.

Under Father Cavanaugh's guidance, his tolerance in some cases and his autocratic rule, Notre Dame gained national exposure and fame through sports — primarily football. Judging from the anti-college bias prevailing among some business executives, it is amazing what Father Cavanaugh accomplished with very little outside help. Not only was there a University to worry about, but a high school and a grade school or "minums" as it was generally referred to. All were part of the campus scene. Father Cavanaugh had been in charge of the Seminary on campus prior to assuming the presidency of Notre Dame, and it still remained a part of his concerns.

During his regime, Notre Dame football had four undefeated seasons, seven seasons with only one loss and an overall record of 86 wins, 13 losses and 8 ties. Notre Dame adopted the same scholastic rules that the Big Ten schools had in force and adhered to them, while some Big Ten schools managed to circumvent them to suit their goals.

The "tramp" athlete of that era was one who appeared at the start of the football season. He might have been enrolled or he possibly just came out for practice and played that season and when it was over, he disappeared. If he bothered to enroll it was usually the coach who saw that the tuition was paid for the tramp, although he never attended classes. Alumni were involved in this scheme and the tramp athlete received subsistence from the alumni and other business sources. Coach Fielding "Hurry Up" Yost of Michigan's "point a minute" teams, as they were known when he coached, was accused of using these type of athletes. Because the accusing fingers pointed to him, he then retaliated with the same type of accusations against his rival schools, including Notre Dame. Notre Dame lost a close game to Michigan in 1908 and then in 1909 defeated the Wolverines 11 to 3, after which Coach Yost dropped Notre Dame from Michigan's schedule.

Notre Dame had difficulty scheduling Big Ten teams, which avoided the school until Purdue came aboard for a 1918 game. They were aware of Notre Dame's attempts to join their conference and knew the school had adopted all Big Ten rules in order to expedite any movement that might allow it to become a member. But Illinois, the University of Chicago and Michigan did not want to face Notre Dame's inspired teams and vetoed its entry whenever Notre Dame applied.

Gipp certainly did not fit the description of tramp athlete as it applied to football, for he was a bona fide, enrolled student at Notre Dame. Neither did he fit the dictionary's definition of tramp: "a begging or thieving vagrant." He never begged nor stole anyone's money. On the contrary, he gave money away most of the time when he won a sizable pot. He had a room on campus earned by his efforts on the football field. He also had a room in South Bend's Oliver Hotel earned in trade for services to the hotel. Gipp, a vagrant? Horsemanure! Yet that's what he has been called by some authors.

While college baseball never resorted to the use of a tramp athlete — at least not on records I have checked — there were instances where a "ringer" was brought in to pitch a certain crucial game. An amusing such instance comes to mind. It was told to me by old timer John Cheney, a descendant of a pioneer Orlando, Florida, family.

Near the beginning of the last century, the first World Series in 1892 was a battle for the Temple Cup. The Cup was named for the owner of the Pittsburgh Pirates, William Temple, who sold his team and retired to Winter Park, Florida, to grow oranges, not only as a hobby, but for profit. The tasty, easy-peeling Temple orange was a hybrid creation of his.

Temple was an ardent booster of Rollins College, located about a half-mile from his orange grove. Rollins and central Florida area Stetson University of Deland were bitter rivals in all sports, but Temple, because of his love of baseball, particularly wanted to win the traditional annual baseball game. He got the Rollins coach to agree to use a ringer who would be recruited by Temple for the game.

Temple got the strikeout king of the big leagues, lefty "Rube" Waddell to pitch for Rollins. Waddell had just won a 20-inning shutout against Cy Young, both pitchers going the distance. As John Cheney related the story, "Temple hired Rube to pitch and paid him to make himself visible on the Rollins campus for three days prior to the Saturday home game in Winter Park. Temple wanted everyone to think Rube was a Rollins student.

"So for three days, with a book in his hand, Waddell walked from one building to another, pausing and spitting in front of each, pretending to read his book. Then he'd go to the library and sit there for an hour. The desks in the library had a lid on top which could be lifted to put books in. What Rube did when he opened his desk lid was to spit tobacco juice."

Cheney said that this walking, chewing, spitting procedure was followed by Rube so diligently that there were pools of tobacco juice in front of buildings, on the brick sidewalks, and in almost every library desk. Also empty whiskey pints were in the desks and behind shrubbery. The whole campus was a janitor's nightmare. Rube was a heavy drinker and was referred to by many sports reporters as a "sousepaw" pitcher instead of southpaw. Oh yes, Rollins won 2-0, and Rube registered 15 strikeouts in his first and last collegiate victory.

Father Cavanaugh's goal was "to teach Catholic young

men superbly; foster morality and disciplinary regulations for the welfare of the students." These goals were aimed at every Notre Dame student, be he Catholic or Protestant or any other belief, but the accent was on Catholic.

The weight of mitigation and common sense was applied in regard to students' problems. There were situations where athletes without high school diplomas were allowed an entrance exam (an opportunity that was also available to non-athletes) — not only at Notre Dame, but at many other schools of higher learning. If that option wasn't available at Notre Dame, both Rockne and Gipp would have to have gone to high school again to earn their diploma since neither had one when they entered the school.

While there was a rule regarding class absences, Father Cavanaugh had provided room for mitigating circumstances that allowed a young man to catch up with his class work in spite of absences. The reasoning was,"why repeat the same subject you already know," which saved tuition money and time.

There were many schools in that era that were licensed by the state, but not accredited, from which one could get a degree. A person could go to a school that taught one subject such as law and be qualified with that degree to take a bar exam. That's why many business executives Father Burns encountered in search for donations felt that going through a college system was a waste of time and money.

Father Cavanaugh was flexible on occasions whenever a situation that was contrary to the rule arose. Hunk Anderson remembered that Cavanaugh by-passed the Faculty Athletics Board in the case of Frank Thomas, a Notre Dame

24

substitute quarterback, and gave Frank a re-exam after Frank flunked a civil engineering class test. Frank was hit hard in practice and had a concussion which sent him to the infirmary and he missed two days of classes. On the day of his return, there was a test given which he flunked. On the re-take, he passed, as Hunk Anderson put it, "with my help."

Yes, Hunk admitted that he and the future head coach of the Alabama Crimson Tide cheated. Father Cavanaugh got the exam from the Engineering Department and gave Father Pat Haggerty the chore of giving it to Frank Thomas. Father Haggerty had a full schedule of his own in his office, so he placed a classroom desk in the hall with the door open and with Thomas sitting in front of the doorway, leaving room enough for someone to enter and exit. Hunk was hanging around near the stairway and watched for someone to enter Father's office on business. When a priest came to Haggerty's office, Hunk got Tom Meehan (an amateur magician) to slip two blank sheets of paper with one hand and pick up the Thomas exam papers with the other hand as he passed by. Hunk then went downstairs and did the exam, missing two items on purpose, and then came upstairs. When someone else came to see Father Haggerty, Tom again walked by, dropping the exam on Thomas' desk. If they got caught, all three would have been expelled, for it was known by the students that Father Cavanaugh did not tolerate cheating.

Frank Thomas was the quarterback on Gipp's freshman team who called for a punt, but Gipp crossed him up when he kicked a 62 yard field goal instead. Playing Western State Normal of Kalamazoo, Michigan, and tied 7-7 with only a few minutes to go late in the fourth quarter, the ball rested on Notre Dame's 38 yard line with a lot of yardage to go. When Thomas called for a punt, Gipp argued with Thomas. "We don't want to settle for a tie, let me drop kick...I know I can make it." Thomas insisted that it was too far and too risky. And it was.

Pete Bahan, who started the game at quarterback but got hurt and was replaced by Thomas, told me that people don't realize what a great effort that was on the part of Gipp. It started snowing before the first half ended and it had gotten worse in the second half, causing both teams to slip, slide and fumble. The ball was wet and center Frank Coughlin had the ball get away from his grip on the snap, resulting in a bad snap which Gipp had to jump high to catch. The team blocked long enough for Gipp to drop-kick the ball accurately for three points.

One thing Bahan was sure of, was that Gipp lined up deep in punt formation, and it would have been safer to punt the ball than to drop kick it. There was no doubt Gipp was going for the win and lining up deep was a ruse to fool the defense and Thomas.

Young quarterback Thomas was angry that Gipp didn't follow instructions. He wasn't aware of the bad snap until Pete told him. Gipp and Thomas seldom spoke to each other on the field and off the field. Gipp ignored him. Grover Malone had words with Gipp in the locker room at one time, but the rest of the team liked Gipp and admired his ability.

Bahan said that the kick was actually a 75-yard field goal if field goals were counted from the spot of the kick as they are in modern football. In that bygone era, field goals were measured from the line of scrimmage.

When the war began in early April of 1917, students, in anticipation of going into the military, began dropping out of school. Even more left after the Draft Act was passed in May, many not even waiting for final exams. So Gipp missing his finals wasn't such a big deal. At the start of the fall term the enrollment dropped off considerably. When the Selective Conscription Act was passed, almost 10 million men registered and almost a million men were called up immediately. Those in college waiting to be drafted got a break and were recipients of a reprieve because the government established the Students Army Training Corps which permitted students to remain in school and continue with their studies while undergoing military training.

Gipp did not pass the physical for the SATC and since he had a temporary stay from his local draft board pending a second exam on his ailing leg, Hunk said that Rockne asked Lt. John Kirkrohr of the SATC to send the results of the physical exam Gipp flunked to his local draft board. Gipp never did hear from the draft board about a re-exam after that report.

It was Rockne who urged both Gipp and Bahan to join the SATC immediately upon arriving on campus. Rockne was named head coach replacing retiring Jess Harper in 1918 and wanted to make sure he had a team when he got back from Fort Sheridan, Illinois. Rockne had been drafted for the summer to help in the physical training of the SATC officer candidates at Fort Sheridan, among them, Joe Brandy, who got discharged in 1919 in time for football that year.

Captain-elect Pete Bahan got a second Rockne letter from Headquarters Company, Fort Sheridan. Rockne wrote that he would be arriving late for fall football practice and that he wanted Pete and Gipp to take over practice until he arrived on September 17. In urging Bahan, Gipp and all returnees to join the SATC, Rockne concluded in the letter to Bahan: "Don't forget, we wear uniforms next year and belong to the army." Rockne had lost most of his starting team to the army via the draft and voluntary enlistments, because the SATC program came a bit too late for them.

If the SATC players belonged to the army, so did Notre Dame in toto. Francis Wallace, in his book "Notre Dame - Its People and Its Legends," described the army takeover: "As the campus became an armed camp, ordinary college routines were subordinated and all was not salubrious for the academically oriented..." And Father Cavanaugh was pleased with the income that the SATC brought to Notre Dame, because being in a situation of declining enrollment meant near bankruptcy for the school without the government program.

The tuition was paid for each student, which was $120 a year, as well as $30 per month for room and board. It was a complete takeover by the army. Even the residence halls were referred to as barracks and were numbered. Notre Dame saved money on janitorial services because the SATC trainees had posted duties they had to perform before or after classes and as punishment. Once football practice began, football players managed to escape the "work sheet list."

It was somebody else in charge at Notre Dame and not the priests. When the program ended in January of 1919, Father Cavanaugh wrote a friend, "...Notre Dame is perfectly herself again. It is the sweetest miracle of my life."

Gipp was one of the few students who did not belong to the SATC program. In an environment that was not normal, Gipp got away with some rule breaking that he ordinarily would not have. The upheaval that cast aside normalcy in our country and permeated most campuses began from the second half of the 1916-1917 school year and lasted all the way through the 1918-1919 school year and had a great effect on Notre Dame.

Besides fighting World War I, our country and the world were ravaged by the "Spanish Flu." Maybe a comparison with a recent event can give the reader an idea of what an enormous problem our country had to cope with in that period. More than 3000 innocent lives were lost in the destruction of the World Trade Center in New York and the Pentagon hit on 9/11/01, with the psychological wounds possibly never to be healed. With that in mind, we can appreciate the earth-shaking events of the Gipp era which our country and colleges faced.

The war in Europe was taking young American lives. This was compounded by the virulent Spanish Flu which, even today, is called history's most horrific disaster. In the wake of the WTC 9/11 terrorist tragedy, the Orlando Sentinel of September 23, 2001 recounted the damage and terror the flu had caused around the world. It was pandemic, with figures of lives lost worldwide estimated as being as many as 40 million. In the United States, more than two million had the flu, which caused more than 620,000 deaths, a staggering sum.

The great flu epidemic of 1918, which began in the spring, tapered down only to intensify in September and caused grave concern on campus. Some students did catch the virus and after treatment at the infirmary were confined to their rooms, thereby missing classes. Those in the military program were not charged with missing classes and apparently neither were the non SATC students. The widespread epidemic of Spanish influenza in 1918 caused many attendance problems for all institutions of learning.

A directive from Washington urging people to stay away from large assemblies and events where crowds gathered, coupled with new government travel restrictions, made Notre Dame's first 1918 game its last for a whole month. Notre Dame played Case Tech in Cleveland on the 28th of September and after falling behind 6-0 early in the game, managed to win comfortably 26-6 with Gipp scoring two touchdowns.

Notre Dame was forced to take a hiatus for the month of October but as the flu abated and the war in Europe looked like it was going to end almost any day, Athletic Director Rockne hurriedly scheduled games for November, with a game against Wabash on the 2nd which Notre Dame won easily, 67-7. In a home game, a 7-7 tie against a star studded Great Lakes Naval Training Center boasting of several ex-collegians was a moral victory. Notre Dame scored early on a long drive with Gipp going over for the score, but the Lakers came back to tie the game. Great Lakes went on to play in the January 1, 1919 Rose Bowl game against the Mare Island Marines, another military team loaded with college stars. Great Lakes lost 19-6.

The next game was Rockne's first loss as Notre Dame's coach. The South Benders played Michigan A&M

(Michigan State) away from home and lost, 13-7. Gipp played well, and although he was used sparingly in all the games, in this one he went almost all the way. His leg was hurting and his right foot had open bleeding skin between the toes from athletes foot. My cousin, Gene Basker, said that Gipp had that problem in 1919 as well, and his father, my uncle Frank Koszewski, who in later years Anglicized his name to Basker, treated Gipp in the Oliver Turkish Baths for it. Frank told Gipp that after taking his shower he should wipe down thoroughly with one towel and then, with another clean towel, dry his feet well before putting on clean socks. And that towel was the cause of his rift with Grover Malone.

Gipp had asked a student manager to put another towel on Gipp's chair by his bench and as he came out of the shower, he caught Grover taking the towel. An argument ensued with Gipp wresting the towel away from Malone. Pete Bahan said that Malone, after spending two years in the army, was resentful that he should end up being a substitute for someone he called a "slacker." Only Bahan's grabbing Gipp's arm poised to strike prevented a brawl as Malone then prudently walked away.

Gipp never told Rockne he had any problems with his leg or his foot. He only told his buddy Hunk and then cautioned him not to tell the coach.

While this episode occurred in 1919, the years 1917 and 1918 were unusual to say the least. Researchers failed to find a paper trail of Gipp's records as to grades and attendance. Immediately there was an assumption that they were purged from the files by Notre Dame officials. Surely Notre Dame wasn't worried about it at the time he attended classes, knowing that he wouldn't get a degree without fulfilling requirements. And why should any post-Gipp official worry about an era that has been long gone?

It is more logical to assume that those items regarding Gipp became a memento of some hero-worshipping student who worked in the office — and there were many of those through the years. Since biblical times, the garb, bones and organs of saints were relics cherished by individuals that eventually were given to the church. In modern times, the same infatuation exists with sports and entertainment icons, but not all memorabilia is preserved beyond the original collector. Remember the hundreds of wooden goal posts that have been torn down after a victory and broken into pieces by the exited mob? Can anyone find a tub full of them anywhere...or, for that matter, a piece of one? The heirs, not having the same affection for their fathers' heroes, probably found the portion of a goal post to be a good starter wood for the fireplace.

There has been some memorabilia of Gipp's that reached Notre Dame's Sports Heritage Hall. The Gipp monogram sweater that raised great controversy when President Ronald Reagan greeted Lou Holtz and his 1988 National Championship team at the White House is one item. Holtz gave the President an autographed football and Notre Dame's president, Father Edward Malloy, presented him with Gipp's sweater. John Cackley, a 1937 grad and former president of the Notre Dame Alumni Association, complained bitterly and nationally about the gift to Reagan.

Previous to that incident, I had been in contact with Cackley on rumors concerning Notre Dame's possible disposal of items that belonged to the International Sports and Games Research Collection. I felt, as he did, that the sweater might not receive as much exposure at Notre Dame as it would in a presidential library, but that the sweater belonged to Notre Dame where it would be viewed with reverence.

I did ask Cackley if he was a Democrat and he said he was, but he added that even if he were a Republican he would feel the same way. He repeated what he said nationally, that the sweater was given to satisfy egos at Notre Dame and in the White House.

Few writers ever mention Gipp's generosity, and if they do, it is only to say examples of it were fiction. Percy Wilcox, another Laurium buddy of Gipp's, finally made the ND scrub team in 1920. Gipp knew that Perce would cherish wearing a Notre Dame monogram, so he gave him his own sweater. When Wilcox died, his widow gave it to Wilcox's classmate Tom Lee. Lee, after basking in bragging rights for a few years, passed it on to Cackley.

Another piece of memorabilia of Gipp's is really a joint ownership edition. Although Rockne in a letter to Bahan was asking that both he and Gipp get to Notre Dame early in 1918 to conduct the pre-season practices until Rockne got back from Fort Sheridan, both he Gipp were late arrivals and the uniforms were given out on a first-come basis. There was no new equipment available due to the war, so both players got some bad fits.

When the curtailed 1918 season resumed, both men still had their original selections of gear. During practice after one of the games, Rock ran the first string through its paces and then gave them a breather. Bahan and Gipp left the field together, throwing their helmets down. When Rockne called for the first string to return, Gipp and Bahan accidentally grabbed each other's helmet only to find they had a better fit. So they traded. This Gipp helmet is at Notre Dame with other mementoes that belonged to Pete Bahan.

There are other Gipp relics but not at Notre Dame. The gold watch charm football with 1919 Western Champions inscribed, which Gipp wore on his pocket watch chain, he gave to his girlfriend Iris Trippeer. She wore it around her neck but eventually made it a bracelet ornament. It is currently in possession of her granddaughter.

It has been written by all who have chronicled Gipp that he never took notes in class. This statement was proclaimed by its authors to be as solid as concrete. A few said he was so smart that he didn't have to take notes. The majority, however, said that he was plain lazy and disinterested, so there couldn't be and there wasn't a notebook.

Well, there is a notebook with class notes that did belong to Gipp. Vincent Gratzer, who is a researcher for the movies, has the notebook. As a sideline, Gratzer has a web site on which he buys, sells and trades Notre Dame memorabilia. The notebook has been authenticated as having belonged to Gipp. Gratzer inherited the notebook and, as a researcher, he has traced the history of its whereabouts.

Perhaps one day Gipp's record of grades and absences will show up. Perhaps the wartime era record wasn't totally recorded. One thing is sure — Notre Dame had a program that was scholastically equal if not superior to the Big Ten and other schools engaged in intercollegiate sports.

Compare that with today's programs of the big football powers. Michael Vick of Virginia Tech, who was a preseason favorite for the Heisman Trophy for the 2000 season, was interviewed by an Orlando Sentinel reporter prior to the football season. He couldn't name all the subjects he was taking and when he did name one and was asked what it was about, he said he wasn't sure.

A professor at the University of Tennessee blew the whistle on a situation where tutors did the exams for football players. And stacking chairs is a science course there. At Florida State, besides the many football players who have gotten into trouble with the law, there are modern day class-skippers that would put Gipp's efforts to shame. While a "student," Deion Sanders did not attend classes from August to bowl time in January and even got into trouble with the law during that period, yet he played in every game, including the bowl game. His coach, Bobby Bowden, said that nothing could be done about it until the grades came out in January.

What probably shocked everyone was the announcement of a great pro football lineman of the Washington Redskins who retired. He said he was going to go to school so that he could learn to read. How could anyone go from kindergarten to college in our public school system without knowing how to read? Who did the work for him in grade school? High school? College?

As it has been said before, Gipp's indiscretions are blown out of proportion. If comparisons are used, he might end up a candidate for sainthood.

# 2

# HOW GIPP BECAME
# "THE GIPPER"

It's difficult to disassociate Gipp from his almost legendary nickname, "The Gipper," but there is a coterie of writers who have taken the position that Gipp was never called "Gipper" during his lifetime, either in person or in the media. Let us examine what has been written about the subject.

Author-Professor Murray Sperber, who has questioned many if not all of Notre Dame's legends in his books, states flat out in two of his tomes, "Shake Down the Thunder," published in 1993, and "Onward to Victory" published in 1998, that "...no one called Gipp by that nickname, nor did he ever use it himself."

Following Sperber's lead, Ray Robinson, in his 1999 book "Rockne of Notre Dame," writes, "Nobody had...heard Gipp referred to by the nickname of 'The Gipper.' Certainly

Gipp never used that name himself." Well, in spite of Sperber's and Robinson's concrete assurances, I have proof that Gipp was referred to by close friends and even sportswriters as "Gipper" and I will also reveal in this chapter how Gipp got that nickname.

Robinson contends that the first use of "The Gipper" can be traced to Harry Stuhldreher's book, "Knute Rockne, Man Builder," which was published in 1931, soon after Rockne's death. Stuhldreher, who was a member of the legendary Four Horsemen backfield which played for Notre Dame in 1924, admits in the book that he never knew Gipp personally, but he titled his chapter on Gipp, "The Gipper." He writes that Johnny Mohardt and Norm Barry, who substituted for Gipp in the 1920 Indiana game, said they had to "win the game for The Gipper," who was injured. (Gipp subsequently entered the game and helped turn a 0-10 Notre Dame deficit into a 13-10 victory.)

Robinson says that Barry later denied using the term "The Gipper," and in actuality claims he and Mohardt never even mentioned Gipp in discussing what they had to do to win the game.

Adding fuel to the non-believer's arguments is a declaration in Michael R. Steele's book, "Knute Rockne, A Bio-Bibliography," published in 1983, that Chet Grant and Paul Castner, two contemporaries of Gipp's, said that Gipp never referred to himself as "The Gipper." They did not say if others used the term, however.

So, if we're to believe the above-quoted gentlemen, not only did no one call Gipp "Gipper," no one even heard the expression during George Gipp's days.

Robinson says Stuhldreher introduced the word "Gipper" into the Notre Dame lexicon. But that assumption is debatable, because Knute Rockne first divulged Gipp's now famous death bed request to "win one for *The Gipper*" in an article for Collier's Magazine that appeared in 1930. That same article eventually became the chapter entitled "Gipp the Great," which was published in 1931 in Rockne's posthumous autobiography. So, if anyone "invented" the term, "The Gipper," it would seem it had to have been his coach, Knute Rockne.

Or was it?

Granted, none of the newspaper articles of Gipp's day which covered his games referred to him as "The Gipper." One would think the phrase might have been used somewhere along the line, but apparently it was not. So, again, the finger points toward Rockne. Rockne wrote that Gipp asked the team to "win one for *The Gipper*." He could have just as easily written that George asked the team to "Win one for *Gipp*." But why would Rockne quote Gipp as using a nickname that, according to the dissenters, had never ever been used by anyone, especially Gipp?

That question gets us back to the original point. Was Gipp called "Gipper" by anyone during his lifetime? A newsman who was a good friend of Rockne's, Robert Harron, writing in his book, "Rockne: Idol of American Football," published in 1931, flat out states that "Gipp's teammates called him Gipper." If true, that could explain why Rockne chose to report the "win one for The Gipper" request rather than "win one for Gipp." Gipp and Gipper, according to no less an expert than Knute Rockne, were synonymous.

Ken Rappoport, in his book "Wake Up the Echoes," published in 1975, details a report by Dutch Bergman, a teammate of Gipp's, who says that Rockne occasionally greeted Gipp with, "Hello, Gipper...," although it has been written that Rockne preferred calling Gipp by his first name.

Hunk Anderson had an interesting theory as to why Gipp wasn't called "Gipper" very often during his lifetime. Hunk felt it was because Gipp was a loner and rather aloof. People didn't call him by the Gipper nickname out of respect, possibly because they were a little in awe of him. It must be remembered that Gipp was older by almost five years than other team members. And he was a bona fide superstar. He wasn't the type of person you got too close to, so the reluctance to call him by a nickname is understandable.

In any case, it would be more comforting to the "Gipper" proponents if something in writing had appeared before 1930, some ten years after Gipp's premature death. And, apparently, there is just such evidence.

Francis Wallace, who was a student at Notre Dame while Gipp was there, and who became a prolific writer of books and articles, wrote a book entitled "Knute Rockne," in 1960, which was replete with first-hand accounts of Rockne and his players. In writing about the escorting of Gipp's body from the funeral home to the railroad station, which took place on December 15, 1920, Wallace quotes from his article which ran in the South Bend News-Times and said that Notre Dame students "...bowed their heads to the snow as the body of their *'Gipper'* went on to its appointed end." Robert E. Burns, in his book "Being Catholic, Being American-The Notre Dame Story, 1842-1934," writes that "A reporter for the

South Bend Tribune used the word 'Gipper' in a story published on December 17, 1920, about the progress of the Gipp cortege from the McGann Funeral Parlor to the Union Station," but doesn't credit the writer.

Based on the above, it would seem that as early as 1920 and probably before, the term "Gipper" was a familiar nickname for Gipp. The same reasoning with both Wallace's newspaper piece and Rockne's Collier's article can be used — why would either of them use "Gipper" if it was an unknown sobriquet when "Gipp" could have been used just as easily in its place?

Nevertheless, one would like stronger evidence over the use of "Gipper" if it was obtainable. I came across that evidence via a rather circuitous route.

When I was working with Hunk Anderson on his autobiography, which was published in 1976, I naturally was curious as to how Heartley Anderson got the nickname "Hunk." Certainly the modern usage of the name fit Anderson, because he was a "hunk" in the true sense of the word. Ruggedly handsome, he was one of the best linemen ever to play for Notre Dame. Small even for that long-ago era, Anderson stood only 5'10" and weighed 170 pounds, which was positively diminutive when compared with today's 300 pounds-plus behemoths who man the front lines for college and pro teams alike. In fact, when playing on offense at guard, it was Hunk's job to help open holes for backs such as Gipp, although he was smaller than Gipp, who checked in at just over 6-feet and 180 pounds. But Hunk was tough, dogged, skillful and football smart — attributes that contributed to his greatness as a lineman who played both offense and defense and to his future career as a coach. So it's easy to assume that was why he was called "Hunk." He was a hunk no matter how you define the word. But the nickname didn't come about that way. Here's what Hunk told me:

He said that when he was a kid growing up in the Calumet, Michigan area, he was involved in a lot of neighborhood fights with kids of all sizes. The fight was over only when the kid getting the shellacking yelled, "uncle." As Hunk put it, "I handled myself pretty well and made so many kids yell uncle that they began calling me 'Unk,' a shortened version of uncle. Then, in a scrimmage in high school, our tackle on defense tried to tackle me *(Hunk was a running back in high school)* and I ran over him and got out in the open. The coach gave the tackle (Cameron) hell and told the offense to run the play again. We did and again the tackle managed to slip off the blocker to hit me high and I carried him for 10 yards before the secondary helped him down me.

"When we got up, Cameron quite loudly said, 'Hell you're no Unk, you're just a big unstoppable hunk.' From then on, everyone called me Hunk."

That having set the record straight regarding "Hunk," it occurred to me at the time that Anderson might know how the term "Gipper" came about. After all, Hunk was not only Gipp's teammate at Notre Dame, they were from the same home town in Michigan and were considered best friends.

When I asked Hunk if he knew how Gipp got his nickname, "Gipper," Hunk replied, a bit to my surprise, "Yeah, he got it in baseball."

It seems that Joe Swetish, manager of the Laurium, Michigan baseball team, was going through the lineup to answer a questioner as to how many extra base hits the team got and who got them. When Joe got to Gipp's name, he said, "And we have a double and a round tripper for the Gipper."

Someone turned to Gipp and said, "Hey, Gipper, Joe's a poet." From that time on everyone on the team began calling George, "Gipper." Hunk said that during practice at Notre Dame one could hear Ojay Larson or Perce Wilcox call Gipp by that nickname...even Rockne at times used it, although Hunk agreed with those who say that he usually called Gipp, George.

So there it is. Right from someone who knew Gipp, played ball with him and was there when the nickname was born. It stands to reason that the name just didn't appear out of the blue in a Francis Wallace newspaper article or in Rockne's or even Harry Stuhldreher's writings. If we're to believe Hunk Anderson, "The Gipper" sprang from Gipp's prowess as a baseball player. "A round-tripper for The Gipper."

It makes sense.

# 3

# GIPP'S HEALTH AND PREMONITION

George Gipp, standing a fraction over six feet and weighing anywhere from 180 to 185 pounds during his Notre Dame career, was considered to be on the "big-man" side in football in his era of the game. Hunk Anderson, who was an All-State fullback in high school, told me that in the semi-pro games he and Gipp played in Calumet, the manager used Gipp in the line while the 165 pound Hunk played fullback. It was Gipp who got the Notre Dame scholarship for Hunk when Rockne took over in 1918.

When Hunk arrived in South Bend to begin his career at Notre Dame, Gipp met him at the Michigan Street depot and was going to hail a cab for Hunk and the large trunk filled with clothing that Hunk had brought from home. They bumped into Rockne, who had just come out of Hullie and Mike's, where Rockne usually bought his cigars. Gipp introduced Hunk to Rockne and Rockne then asked Hunk what position he played."Fullback," answered Hunk.

"Well, we don't need any fullbacks...we need guards."

"You're looking at the best guard you'll ever see," countered a confident Hunk.

"I hope so," said a smiling, cigar smoking Rockne. "See you boys on campus."

For the Aristocrats, a team in Calumet, George played tackle and for the Calumet Athletic Club, he played center. George was well coordinated and had a consistent head-on speed between 10.2 and 10.4 running the hundred-yard-dash in uniform at Notre Dame. He was the fastest man on the team according to Pete Bahan. Most teammates thought that Arthur "Dutch" Bergman was faster, yet Dutch timed fractions of a second slower than Gipp. Bahan, who played in the same backfield with both stars for three years, two as team captain, said Rockne used psychology to get Gipp to run so that Rockne could get a good effort from Gipp on his timing.

The players, after classes were finished, would get to Cartier Field individually and not as group and would get out on the field and loosen up as soon as each got his uniform on. Gipp would warm up by drop kicking and punting from midfield. Rock would come up to Gipp and say, "George, why don't you go to one goal line and I'll stand on the other so that I can get a timing on you. Everybody says that Bergman is faster and I just don't believe that. Run when I raise my hand."

Rockne used the same ploy on Bergman, so although it wasn't a head to head race for a timing, both men knew they were competing against each other. Some Notre Damers forget that Rockne was Notre Dame's head track coach up to

1925, when John Nicholson replaced him, so Rockne wasn't just a football coach trying to operate a stop watch...his timing was accurate.

Hunk knew that Gipp was faster than Bergman, who clocked in only once under 11 seconds flat according to Bahan, who watched those sprints. Hunk, in later years and with 35 years football experience, had an answer as to why Bergman would seem to be faster than Gipp to most observers. When running with the ball, Dutch, a smaller target, would run straight ahead and tried to outrun anyone who was about to tackle him. Because of his smaller size — 5 foot 7 and 160 pounds — Bergman had to pump his legs rapidly more often than Gipp to cover the same distance. Gipp on the other hand, possessing a long stride, preferred to head feint, sidestep and pivot to elude a tackler.

Bahan, playing in the same backfield with Gipp, had the answer as to why Gipp was one of the few passers of their era of football who could throw a perfect overhand pass for a great distance and for accuracy. The fat football in those days wasn't easy to grip. Some passers flattened their palm, placed the ball on it, and with the other hand to steady it, raised it up to throw it overhand. Some tossed it in shot put fashion; others merely threw it sidearm. Gipp sometimes threw short passes sidearm to the flat zones to avoid a blocked pass by defensive rushers.

But what Bahan noticed was the extreme length of Gipp's fingers. Evidence of that observation by Pete can be seen in a picture of George punting a ball and his arm coming across his chest. The hand seems to have very long fingers...even his small finger looks like an index finger. This explains why Gipp could grip the ball and throw a perfect overhand pass. Hunk once mentioned that Ojay Larson kidded Gipp about how George could make a lot of money as a pick pocket.

No doubt that Gipp was a perfect model for the perfect football player. He had the physique, talent, brains, speed and coordination. But most importantly, he had poise. Nothing seemed to rattle him, on or off the field. Yet the Gipper had health problems that began in his childhood and this seemed to affect him subconsciously. He was a victim of the dreaded infectious disease that some children are unfortunate to acquire — rheumatic fever.

The disease, for the most part, strikes children in the three years to 15- years-old age group, although young adults can be afflicted by it as well, especially those who had the disease previously. There usually is a lot of pain in the joints, but the silent damage in severe cases is usually done to the heart due to the swelling caused by the invasive bacteria. While any part of the heart can be damaged, the mitral valve is usually the part of the heart that is affected.

In Gipp's day, the remedy was treatment with salicylate and the painful joints were treated with topical applications of wintergreens. Bed rest and a high caloric diet were also part of the old treatment. There is a vagueness about the causes, but generally, tonsillitis and strep throat — either individually or severally — are considered the culprits from which the bacterial toxins spread to the heart.

It is possible that Gipp had been living on borrowed time and his life would have been shortened, anyhow. It is not known if his heart had been damaged to any degree dur-

ing his childhood bout with rheumatic fever. Gipp's procras-
tination regarding having something done about his bad tonsils made him a candidate for a recurrence of that rheumatic
fever, which can be fatal the second time around. It is almost
certain that his doctor warned him about the consequences if
Gipp got the same malady again.

Hunk Anderson said that Gipp worried about his
health. Yet it seems though that Gipp shied away from a reg-
imen and life style that would enable him to stay healthy. On
several occasions he told Anderson he thought he had consumption. In Gipp's time that was the name frequently used
for tuberculosis. Hunk didn't know what symptoms Gipp had
experienced to diagnose himself as having TB. Usually, a severe weight loss occurs, yet Gipp appeared normal. It must
have been a prevalent disease because the Healthwin Hospital in South Bend opened its doors for the first time in 1920
specifically for treatment and care of tubercular patients
only. It became the city's third hospital.

At a practice session on Cartier Field, Rockne wasn't
satisfied the way a certain play was being run. Rock had
worked the first string hard with a scrimmage of long duration, so he decided to rest them for a few minutes and then try
again to get the team to run the problem play to his satisfaction. Gipp, after taking a ladle full of water from the bucket
and spitting it out, started for the gate. Hunk ran after
George and caught up with him. Hunk thought that Gipp
misunderstood that Rockne merely wanted to give the first
stringers a rest and did not mean for them to go in for the
day.

"I know what Rock meant, I'm going in anyhow," Gipp

told Anderson. "I'm spitting a helluva lot of blood, Hunk."

"What happened...you got a cut in your mouth?"

"Naw, I think it's coming from deep inside — it's something else," replied Gipp.

"What do I tell Rock if he asks," Hunk wanted to know.

"Tell him that I just remembered that I have an important business date downtown," replied George.

As Hunk approached the scrimmage area, Rockne went out to meet him, so as not to be within earshot of the rest of the players.

"What's with George?" Rockne asked Hunk.

"He says to tell you he's got important business downtown, but his mouth was bleeding pretty good, coach," Rockne winked at Hunk, trying to suppress a knowing smile and said, "Get into the huddle Hunk, we've got lots of work to do."

Whether it was a psychological subconscious awareness of a latent health problem or a premonition that affected his behavior, only Gipp knew. He seemed to feel that he was destined for an early death. It was nearing the end of Hunk's freshman year at Easter and classes were out for Holy Week. Ordinarily, the Laurium group would stay on campus, but Gipp won big playing pool and treated his buddies to a trip home and back. Gipp also had two cases of whiskey — one he took in lieu of an on the spot debt that an ex-whiskey salesman incurred playing pool and the other suitcase of whiskey he bought from the same man for a bargain price because the fellow needed cash to get back to Kentucky.

The 19th (Prohibition) Amendment wasn't ratified yet, but the wartime act by Congress in 1917 prohibiting the manufacture and sale of whiskey, only, made whiskey an item of contraband. Apparently the salesman stocked up on his company brands. So this whiskey wasn't bathtub gin or white lightning made in a cow-barn still. This was the real thing. The salesman was trying to sell it to the South Bend speakeasies, but they had their own suppliers and because of the brand names, they felt that he might be a part of an entrapment operation. Hunk said the man told Gipp that he went to Indianapolis first, but there was rigid enforcement for the wartime ban locally, so he tried South Bend.

Although South Bend is only seven miles from the Michigan border and 11 from the city of Niles, the quickest and best route to Michigan's upper peninsula was through Wisconsin. Some trains going through Wisconsin went to cities that were close to the Canadian border. Inspectors riding on trains going through Wisconsin had the duty to exam suspicious luggage for any war time contraband and they had the power of arrest and confiscation.

When the inspector got to their seats he looked at the suitcases, looked at Hunk and Ojay, then looked at the suit cases again and asked what was in them.

"Just our dirty clothes we're taking home to be washed," replied Hunk.

"Oh, college kids, eh?" And with that remark the inspector went on about his business.

When the inspector was out of sight, Gipp took a bottle of whiskey out of one of the suitcases. Ojay went to get the cone shaped paper cups at the car's water fountain and the boys had their drinks.

As the bottle's contents neared its bottom, the train

passed a huge cemetery quite visible from the train's window. Gipp stared at it for a minute.

"That's the place where I'm gonna be going," said George.

"Hell, George, we all will be going there someday," answered Hunk.

"For me it's sooner than you think," insisted Gipp.

"Cut that crap out, you guys...gimme that bottle," was Ojay's irritated comment as he poured another drink.

Johnny Jegier told me of another instance of Gipp's preoccupation of an early death. I listed one of Gipp's attributes as his on and off the field poise. When it came to his personal health problem that was gnawing at him incessantly, Gipp had trouble coping with it.

Johnny picked Gipp up at the Oliver Hotel for an evening of pool and cards at Goldie Mann's — at least Goldie's was to be a starting point in a search for big stakes. Gipp asked Jegier to detour a few blocks. Gipp wanted to stop by a carnival, which was to be the last of the season before the carnivals and circuses folded up for the winter.

The "Circus Grounds" was a plot of acreage with railroad siding located on the southwest corner of Prairie Avenue and Sample Streets. Because it had the railroad siding on the inside edge, it was ideal for circuses. It was used to park boxcars and flatbeds by the railroad company that was bringing in materials to the Studebaker auto plant. A Studebaker steam engine would then bring the boxcars across the street into the Studebaker yards.

Parking their car on Sample Street, Jegier and Gipp then went directly to the sideshow concessions, avoiding the carnival rides. The reason Gipp wanted to attend the carnival was his desire to throw baseballs at the wooden milk bottle pyramid atop a square pedestal. These milk bottles had lead bottoms and they not only had to be knocked down, but also completely knocked off a very abrasive base on which they sat in order to win the prize.

On the first try with three shots at the target, Gipp knocked the bottles down, but not off. The baseballs he threw were very soft and Gipp, a veteran of this type of carnival game, asked the carnie to see the bucket of balls he had underneath the counter. The guy denied having them, but when Gipp leaned over the counter to look, the carnie brought the bucket to Gipp.

George managed to find three suitable balls and with the first throw knocked the two top ones off the base and the bottom ones down. With a great arm and accuracy, Gipp managed to knock the remaining bottles off the pedestal and won a large Teddy bear. His next attempt resulted in winning a doll and before the concessionaire could tell George that was all for him as he handed him the doll, Gipp just walked away. Spotting a lady with two young children, Gipp gave the doll to the little girl and the Teddy bear to the boy, and was thanked profusely for it by the mother and the kids.

Jegier said that Gipp wanted his fortune told and they both went into the Gypsy fortune teller's tent. When she told Gipp to be careful because in the cards she saw death hovering around him, Gipp stormed out, not waiting for Johnny, who dashed out after him. When he caught up with Gipp, Jegier asked, "What happened, George?" Gipp replied that she saw an early death for him.

There was silence as the two walked toward their parked car. As Johnny started toward Goldie Mann's down Sample Street, Gipp asked Johnny to turn around and take him back to the hotel. Although he could have purchased a bottle at the hotel, they stopped at a neighborhood saloon off Prairie Avenue where George went in and bought a pint bottle of whiskey, showing that even small saloons had whiskey available. (The wartime prohibition act was still in effect.)

Gipp had great sensitivity regarding illness and death. Anderson told about the time a classmate of Gipp's died in the hospital from a severe case of carbuncles. It seems that when his classmate got to the hospital, it was too late because the boils had become infected. Perhaps he correlated the victim's case with his tonsillitis. The term "poisons" was loosely used in that era and the account of the boy's illness in the papers said that the poisons spread and killed him. Gipp certainly remembered that Dr. Roche, when urging Gipp to have his tonsils removed, would use the term poison in saying that it could be serious if the poison spread through Gipp's system.

Gipp seemed obsessed when the news of his classmate's death reached him. Hunk Anderson said that Gipp would talk about it to anyone who would listen. Hunk told him there was nothing he could do about it, so he ought to get it off his mind.

It upset Gipp so much that without a word to anyone he left school and went home to Laurium. Although it was the end of May and near the end of the school term, Gipp just took off without waiting to take his final semester exams. Hunk speculated that Gipp made up his mind to go home and have his tonsils taken out, but when he got to Laurium, he again got cold feet and put it off for another time.

Behind Gipp's premonition of an early death undoubtedly were his past and his latent health problems. Yet Hunk thought there was one time Gipp came close to death by asphyxiation. Gipp and Anderson were playing a Sunday morning baseball game in Calumet and Hunk didn't bother to eat breakfast before leaving home. After the game Hunk wanted something to eat and Gipp suggested the Michigan House restaurant where Gipp had friends working. This was a little after lunch time, but in those days in most families the noontime meal was "dinner," a big meal, and the evening meal was supper, a much lighter repast.

They both ordered a beef plate with all the trimmings and just as Gipp began chewing his meat, a friend passing by his table and without realizing the situation, greeted Gipp with a slap on the back. Gipp's meat lodged in his throat and he began choking, clutching his throat and trying to cough the meat out. Gipp was on his feet but the friend didn't help, standing paralyzed and dumbfounded. Hunk had gotten up, but in trying to rush over to help, tripped on his own chair and catapulted about 10 feet, sprawling out on the floor.

A waiter finally noticed what was happening, but before he could reach Gipp, George with a great effort expelled the meat from his throat with a gush that sprayed the next table near their's.

"George's face was red," said Hunk, "and it could have been from the choking, but I'm sure he was mad as hell, too. The guy was apologizing all over the place."

Hunk said that Gipp lightened up a bit when he saw

the waiter wiping up the "damage" at the next table and as the "friend" continued with his apology, Gipp sat down waving for him to go without saying a word. When they finished eating and asked for the bill, the waiter said that Gipp's friend who caused the problem paid for everything.

At that time, the method one used in a situation like that was to try to dislodge the tracheal obstruction by using a finger to move the obstruction sideways or out while trying to cough and the other was for someone to slap the choking person at the shoulder blades. This sometimes helped and sometimes made the situation worse as happened to the great home run hitter, Jimmie Foxx, who choked to death in a restaurant. Also, Mama Cass of The Mama's and The Papa's singing group allegedly died that way. This was before the discovery of the Heimlich maneuver now recommended as a far better method of dislodging obstructions.

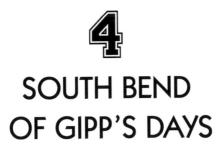

# SOUTH BEND
# OF GIPP'S DAYS

George Gipp came to Notre Dame to play baseball. He had no desire to get a degree, but he realized that there was a certain amount of book learning to do in order to stay in school and that became his biggest obstacle. He was smart enough to handle the books, but he did not care to "waste" his time studying and therefore he would expend only enough effort to just get by.

So why did he come to South Bend just to play baseball when he was doing it in and around his home town in the Laurium/Calumet area? He discovered that playing locally or in a factory league was the hard and long way to get noticed by the big leagues. But a friend gave George a short cut to reach his destination.

The friend was Wilbur "Dolly" Gray, a 1914 Notre Dame graduate and baseball star, who convinced Gipp that

Notre Dame was one place to be if he wanted to get noticed by the major league scouts. Dolly buoyed his contention by pointing out that Adrian "Cap" Anson, who was to become a charter member of the Baseball Hall of Fame, was a Notre Dame man. Although Anson played only inter-hall baseball because Notre Dame did not offer inter-collegiate baseball while he was in school, he still was noticed by the Chicago Cubs.

Dolly Gray pointed out that there had been 23 Notre Dame baseball players who had made the big leagues and that the Notre Dame campus had become a good hunting grounds for major league scouts because of the quality of Notre Dame players. Cap Anson led the National League in hitting in 1887 and 1888 and played on teams that won five National League pennants, feats that helped pave the way for future Notre Dame baseball players to become major leaguers. Jess Harper, Notre Dame's athletic director and football coach, was also the baseball coach. Dolly had informed him about Gipp and Jess agreed to give Gipp a baseball scholarship on the basis of what Dolly told him about Gipp's talent. Gipp, like Knute Rockne, did not have a high school diploma and had to pass an entrance exam, which he did with little difficulty.

Upon arriving at Notre Dame, Gipp had two obstacles to overcome: the lack of money and an uneasiness of being among students who were a lot younger than he was. (Gipp was 20 when he entered Notre Dame.) George found a solution that dealt with both of his problems — downtown South Bend.

Gipp's skills at pool and poker became well known in the local cigar store establishments that were fronting the more lucrative business of pool, beer, whiskey, in-house gambling as well as betting on outside sporting events. After a semester in Brownson Hall, rooming with Elwin "Dope" Moore, Gipp decided to break away from campus regimentation and to use that freedom to augment his meager or non-existent finances in downtown South Bend. Moore, who got the nickname "Dope" because of his amazing knowledge of baseball players, statistics and horse racing, gave Gipp a thorough orientation of South Bend during that first semester.

Moore hailed from Elkhart, Indiana, a city only 17 miles from South Bend and played baseball in South Bend before he entered Notre Dame. He knew South Bend well. Although Gipp was an exceptional pool player, it was Moore who taught Gipp the fine points of three cushion billiards which "art" enabled Gipp to become the house player at the Oliver Hotel. That position was bartered for free lodging for Gipp.

South Bend in Gipp's time was a rapidly growing manufacturing city with many diversified industries. The biggest of these were the Studebaker Corporation, the Oliver Chilled Plow Company and The Singer Sewing Machine Company. The ethnic composition of South Bend residents was just as diversified as its industries. The 1920 census figures pegged the South Bend population to be 70,983. There were banks, six to eight-story buildings for professional and business offices, theaters and many fine department stores along with five and dime stores, shoe stores, various specialty shops, restaurants — everything you'd expect in a large city.

Forms of public transportation in South Bend were trolley cars and 24-hour cab service with three vying companies accommodating customers. There was the New York Central depot whose tracks were adjacent to the Studebaker assembly plant a bit south of the downtown boundary (Division Street, now named Western Avenue) and on that very same boundary at the South Michigan Street corner was the Grand Trunk depot. Its trains rumbled in the center of Division Street as far as Laurel Street where they then turned to meet the main rail system on the south side of the Smogor Lumber Company and the J. D. Oliver athletic field. This is the field where many a Notre Dame footballer moonlighted under the lights, coaching a South Bend pro football team. Incidentally, on a triangle of the corner where the train turned in to meet the main tracks, a gas station was owned by Baseball Hall of Famer Stanley Coveleskie, who was the first pitcher to win three games in a World Series.

Shortly after 1920, a third method of getting out of South Bend toward Chicago and points North into Wisconsin and Northern Illinois emerged. It was the South Shore electric train with its small depot on the corner of LaSalle and Michigan streets, downtown. The South Shore is still in operation while the Grand Trunk line along with its tracks on Western Avenue is long gone.

There were saloons, but when Gipp arrived on the downtown scene they were fronted by cigar stores and lunch counters — a facade for "speakeasies" in the back rooms. George Hull and Mike Calnon bought a saloon at 112 South Michigan Street in 1905 and it became a Notre Dame student hangout from that time on. Hullie and Mike's was a favorite downtown hangout of Notre Dame students because of reasonably priced food, a spot to place bets and a "Grid Graph," which was a background of glass or wood with demarcations of a football field. As the play by play account of the game came in over the wire, symbols were hand-moved to denote the advance of the ball. The Oliver Hotel was first to use that system and Hullie's adopted it upon learning of its use by the Oliver.

If Hullie and Mike's was a favorite spot for Notre Dame students, it really wasn't one for Gipp. He did frequent it in his freshman year, but after that it was only for important pool tournaments, big poker pots and perhaps a personal challenge with a bet on the line. One reason for George eschewing Hullie and Mike's was the very fact that it drew Notre Dame students. Seniors only, at Notre Dame, were allowed to go into town on school days during the week. They had to be on campus by ten p.m. with lights out for everyone at eleven. Students who were not seniors sometimes sneaked off campus and got back before curfew. Rockne, Gus Dorais, Hunk Anderson, Pete Bahan and Gipp had done this occasionally.

Hullie and Mike's drew the scrutiny of the Prefect of Discipline, Father James Gallaghan, who patrolled the downtown streets to nab any curfew breakers. Those caught were "campused," which meant the denial of the privilege of going into town for a certain period of time. This tough policy existed well into Father Theodore Hesburgh's presidency, which began in 1952.

While Gipp risked expulsion, if caught, by frequenting off-limits establishments such as Goldie Mann's and the Tokio Dance Hall, a dime-a-dance facility on Main Street, he certainly didn't want to chance getting caught breaking curfew at Hullie and Mike's, where the odds were greater to be seen by the Prefect. Besides, the monetary returns were usually larger at Goldie's than at Hullie's and worth the risk.

Father Gallaghan had difficulty trying to patrol those establishments because they had back alley exits. Also, Goldie Mann gave orders to his workers not to allow Father Gallaghan to enter and tarry without buying cigars up front or a drink in the back room. If Father Gallaghan showed some reluctance to move on, old Muggsy, an ex-pug bartending in back, would be summoned and rather than get a regulation growl at best and who knows what at worst — perhaps a public nuisance or trespass charge — Father Gallaghan would leave the premises. So his spying was casual and infrequent in that part of town.

Goldie Mann owned several establishments but the ones on South Main and South Michigan Streets were the rough ones, perhaps because the poker stakes and pool bets were in big money and sore losers with bad tempers were involved.

The Tokio Dance Hall was off limits because the good Fathers at Notre Dame assumed it was a den of iniquity because one had to pay a dime to dance with a female. "What else can you get there for money?" was the barbed question Father Cavanaugh, who made Tokio off limits, would offer when asked "why?" Charlie Davis, who would sneak out after class to play his trumpet in the band at the Tokio, said the Fathers were wrong. "It always was a good, clean place," said Charlie, who paid his way through four years at Notre Dame by playing at the Tokio. We shall revisit Charlie Davis a bit later in this book.

Jake Engle's speakeasy differed from the cigar store front speakeasies. His was a drug store selling patent medicines and cosmetics up front, a soda fountain counter and tables in the middle and the omnipresent "back room" in the rear. It was located on the corner of Michigan Street and Division Street. This last vestige of an era of speakeasies was razed in 1997.

South Bend wasn't a dry town when conversion into speakeasies began downtown. It had the Muessel Brewery and the nearby Mishawaka, Indiana-based, Kamms-Schellinger Brewery operating. Going dry was a defensive move in anticipation of things to come.

Probably a bit of background is necessary at this point. From as early as 1880 there had been a growing movement by churches and women's groups for legislation to bar the manufacture, sale and consumption of alcoholic beverages and by 1916, 24 states had passed prohibitory laws. The remainder of the states had local option and only three had no liquor-prohibiting laws.

With our entry into World War I in 1917 and Congress being goaded by the Prohibitionist movement, a law forbidding the manufacture of all liquors except beer and wine was passed. Politically sensitive lawmakers said the law prohibiting the manufacture and sales of hard liquor was necessary to preserve grain for the war effort. Prior to that law, a resolution was passed by Congress for a national prohibition amendment to the Federal constitution and ratification, requiring the approval of three-fourths of the states, was underway. That was done and Congress in 1919 passed the Volstead Act over the President's veto. The Volstead Act set the maximum amount of alcohol content allowed in non-intoxicating drinks. Enforcement provisions were included in the law. A short reprieve occurred when the law and amendment were challenged in the courts. In June of 1920, the U. S. Supreme Court upheld the validity of the 18th Amendment and the Volstead Act. Total Prohibition was now a reality.

South Bend started remodeling downtown saloons into cigar store speakeasies long before the congressional act barring manufacture and sale of hard liquor and the ratification of a national prohibition on all alcoholic beverages.

In 1908, Studebaker Brothers Company acquired the Everett-Metzger-Flaunders Company of Detroit that handled business assets and sales strategies. Upon the buyout agreement being fully consummated, involving a stock tradeoff, the combine became the Studebaker Corporation in 1911 and its Detroit experts were authorized to make decisions for the company.

When Henry Ford introduced assembly line production in 1905, many of the workers he had were immigrants from Europe with an agrarian background. The speed of a moving assembly line, and the monotony of doing the same operation over and over in a 10 hour day, drove many workers to drink. While drinking was quite a problem in every city in the country, in Detroit it was of epidemic proportions.

You can't run a factory when a man doesn't show up for work or if he does show up but is half drunk and can't do the job properly. Henry Ford had them fired on the spot. He had a squad entering homes at supper time almost like a SWAT team and if there was wine on the table, the man was fired in his own home. Just think of the deluge of law suits that would be filed if it happened today!

Ford supported all congressional candidates financially if they were for prohibition. In 1915 he had the city of Detroit close all its saloons. This is what worried South Bend saloon owners. Upon hearing what happened in Detroit and knowing South Bend was a similarly industrialized city, with Detroit people in charge of manufacturing policy at the Studebaker Corporation, they took measures before local industry could pressure them to close the saloons. Saloons became cigar stores and snack shops with pool and cards in the back rooms.

Goldie Mann was ahead of the pack. He was thinking in terms of total prohibition eventually coming in with the ratification of the 18th Amendment. In the back rooms, Goldie put a hole in the floor for a trap that had a narrow ladder and a playground slide going into the basement, the slide being a way of disposing of boxed and tubbed liquor in the main floor bar.

To hide the trap door, there was a card table over it. The floor was covered with butcher's sawdust. There were a lot of tobacco chewers around in those days and many missed hitting the spittoon, hence the sawdust.

South Bend had two hospitals — St. Joseph's and Epworth. In 1920, Healthwin, a tuberculosis hospital, opened its doors. And yes, South Bend had at least two brothels operating openly. According to old timers, one was directly across from the train depot on South Street and the other did business on Division Street.

There were 16 hotels in South Bend in Gipp's time, but all were small except for the Oliver, which was six stories high. The Oliver House, a two story hotel was razed in 1898 and the new Oliver was built on that land. The new Oliver opened its doors with a gala celebration on December 21, 1899, ten days short of the new century. The management invited prominent people to the affair not only from South Bend, but Northern Indiana and Southern Michigan, as well. Arriving carriages received valet service with an attendant opening their doors and assisting occupants as they exited. Valet service was given with a numbered claim ticket for each carriage. The Oliver was called the finest hotel built in America and the owners were determined that from its first impression on, it would live up to that accolade.

The J. D. Oliver family spared no money in making the hotel first-rate. It featured the latest technological advancements — it generated its own electricity; its own water supply was furnished by two artesian wells in the basement and there was refrigeration for food storage and ice making machines. Laundry machinery in the basement, steam heat, hot and cold running water in each room were some of the hotel's features. It was also fireproof.

The interior lobby, banquet room and dining room were of palatial splendor. Mosaic and terra cotta tiles, imported marble, East India mahogany, murals and tapestry accented the architectural design of the interior. The ornamental details resembled French Renaissance while the exterior design had Bedford limestone and Roman brick comparable to Italian Renaissance features.

The Oliver's facilities were to be available not only for the hotel's guests, but also for all the social strata of the community. There were telegraph offices, a barbershop, beauty parlor, ticket office, lavatories, pool rooms and a Turkish bath. A bank occupied a section of the building fronting the corner of Washington and Main Street.

This was the same Oliver Hotel that Gipp occupied some 17 years later. It remained just as elegant then as it was when its doors were first opened.

# GIPP'S OFF CAMPUS VENUES
# AND ACTIVITIES

As a freshman, Gipp couldn't readily adjust to campus life and didn't particularly care to mix with the younger students. He was almost always alone in the recreation room, shooting pool by himself. His teammate-to-be, Walter Miller, said that he watched Gipp many times knock about 80-90 balls into the pockets without a miss and without saying a word to anyone. When he got to know South Bend, he decided to try his skill in the downtown pool halls of the speakeasies.

Gipp did not have many close friends. Although he had a friendly disposition and a good sense of humor, he was quite withdrawn. His best friends on campus were Hunk Anderson and Ojay Larson. In South Bend, he really had one friend who could be called close and that was Johnny Jegier.

Johnny Jegier played football for a South Bend independent team that was actually a pre-NFL pro team of that era called the Arrows. The Kamms and Schellinger Brewing Company sponsored the team and paid the players, which was unusual for 1919. The players usually relied on gate receipts if playing in an enclosed baseball park with the diamond converted into a gridiron. They also got money from opponents' guarantees, personal bets and sideline hat collections on the field of an open park.

In the game lineups, because the Polish "J" is pronounced like an English "Y," Jegier's name would appear in phonetic spellings — Yeager, Yeahgar or Yager. Jager also was another way the name appeared. His relatives owned a soda pop bottling company on South Bend's west side and he had access to a panel truck and he owned an old car in which, at times, he transported Gipp, mainly to outlying towns such as Mishawaka and Elkhart for poker and pool. Jegier preferred playing poker over pool, so he would watch Gipp's pool expertise as he "cleaned" the tables of balls and his rivals' pockets of money.

Sometimes they would go to one of the many dances that were run during the week in parish halls or by fraternal and private clubs. As for the dances at the Oliver Hotel, Gipp usually had a date for those and the girl he would escort more than likely was the young lady who worked in the Oliver beauty shop.

While attending Notre Dame, Gipp played in only one pro football game. Because of that and because my dad, a South Bend Arrows player, played in it with Gipp and five other Notre Damers, I feel I'm obligated to give full details.

The South Bend Arrows in 1919 were coached at

night, three times a week, by Rockne's assistant coach, Gus Dorais. Gus needed a line coach, so he gave the job to Notre Dame's center, Edward "Slip" Madigan. Besides assisting Rockne in football, Dorais was also the basketball and baseball coach for Notre Dame. In order to prepare Notre Dame for the coming basketball season, Dorais gave up the Arrows job with two games remaining and Madigan took over the coaching job without help.

Playing in a pro game would have brought immediate suspension from athletics or expulsion from school for a Notre Damer if caught, and the criteria as to which punishment applied was "admission and contrition." If a player denied playing in a Sunday afternoon football game for money and the person reporting it was one of reliability, the Notre Dame player was expelled from school. Two future pro football hall of famers were kicked out of school for that reason — Curley Lambeau in 1918 and George Trafton in 1919. Notre Dame, however, did allow its players to coach football for money. That was considered legitimate employment.

Coaching South Bend pro teams by Notre Dame players started in Rockne's senior year. As a method of advertising, the Muessel Brewing Company in 1913 fielded a team of young players and asked Notre Dame's captain, Knute Rockne, to coach the team to the extent of his availability. Rockne coached the Brewers at St. Stephen School's playground on Thomas Street at night from Monday to midweek. In his first coaching effort, Rockne had an undefeated season, marred only by a tie with the South Bend Century Club.

Madigan, who hailed from Ottawa, Illinois, was now the Arrows sole coach after Dorais departed. He had been contacted by George Kitteringham of Rockford, a relative by a family member's marriage, who asked Slip to recruit some Notre Dame teammates to play sub rosa in a Rockford city championship game. The annual series of the winner of two out of three games being the champion began in 1916. The series was between the Grands and the Rockford Amateur Athletic Club teams. The "Amateur" was in the founding name, but by 1919 there were no true amateurs playing for the club.

Madigan responded well with his recruiting. Gipp was in the backfield with Dutch Bergman, Fred Slackford and Joe Brandy. Bernie Kirk was at end and Slip was the center. Also in the line Madigan brought in two of his South Bend Arrows tackles, John "Curley" Klosinski (my father) and Tommy (Grzegorek) Gore. Because there would be three Rockford linemen playing, Slip felt he needed someone in the line who knew the Notre Dame signals and plays, which when called, would have to be relayed by a coded gesture to the two guards and end of the Grands team. In the Notre Dame system of that era, the quarterback called the plays on the line of scrimmage without going into a huddle. These days, the so-called audibles are generally used toward the end of the half or near the end of the game to conserve time.

As the series began, the Grands won the first game on a last-minute pass from quarterback George Kitteringham, who also was the club's manager and coach. After that game, the rumors around town were spreading that the A.A.C. team was going to "load up" in the second game with ringers from the pro ranks, some being ex-collegians. Walde of Purdue playing for the Fort Wayne Friars and Don Oliver from Illinois, starring for the Chicago Cardinals, as well as the Falcon brothers with the Hammond Bobcats were mentioned frequently in the rumor. The Rockford A.A.C. felt that this had to be done to stay alive in the short series.

Kitteringham wasn't about to be torpedoed by a bunch of pro football ringers. When he contacted Madigan, he promised two hundred dollars for each Notre Dame player who would play. He also said he could double that if a player chose to bet on his own team to win. To digress for a moment for a bit of background as to what was in store for the Notre Damers. After World War I ended, many ex-soldiers without a job, but no longer bumpkins, having been schooled in the vices of the world while in the Army and in Europe, became professional gamblers. Gambling and gamblers thrived and even invaded major league baseball's locker rooms.

The Chicago White Sox of 1919 going into the World Series against the Cincinnati Reds were then called the greatest baseball team of all time with players such as Shoeless Joe Jackson, Chick Gandil, Happy Felsch, Eddie Cicotte, Claude Williams, Buck Weaver, Fred McMullin and Swede Risberg in the Sox lineups.

Before the start of the World Series, the odds were heavily in favor of the White Sox until two days before the first game, when they began slipping. Then, on the eve of the Series start, the sports world was stunned as the odds swung to favor Cincinnati. Both the gamblers and the cops knew that the "fix" was in.

Things got hot in Chicago immediately after the Sox lost the Series. The police in every Chicago ward made it miserable for the gamblers, hustlers and racketeers, arresting them on "suspicion" of minor or imaginary infractions. It looked like a lawyers convention in the Chicago police stations as they bailed out their clients. According to Hunk Anderson, a pool and card player named Cheesy Schultz told Gipp that he was in jail and bailed out three times in one day. Gipp played pool and cards with some of the displaced hustlers and gamblers who came to South Bend to get some "action." As soon as things got hot after the Series loss by the Sox, these police "targets" decided to get their action where the situation was "cool." Many chose outlying but promising areas such as South Bend and Rockford. The A.A.C.- Grands game was an ideal plum for the displaced Chicago gamblers.

Notre Dame played Purdue that Saturday in West Lafayette, and when the team arrived in South Bend after the game, it was late, about 1 a.m. Sunday morning. The six players, with their gear stuffed inside their football pants, broke off at the train depot. They took cabs to the other R.R. station for a train to Chicago. From Chicago, a change of trains to Rockford made the trip sleepless and very tiring, especially after getting banged up by a big Purdue line. Although Notre Dame won 33 to 13, it was a bruising battle.

About noon on game day, the South Bend Arrow tackles were already at the Kishwaukee Park when the Notre Dame group arrived with Kitteringham. The Notre Damers were told to pick a black and orange jersey that fit from a pile stacked on a bench. As for the official lineups, Kitteringham used the names of his displaced Grands players for the newcomers in the line. But for the backfield, where the visibility was focused and greater, Kitteringham came up with aliases: Brandy was "Boyd," Bergman was "Smith," Slackford was

"Scone" and left halfback Gipp was "Baker." The decision in the locker room conference between Kitteringham, Madigan and quarterback Brandy, was to run the ends as much as possible in order to use the speed of Gipp and Bergman. Slackford was to be sent into the middle when short yardage was needed. On the opening kickoff, Kirk made a short return. Gipp, called to run the end on the first play, had to cut over tackle because the Grands guard was slow in pulling out, and he burst out into the open for 30 yards, being knocked out of bounds by the safety. The play was called back and a penalty assessed. That became the scenario for the game...Gipp and Bergman making long gains and the play being called back. There was no doubt in the minds of the Grands and their fans that the officials were bought off by the gamblers. Still, the Grands managed to reach the A.A.C. 28 yard line. Being stalled by Slackford losing a yard over center, a Gipp gain nullified by a penalty plus two incomplete passes, a field goal attempt by a rushed Gipp went wide. The Rockford Gazette summarized the first quarter: "The ball see-sawed back and forth with the Grands receiving a penalty on nearly every other down."

In the second quarter, end Thissel of the A.A.C. dropped off the line and intercepted a Gipp pass in Grands territory. Three running plays into the line were stopped by the Arrows tackles and rather than try a field goal, the A.A.C. punted for the coffin corner.

The Grands couldn't move the ball, being hampered by the usual penalties. After an unfruitful series for each team, the Grands found the needed spark. In spite of penalties, Gipp ran and passed the ball to the A.A.C. 10-yard-line.

On a Bergman delay, Gipp passed to Bergman in the end zone for a score and kicked the extra point for a 7-0 lead for the Grands.

An onside kick was recovered by tackle Klosinski on the 50-yard-line, but a first down pass of Gipp's was intercepted when the intended target, Kirk, making a cut, slipped and fell. The interception brought the ball to the Grands 40 yard line.

With time running out in the first half, the A.A.C. lined up for a field goal, but the Notre Dame secondary of the Grands, thinking it was a fake because of the distance, played the defense normal. It was a kick, however, and kicker Ericson being harassed by charging linemen, sliced a line drive to the left into Dutch Bergman's hands and he ran 75 yards unmolested for a score. Gipp added the extra point as the half ended with the Grands leading 14-0.

Just as the half ended, Kitteringham confronted referee Holderness, umpire Gardiner and head linesman Graves and accused them of doing the gamblers' bidding. Statistics showed that the Grands were penalized 125 yards in that first half. Angry Grands fans jeered the officials as they retreated to the safety of their locker room.

The first half was close but the Grands' last minute drive engineered by Gipp plus the half-ending score by Bergman on a lucky break gave the tiring Notre Damers some breathing room. The second half was even closer than the first.

The Grands' Notre Dame backfield lost some of its spryness and looked tired, having little or no sleep on the train, playing a bruising game for the second day in a row and wasting energy on plays that were being called back because of a penalty. Gipp and Bergman were being stopped effectively. Slackford had trouble hitting the middle for a gain and Brandy gained very little on sneaks and keepers. It was evident that the two regular Grands guards weren't of much help to Madigan at center. The Grands seem to be getting weaker and the A.A.C. was getting stronger and the tide began to turn.

Brandy fumbled a kick into the end zone and luckily fell on it in for a safety, thus preventing a touchdown because a sea of blue and white jerseys thundered on top of him. The two points on the board awakened the A.A.C. supporters. The after-safety punt by Gipp sailed to Oliver on the A.A.C. 25-yard-line and he brought it back for 10 yards, being hit and downed by the Arrows tackles who seemed to be the freshest ones on the Grands team. It was late in the fourth quarter but the A.A.C. had momentum.

Ericson began throwing passes over a charging Grands line, reaching the Grands' nine yard line. A fake plunge into the line made Grands safety Joe Brandy go for the fake and before Joe could recover, Ericson lofted a pass over his head to end Thissel for the score. The extra point made it 14-9 and the A.A.C. followers were delirious, as must have been the gamblers.

In the huddle before the kickoff, Gipp told Brandy: "Cut out calling end runs, Joe. Dutch and I are getting smeared without much gain and we're getting awful tired. Use our tackle and pass plays. We've got to start moving the ball or we're gonna get our butts kicked."

After the kickoff, which Slackford fumbled but recovered, Brandy called Gipp's number off tackle and Gipp responded with an 18 yard run. As he got up after being tackled, Gipp looked at the officials for a call. No penalty! The play wasn't called back. Maybe Kitteringham's talk with the officials at halftime worked. However, up to that point there were no long runs in the second half, so perhaps this one caught the officials napping. Also they may have been wary of the consequences if they continued so obviously, because Gipp again carried for a good gain and then on a reverse from Bergman, "workhorse" Gipp gained 14 yards. Then a pass to Brandy coming out of the backfield brought the ball deep into the A.A.C. territory.

To give Gipp a rest, Brandy called his own and Slackford's numbers for short gains. Gipp then went back to pass but a guard broke through, and rather than throw a bad pass, Gipp plunged into the line for four yards, which wasn't enough for a first down. Gipp then calmly kicked an 18 yard field goal making the score 17-9 and putting the game out of reach for the A.A.C. with only a minute left to play.

It was fortunate for the players that news of this game had not reached Notre Dame authorities. When the Notre Dame bunch arrived in the locker room, the displaced Grands players were there too, and decided to get even by going to the A.A.C. sideline and telling Coach Tony Haines that his team was playing Notre Dame. As for the Notre Dame/Arrows group, they showered and dressed and before they were ready to leave, Kitteringham brought $400 for each of the eight men. Coaches Kitteringham and Haines handled the bets for the players.

An editorial in the Rockford Register Gazette addressed the situation: "Following Sunday's game, the second of a series heralded for the city championship, local football fandom has been wandering through a maze of speculation concerning the identity of Grands football players who put over a victory on the A.A.C.

"It was no ordinary bunch of gridiron talent that had been imported for the fray. That much was evident after the smooth working Grands backfield had been in operation for two plays. The backs played too well not to have been in operation all season, and they maintained this pace through all quarters, showing some of the niftiest football that has been seen on a local field in many a day!

"Claims were made by the A.A.C. camp that the Grands for the greater part were made up of University regulars disputing the middle west championship with Illinois.

"A.A.C. men insist that a regular varsity backfield, the regular center and right end was used. This sextet, reinforced by five other players, not over three of whom were Rockford men, proved too fast for the blue and white. The only wonder is that the score was not of greater proportion, and many neutral fans along the sidelines marveled that coach Haines' aggregation could hold the Grands to as low a count as it did.

"As far as settling city honors, the scrap did nothing of the kind, for not over 50 percent of the talent engaged were Rockford products."

In that Rockford game the gamblers operated in the background. In South Bend, Gipp had experienced personal confrontations with gamblers and a variety of unsavory characters. Johnny Jegier told how he, Ila "Babe" Shafer and Leo Sobieralski saw Gipp handle a Chicago pool shark. It was at

Goldie Mann's place not far from the Grand Trunk and New York Central depots, which made it convenient for the Chicago gamblers to ply their trade at Goldie's when they got off the train.

While Babe and Leo were eating the bar's freebie sandwiches, Jegier and Gipp played a friendly game of pool. Gipp saw that a well groomed hustler was watching him play. He eased off on his buddy Johnny by missing some easy shots but still won clumsily by calculated intent.

The hustler then challenged Gipp and Gipp accepted. Gipp lost about four games at five bucks per and the hustler suggested they play for higher stakes "so that you can win some of your money back." Gipp did agree and won about three to the hustler's one game. The ante was raised to a hundred dollars. And now Gipp got serious. The hustler kept losing to Gipp, who cleaned the table off after the break in his last effort without the shark getting a shot. The hustler was angry and began swearing and making accusations.

According to Jegier, the guy accused Gipp of being unfair by playing possum about his skills in order to lure the hustler into playing for higher stakes. When Gipp replied that all was fair in love and "pool," the guy took brass knuckles from his hanging-coat pocket and came at him swinging. Gipp ducked under a roundhouse right, and as he came upward, he took his cue stick with both hands on the ends, stuck it under the hustler's chin and drove him up against the wall. Muggsy, the bartender and former boxer, observed the squabble and was there almost at the moment that Gipp had pinned the guy against the wall. He whacked the guy with a leaded sap and the hustler fell to the floor. Muggsy asked

Gipp if he got the last stake he won and when Gipp said no, Muggsy took a hundred from what was left of a dwindled bankroll, and tossed the guy out into the street and his coat after him. They never saw the hustler again.

Jim Beach, in his first book about Notre Dame, wrote about Peaches Donnelly teaming up with Gipp as both rented a suite of rooms at the Oliver for poker games. Actually Donnelly rented a room adjacent to Gipp's room, which was rent free for Gipp's house-player services. Peaches was a promotor of card and dice games and prevailed upon Gipp to become a partner. Gipp preferred to gamble solo but he did agree to be a partner with Donnelly.

The union was short termed. My cousin, Gene Basker, told how his father, my uncle Frank Koszewski, came in early Monday morning to open the Turkish baths in the Oliver Hotel basement, only to see a couple of broken chairs, lamps and a dresser mirror piled near the bathhouse door for disposal. In questioning the janitor, Frank was told that the debris came from Gipp's room where there had been a poker game with a couple of gamblers. When Frank bumped into Gipp that same Monday, he didn't see a scratch on him and thought to himself that either Gipp was not involved or if he was, he sure handled himself well. Later Frank found out from the hotel's night manager that Gipp actually broke up the fight and made amends. Donnelly was caught cheating. There was some chair throwing as evidenced by the hole in the wall and the broken mirror. Peaches was bloodied up, as was one of the gamblers. It seems that Peaches had a case of sealed card decks in his room that were specially manufactured for him. These marked cards were the ones he furnished whenever he hosted a game.

Needless to say, Donnelly was kicked out of the Oliver on the spot and Gipp was given another room.

Playing cards and pool wasn't the only recreational activity of Gipp's. He knew that Hunk did not receive money from home because Hunk's sister was attending a teacher's college and she got financial priority from his folks. So when baseball season got into full swing, it was Eddie "Goat" Anderson who arranged for Gipp to play in Sunday baseball games and Gipp naturally got Goat to see that there was an opening for a catcher and that would be Hunk. They'd play in nearby little towns that had a crucial game to win for the home town honor plus the ever present "pot" that went to the winner. Towns like Bristol, Waukarusa, Nappanee and Argos were some of the teams Gipp and Hunk got involved with through the courtesy of Goat Anderson. The money Hunk earned helped him achieve a modest social life and buy personal necessities. Depending on the importance of the game, Hunk and Gipp earned pay that hovered from five dollars to fifteen. Gipp would tell Hunk to meet him early Sunday morning at Jimmie and Goat's place only to find George Gipp was a "no show." Gipp would turn up though when Goat told him they'd get $15 to play.

A humorous incident revealed by Hunk occurred when both played a Sunday game for Nappanee. It was a small baseball park in which they played with a miniature grandstand in back of the home plate screen. The roof covered only half of approximately 12 tiers of seats. Apparently that was where they sold refreshments. There was some seating along the first and third baselines but in the outfield, there was no seating and no fence separating a farmer's herd of grazing cows from the ballfield. More often than not, a cow or two strayed away from the farmer's confines and grazed in the outfield during the week. During game day, the farmer kept his cows near the barnhouse for he was a rabid baseball fan and supporter of his home team.

Gipp, in chasing a fly ball for the final out of the inning, stepped into a splatter of cow manure that still had a generous amount of freshness. As the team got back to the bench for its turn at bat, everybody started sniffing and looking at each other. Hunk with his nose sniffing up a storm, yelled, "All right...who went in his pants?" Finally Gipp realized that it was his shoe that had the stuff, so he walked off to clean it off as best he could.

When Gipp got back, Hunk started sniffing around Gipp to check if Gipp did a good job. Before Hunk could say anything, Gipp blurted out, trying to suppress a smile, "Look, 'Big Nose', I did the best I could with what I had. There's a cigar and a pack of cigarettes in my jacket hanging on a nail in the corner. Light one of them up and stop sniffing me like a dog in heat."

Gipp didn't always play pool and cards. Across the street from his hotel was the Oliver Opera House, which saw less of opera in post war South Bend and more of moving pictures and vaudeville. He would take in a movie and a stage show on many occasions and next day describe to Hunk some of the funny routines performed on stage. Sometimes he went to the Elks Club, which usually featured boxing's newcomers. The big pro fights were held at the Auditorium which also served as a movie house. Besides the Oliver Opera House and

Auditorium, Gipp would try to attend a movie — at times a matinee — if there was a Western playing at the Blackstone, the Orpheum, LaSalle, or Castle theaters.

Gipp loved to dance. The Jules Stein orchestra usually got gigs at the Oliver Hotel Cafe Room. There were dances also held in the Tapestry Room and the Ballroom, sometimes in competition with each other. The Oliver believed in alternating different orchestras, so Stein freelanced the local fraternal clubs' dance halls. Gipp asked Hunk to go with him to the Kosciuszko Club...yes, on Kosciuszko Street, where Jules Stein's orchestra was playing that night.

"Ain't that a Polish Club — what are we going to do there?" asked Hunk.

"Do what they do. Remember, Hunk, when in Rome do as the Romans do," replied Gipp. Then he went on to explain that he was actually going there because Stein's orchestra was playing and that he loved Stein's music. Gipp would sometimes hum a catchy tune under his breath while waiting his turn to shoot in pool. Research shows that the big hits of the season, according to record and music sheet and piano roll sales, were tenor John McCormack's "When You and I Were Young," "Whispering," by John Steele and "The Japanese Sandman," by Olive Kline.

Just as Gipp and Hunk arrived at the club, Stein had finished playing a standard tune and two girls who had danced with each other were coming off the dance floor. Gipp said to Hunk, "Let's split 'em up and it's your choice."

Hunk, trying to be funny, used a Gipp expression, "That's Jake with me."

Just then, as they were walking toward the sitting

girls, Stein began playing a polka.

"Hell, I don't know how to do that," complained Hunk.

"You just hop, skip and whirl," advised Gipp. Both asked the girls to dance and Gipp wasted no time to get "jumpin'" as he swept the girl off the floor in rhythm with the music. Hunk hesitatingly got on the floor with his partner but he said that he explained to her midway through the tune that he couldn't do the polka and asked her if she'd care to sit and she agreed. Hunk said she was as relieved as he was and they watched Gipp put on an excellent performance while the orchestra segued into another polka.

Coming off the floor, Hunk noticed that Gipp was limping slightly and surmised that his bad leg bothered him.

"I didn't know you could polka so good, George," said Hunk as he greeted him coming off the floor.

"Neither did I,"replied Gipp

"Oh, he's a marvelous dancer," chimed in Gipp's near breathless partner.

No, they didn't escort the sisters home. Just as they were about to ask, the girls' "big" brother appeared to do just that.

Gipp was a good dancer. He won a gold watch for dancing in a contest held at the Oliver Hotel in the Tapestry Room on the mezzanine floor. His partner was the young lady who worked in the Oliver beauty salon and she won a pearl necklace. This was at a time Gipp was having problems — which began in the summer — with his Indianapolis girl friend, Iris Trippeer.

The Gipp dance triumph was reported by Gene Kessler in his October 20, 1920 Tribune column, "Serving the

Punch." The contest was promoted by dance instructor Charlie Gates, but he was only one of three judges, thus adding legitimacy to the decision. Jules Stein played the Tapestry Room that night and made the award presentation.

Gipp wasn't an easy fellow to know, but he took kindly towards the young fellow who idolized him and tried to help by doing things for him. Herb Juliano called such a person a "stooge;" I. I. Probst, a 1926 Notre Dame graduate and columnist for the Notre Dame Magazine at age 97, says "Man Friday." Others call him an "assister," or "gofer." In South Bend, as previously mentioned, Notre Dame student Charlie Davis, class of '21, racked the balls up and ran gofer errands for Gipp at Hullie and Mike's and Goldie Mann's. He did this for Gipp while waiting to go to work. As mentioned previously, Charlie played trumpet at the Tokio Dance Hall, the dime a dance place that was off limits to Notre Dame students, but Charlie never got caught by the Prefect of Discipline. He managed to find time to play in the school's orchestra, as well.

Charlie Davis led an interesting musical life after graduating from Notre Dame. He formed his own band, toured a bit and at one time or another there were several future music greats who played in his band. Red Nichols, pianist Hoagy Carmichael, Bix Beiderbecke — all stinted in Charlie's band and singer and later movie star Dick Powell joined the band for weekly radio broadcasts. In the larger Indiana Theater in Indianapolis, Davis' band of 19 musicians backed up vaudeville revues that had many stars appearing, such as Ginger Rogers, Ray Bolger, Ethel Merman, Ted Lewis, Eddie Cantor, Bill "Bojangles" Robinson, Bob Hope and others of that era. To keep a promise to his wife, Miriam

— as a condition of marriage — to play 10 years and quit, Charlie Davis eventually left the music business.

While an article on Davis in the Notre Dame Magazine entitled, "Wasn't That a Time" by Joe Carey as well as a book by Davis titled, "That Band from Indiana," mention Charlie "stooging" for Gipp, there is no mention of Charlie ever seeing Gipp at the Tokio Dance Hall although Charlie played there nightly. True, on a crowded dance floor, a trumpet player probably would not notice an individual dancing. But if Gipp was such a frequent visitor as had been said of him by some authors, Davis could have bumped into Gipp during the intermission that gave the dancing girls and the band a chance to catch their breath, as well as for the male customers a time to replenish their ticket supply.

There was one other South Bend "stooge" that hung around Gipp when George played pool at the Oliver Hotel. In his book, "Notre Dame Odyssey," Herb Juliano mentions a stooge who was a midget nicknamed "Jinks." Actually Jinks was Eddie Borkowski, who lived with his parents on Walnut Street, a block away from where my grandma lived at that time. Eddie Borkowski was one of my dad's friends when they were kids. Dad said that Eddie was a strong kid for his size.

As a youngster Eddie had gotten a job at the Oliver Hotel as a bell hop and had no other job during his lifetime nor did he want any other. He was a likeable fellow and apparently Gipp appreciated his presence. It was after Eddie finished his shift that he grabbed a quick sandwich and hustled down the Oliver basement when he knew Gipp would be there, playing pool.

Probst's "Man Friday" for Gipp on campus was Joe

Donaldson. Actually, it was in the locker room Joe managed to do things for Gipp. Donaldson tried out for football as a freshman, but his lack of size and ability cut his football career short. Knute Rockne liked Joe's spirit and felt that spirit around the team, even if it came from an equipment manager, was a plus for Notre Dame. So when Rock asked Joe if he'd like to be a manager, Joe readily accepted .

Joe — class of '22 — was a CEO of his own company. He passed away in March of 1999 but until then he kept in contact with Probst via letter and telephone. Probst learned new details about Gipp's change in demeanor in 1920 and Gipp's injury in the Indiana game of 1920 from Joe.

# AN AFFAIR TO REMEMBER — OR FORGET

ecause there were no one-on-one interviews of George Gipp to probe deeper into his personal life as reporters are prone to do, much of what we know about him came from his family and close friends and usually at a time many years removed from the day of his death. The accuracy and details of some events in his life are clouded by the passage of time that plays tricks on the memories of the best of us recollectors.

Not much was known about the ladies in his life, but as he approached the age of 25 he did get serious about an Indianapolis young woman named Iris Trippeer and did contemplate matrimony. He wasn't aware of what was in store for him in his romance with Iris in an acquaintanceship that lasted approximately nine months.

Before enrolling at Notre Dame Gipp had a girlfriend

named Hazel in Laurium and he did go out on dates with her. In South Bend, he occasionally dated the young blond who worked in the Oliver Hotel beauty salon. But neither young woman affected him as did Iris.

Gipp was quite handsome, and when his picture appeared in the local papers he received letters addressed "In care of Notre Dame" from young ladies seeking to meet him. Some asked for dates with him. This was at a time when Victorian "propriety" still ruled, unlike the bobby socks or rock star era, where "groupies" are more or less the norm.

Iris Trippeer was a mystery woman in Gipp's life and for several years very little was known about her. She was said to have come from a middle class family that was socially prominent and active. According to early information, her father was an Indianapolis attorney of Irish descent, a devout Roman Catholic who hated Protestants (which Gipp was) and despised athletes. As for Iris, she was described as a beautiful, demure, intelligent, soft spoken and sensitive young woman. That was the extent of the information anyone had been able to obtain about Iris up to several years ago.

Then, in an article by Scott Ostler in the Los Angeles Times dated November 25, 1982, a woman named Victoria Adams emerged as the granddaughter of Iris Trippeer. Ms. Adams apparently was the impetus for Ostler's article. There weren't many details about Iris, but the article said Iris was in Gipp's hospital room on the 13th of December when in actuality no one but family, priests and Rockne was allowed to see Gipp as he was lapsing into comas with the end not far off.

The Ostler story stated that as Gipp was in his final hours on the 13th, he gave Iris his miniature gold football that the undefeated 1919 Western Champion Notre Dame team members received from Knute Rockne. Rockne had asked Father Burns to give that added honor to the players but Burns said there were no discretionary funds available and the usual monogram sweaters were sufficient, so Rockne paid for the those gold watch charms out of his own pocket.

Marie Anderson, Hunk's wife, disputed the story about the gold football charm that was supposed to have been given to Iris on Gipp's death bed. I had sent a copy of the Ostler article to her and in a subsequent phone call to my wife Sheila, to inform her of Marie's new address and phone number, Marie made it a point to talk to me about the article.

Marie told me that she and Hunk double dated with Gipp and Iris several times. During that time, Marie was attending college, studying to be a teacher, and Iris was a working girl in Indianapolis, employed by the Indiana State Public Service Commission as a secretary. A requirement for that job was a knowledge of shorthand and that subject was available with other vocational studies in Indiana high schools. However, to work in a state government job up to World War II required political pull.

It was on a double date that Marie noticed the gold football on a gold chain around Iris' neck. She remembered that vividly, because after seeing it on Iris, days later Marie asked Hunk for his gold football and Hunk refused to give it to her.

Further holes in the Ostler story were evident by the dates in the article. Rockne — not knowing that Iris and Gipp had broken up and she now had a husband, as Gipp found out on the eve of the Indiana game — sent a telegram on the

30th of November to Iris saying that Gipp was improving and Gipp wanted to see her. Rockne could had saved a lot of embarrassment for Gipp had he known what had happened between them. According to the granddaughter in a subsequent story by John U. Bacon that appeared in the January 5, 1997 edition of the Detroit News, she said that Iris finally found time and did come to see Gipp in the hospital on the 7th of December. In Ostler's story it was the 13th and Gipp died in the early morning hours of the 14th.

When Gipp was hospitalized, he asked the nun in charge of depositing patient's valuables for safe keeping to give all his valuables to Hunk to hold. The valuables included a gold pocket watch that had a chain on it, to which at one time the watch charm football had been attached. The gold football that Iris had received from Gipp currently is mounted on a bracelet that Victoria Adams has, according to the Ostler story.

Some 15 years after the Ostler story appeared, the granddaughter of Iris Trippeer resurfaced in the article about Gipp by Bacon in the Detroit News. It was a fair article that included the good side of Gipp as well as the bad side. In the article, Bacon not only quoted the granddaughter, whose name now was Victoria Phair (apparently Ms. Adams' married name), but also a niece named Gloria Trippeer Lyons.

Jim Beach, despite being physically handicapped and partially blind, continued to work on his book about Gipp. Beach had someone read him a copy of Bacon's article which I had sent him. Immediately I received a call from Beach asking me to write to Bacon to find out how we could get in touch with either one of Iris Trippeer's relatives. I wrote to Bacon and later Beach tried to talk with him on the phone at the newspaper in Detroit and then at his home in Ann Arbor. There was no response, which, ironically, was exactly the case when attempts to contact Ostler were made in 1982. Not one, but two newspaper writers turned out to be totally unresponsive with regard to articles they had written about Gipp and Iris.

Marie Anderson, who met and observed Iris Trippeer on her and Hunk's double dates with Gipp, pictured Iris completely the opposite of what has been written and said about her. Iris appears to have been a Dr. Jekyll and Mrs. Hyde. On their first double date, it was a dinner and dance outing. Hunk and Marie met Gipp and Iris in the lobby of the Oliver Hotel. Gipp made the introductions and the foursome went upstairs to the dining room. As they got to the top of the stairs — they could have used the elevator but didn't — Iris immediately began displaying affection by wrapping an arm around Gipp's neck and burying her neatly coiffed head into his chest. Walking behind them, Marie told me it appeared as if Gipp was dragging Iris and the expression on Gipp's face when he tried to turn and look at them was of total embarrassment. Iris released the half nelson hold as Gipp stopped to discuss seating sections with the maitre d', whom he knew by his first name. Incidentally, Marie said that on the double dates with Gipp, he was always a perfect gentleman. The granddaughter and the niece also said that Iris told them that Gipp was always a gentleman with perfect manners and total respect for women.

The menu was on the table at each seating and while Gipp began to assist the ladies with their seats, Hunk had already seated himself and began reading the dining fare. Marie said she was quite embarrassed. Gipp must have spoken to Hunk about it later, because on their next date and thereafter, Marie said Hunk always helped her with her chair.

Gipp's embarrassment didn't end at that point. As they were reading the menu, Iris got up, moved her chair close to Gipp and nuzzled him as he tried to read. Marie said that diners in the room stared at them and it was an uncomfortable spectacle. After all, this was 1919! One can excuse Iris somewhat, however, by pointing out that she was possibly getting a somewhat early start on the Roaring Twenties.

At the dance, it was the same scenario. On double dates, Iris seemed to ignore Marie although she did speak to Hunk. When Marie asked Iris if she wanted to go with her to the powder room, Iris declined, only to rise and go by herself when Marie returned.

Hunk said that Iris was "star struck" being out in public with a man about whom she was reading in her hometown newspaper. As for her actions, he thought she might have been jealous of Marie, because he knew Gipp described her to Iris prior to their first double date. Marie was attending college and she was a tall, beautiful, well proportioned blond. I saw a picture of her in that era in an album she showed my wife Sheila and me, and by today's standards...or any, for that matter, she would have been termed a "knockout."

On one double date, Gipp was invited by a prominent South Bend businessman to a party in the businessman's second home on Diamond Lake in Michigan. He told Gipp to bring as many close friends as he wanted. So Gipp borrowed a car and the four of them were on their way to have a good time. Marie said that she and Hunk were in the back seat, appropriately apart. In the front seat, however, Iris cozied up to Gipp so close that it impeded his shifting of gears because cars then had the shift rods coming up from the floor. Hunk said that none of the country roads were paved and there were pot holes and bumps all over a road more suitable for horses than cars.

Going around an undeveloped area of Diamond Lake, Gipp shifted gears and in so doing, hit Iris' leg very hard. As she pulled her legs away in reacting to the blow, the top of her tilted the other way and struck Gipp. This caused him to turn the steering wheel violently and it resulted in the car going down a sloping ditch and almost into the lake.

The girls had to get out and with Gipp behind the wheel and Hunk on bottom of the slope pushing, there was no progress because the wheels were spinning and creating a rut. So Gipp put the gear shift in neutral, shut the motor off and then, with both men pushing, they managed to get the car off the slope. The work for Hunk didn't end there. While standing partially on the slope he had to do the cranking to start the car. Gipp was trying to get a proper adjustment on the spark lever mounted on the steering wheel and Hunk kept slipping as he rotated the crank and it kicked back a couple of times. Finally Hunk dug his feet deep into the now loose soil and the spark adjustment was just right and the car started on his next try. Hunk said, "Hell, I don't think I ever worked so "goldamn" hard as I did that 20 minutes with that "#*.!%ing" car — and I used to chop railroad ties all day for firewood when I was a kid."

Hunk would answer questions about Gipp's love affair or his girl friends if he knew the answer, but he would never give information he knew without being asked. Marie, on the other hand, would volunteer what she knew.

Marie thought that both of the lovers weren't serious in their relationship because she thought Gipp knew he could never marry Iris. She didn't elaborate and my presumption was the difference of each other's religions as the reason for Marie saying so. On the other hand, Hunk thought that Iris and Gipp were madly in love and Gipp would have married her if he could. Marie did say that she knew a St. Mary's graduate who knew Iris, but she didn't say she learned anything about Trippeer from her.

Heartley "Hunk" Anderson passed away in April, 1979. Marie Martin Anderson, Hunk's beloved wife, passed away in June of 1998, one month short of her hundredth birthday.

Now for a shocker for those who have read the many books about Notre Dame football history which featured Gipp's romance with Iris Trippeer. As to the breakup of the relationship, the blame was totally placed on Gipp. The storyline was this: "Iris was a nice looking lady, in an upper class, and had a classically elite manner — she was a lady through and through." Gipp was a ne'er do well and a gambling clod who positively wouldn't meet her parents' approval.

Besides the objections of her parents to Iris marrying Gipp, her niece, Gloria Lyons, said that her aunt had second thoughts about marriage. Said Lyons: "My aunt was given pause because Gipp wasn't sure what he was going to do with himself after school. She wanted him to become a regular person with a regular job and he wasn't that kind of a person."

As usual, blame it all on the Gipper. Bash him, exaggerate, accuse him...he's vulnerable and proper game, you know.

Iris Trippeer from the time she met Gipp in South Bend until she broke the relationship for a reason that only she knew, was never serious about marrying Gipp and as George said after they broke up, she was making a fool out of him.

Jim Beach said she was a married but separated woman when she met Gipp. Jim seemed to believe her maiden name was Dunleavy and that Trippeer was her married name and that her husband's first name was Lewis. Beach further indicated that her father was an attorney from Mishawaka, a small Indiana city abutting South Bend, who received a political appointment to a state job in Indianapolis and the family moved there.

It has been written that Gipp visited Iris in Indianapolis daily. That's stretching the truth. She was a working girl who had to be on the job every morning. Gipp did visit on alternate weekends after the football season was over. Iris tried to keep their relationship secret and his Indianapolis visits and dates with her were confined to a perimeter which extended from the Claypool Hotel to a point designated by Iris. Her excuse to Gipp obviously could have been that she didn't want anyone to see them together because her parents disapproved of him although there is nothing on record that shows the parents ever met him, knew him or knew she dated him.

Soon after Gipp got into trouble by getting expelled, he became pretty well tied up waiting on a final decision regarding his fate at Notre Dame and contemplating alternatives. He had written Iris a letter and she failed to respond. During the summer school break, in June, Gipp and his buddy Pete Bahan went to Flint, Michigan to work at the General Motors plant and to play baseball for GM in a factory league. Gipp and Bahan went out on dates but it was Gipp's obsession for dancing more than a desire for female companionship that served as the reason for it.

Trying again, Gipp wrote one letter to Iris in late June and a follow-up letter in July, but both were unanswered. Around the first of August Gipp got a few days off from his job and went to Indianapolis to see Iris. Upon arriving and reaching her by phone at her job, Gipp then met her at their regular rendezvous in the Claypool Hotel. When Gipp returned to Flint he told Bahan that a problem Iris had with him had been straightened out. Apparently Iris' excuse for giving Gipp the silent treatment was his lack of direction for the future and that she didn't want to be part of it if he didn't set some goals.

Iris apparently was stringing him on because Gipp wasn't aware that there was either a fiance as I had assumed there was, or the obstacle of a husband between them as Jim Beach believed. Actor/writer Jason Miller told Herb Juliano that Iris was a married woman when she dated Gipp but Juliano did not know the source of Miller's information. Although Gipp agreed to accommodate her by changing his attitude and actions, it seems Iris desired to break off the relationship after having sampled her "15 minutes of fame" in

South Bend as Gipp's girl.

It was on the 9th of August that Gipp wrote his first letter to Iris after returning from Indianapolis with the satisfaction that everything was cleared up between them during his last visit.Having had Iris ignore this letter, George wrote again on the 21st of August. Thinking that she might have heard about his dating other girls and perhaps that subject was also brought up when he visited Iris, Gipp wrote this in a letter on August 23rd:

"...I just think of you all the time dear and oh I've been waiting and waiting for some little word. Don't you believe I'm being good?..."

Another letter on the 27th of August was also ignored by Iris as September and the return to school were approaching. It seemed that Iris kept stalling Gipp off and whatever the reason, Iris was not honest with Gipp.

Rockne set September 9 to 11, 1920, as the dates for football players to start arriving. Gipp, after visiting home, got to South Bend as scheduled. In the meantime, he was now making phone calls to Iris at her place of employment, the Indiana Public Service Commission. While her job was prestigious for a woman to have in those days, Iris still had to work and there was responsibility involved.

Sitting in on commission meetings, taking minutes of the meetings and later transcribing them into the record, typing and sending copies to the officials who attended the meetings, taking dictation from her boss and filing papers were some the duties of her position. When a personal call for her from Gipp interrupted a conference or her office routine, Iris had to cope with it while her work came to a halt and her boss probably fumed and stewed. It must have been important for her to get off the phone because she renewed her promise to marry Gipp, thereby continuing with the charade she had been giving him since spring of 1920. In his book, "One for the Gipper," Pat Chelland writes: "George, in keeping his promise to Iris, had settled himself down since returning to Notre Dame that fall. In fact he had become a good student, as we can see from a letter he wrote in October to his friend Paul Hogan in Calumet. In the letter George said that his engagement to Iris was on again despite strong objections from her father. George made a point to mention that everything was fine at school and that his grades were up."

The calls to Iris became so frequent that a final effort by her to make Gipp cease was made when she went to South Bend during Notre Dame's Homecoming Week. It is probable that her supervisor had something to do with the unannounced trip by Iris.

The visit was a surprise to Gipp. The Gunboat Smith-Harry Greb heavyweight fight was on that evening as part of Homecoming Week activities. Gipp, who now lived in Sorin Hall, had rented a room at the Oliver Hotel for the week. Gipp and Hunk were going to see the fight together but now that Iris was in town, Gipp assumed she had accepted his invitation to visit and enjoy events during Homecoming Week. He didn't realize she had another reason. George asked Hunk to get a hurried date if he could with Marie, which Hunk did. Women usually weren't seen at fights and Gipp thought that it would be less embarrassing to Iris if another female attended.

Because of the celebrations going on downtown, the

main event was put on first and the rest of the card followed. Gipp and Iris sat a few rows ahead of Hunk and Marie. It appeared to them as if Gipp and Iris were arguing while the fighters were being introduced.

In an unexpected upset, Harry Greb, weighing only 162 pounds,knocked out the heavyweight contender at 202 pounds, Gunboat Smith, in one round. As a result of the fight's quick finish, Gipp suggested they go to the Tapestry Room at the Oliver Hotel mezzanine for a dance being held there that evening. Iris reminded Gipp that she had to catch her train back at 11 o'clock that same evening and Gipp promised to have her at the depot in time for the train.

When they arrived at the Tapestry Room, Gipp immediately took Iris to the dance floor while Hunk and Marie decided to sit the dance out. Both of them watched Gipp and Iris dance and again it appeared that the dancers were arguing. Marie suggested to Hunk that they leave. After a couple of dances Gipp and Iris returned to where Hunk and Marie sat, and as they arrived, Hunk then told Gipp that Marie wasn't feeling well and that he, himself, could use a little time catching up on his studies. Bidding Gipp and Iris goodnight, Hunk and Marie left, giving the two lovers a chance to be alone.

Then it happened, the following week on the eve of the Indiana game at Gipp and Iris' favorite rendezvous — the two luxuriously upholstered chairs near the mezzanine floor elevator at the Claypool Hotel in Indianapolis. No one knows the words Iris used to break the news that she was married. The story as told in books was that the meeting was short and the message terse: "She said she had married someone else."

Her marriage must have seemed to have been very sudden to Gipp and obviously that "someone else" had been courting her during the months she had been ignoring Gipp's letters and perhaps even before that time. If she had been a married woman and had reconciled with her husband, she may have told Gipp that she had just gotten married to avoid a lengthy and embarrassing explanation to him.

Gipp was going to tell Hunk about what happened when he met Iris upstairs at the Claypool, but Hunk remembered Iris and Gipp's quarrel of the previous week and told him he didn't want to hear about it, that he kept his nose out of other people's business.

Some biographers claim there was a South Bend girl named Irene who seemed to have gotten a lot of attention from Gipp, yet no one is sure if she existed or if she actually was Iris. Because of the similarity of names — Iris and Irene — one could assume, and some did, that the other girl was really Iris, whose name was mistaken to be Irene.

Everything about Irene is sketchy at best, except that Chet Grant added mystery to the Irene story by saying that a woman came to his office in the Hesburgh Library basement at Notre Dame in 1974, telling Chet she was Gipp's girl friend and became his fiancee when he returned from Chicago, just before he died. Chet did not reveal her name because he wanted an exclusive with it in the book he was going to write, but it could have been the elusive Irene. She said that she lived on Harris Street in part of the upstairs of a house that had an outside open stairway as the only access to her door.

Joe Donaldson, who passed away in March of 1999 at

NOTRE DAME — The Untold Story

the age of 101, was Gipp's self-described "Man Friday" as a student manager. Joe "gofered" for Gipp in the locker room and on the sidelines. Joe told I. I. Probst emphatically that Gipp had a South Bend girl friend named Irene.

Frank Leahy in his autobiography added a Rockne preface to Rock's "win one for the Gipper" request. It was, "Years after Gipp died, I met a girl named Irene. She was a town girl that George Gipp would have married. I tried to get her to say something about him that I might not have known, and all she would say, was 'George Gipp was a great gentleman.'"

Jim Beach in his 1962 book about Notre Dame mentioned Irene, a South Bend girl, as Gipp's sweetheart. When asked about it, Jim couldn't remember which of the people he interviewed told him that.

No one knew who the girl was who sat in the St. Joseph's Hospital lobby during Gipp's illness, and when she spotted her friend, who was a nurse, the friend would then update her on Gipp's condition and then the young lady would continue to linger or sometimes she would depart. Could she have been Irene? It can be surmised that Gipp was probably in love with Iris Trippeer until she told him she was married and then he held her in contempt for being made a gullible fool by her.

What about the Gloria Trippeer Lyons' statement that her aunt didn't think she would have stability in a marriage to Gipp? Could Iris have lied to Gipp at that Claypool Hotel meeting that she was married just to stop Gipp's pursuit?

In trying to find the truth in order to be fair and accurate I had the Mishawaka public records checked for both the Dunleavy name and the Trippeer name. Neither name appears on records dating from 1916 to November of 1920. Beach said he found an attorney named Dun*lavy* in Indianapolis Bar Association records of 1920 but no other information about him. Records were checked for South Bend and were unfruitful regarding the two names.

Marion County records were checked for 1919 and 1920 and the city directory revealed an Iris Trippeer married to a Lewis Trippeer, he being listed as a railroad worker and husband and Iris Trippeer listed as wife and a stenographer for the Indiana Public Service Commission. Their residence was at 605 Cottage Avenue in Indianapolis. Here's where a puzzle enters. A check of the U. S. Census of 1920 has the name Loue (*sic*) Trippeer living at 2511 Central Avenue, Indianapolis. His occupation is listed as a brakeman for the railroad. He had a wife named Grace. They had a daughter aged 20 named Iris whose occupation is listed as a reporter for the Indiana Public Service Commission. It appears as if the city directory was in error listing Iris as Louis Trippeer's wife and that the census report was correct in listing Grace as the wife and Iris as the daughter. The address discrepancies may be the result of a change of residences by the Trippeer family.

The census registration date was January 9, 1920, while the directory has listings for both 1919 and 1920. In any case, the two different addresses do remain a question mark.

But some last-minute researching by my son, Marc, uncovered some details that shed an entirely new light on the whole Gipp-Iris affair.

Persistent Marc decided to check counties surrounding Indianapolis' Marion County and, bingo, under marriage licenses in Shelby County, which abuts Marion at Marion's southeast tip, he found the license for a marriage between Iris Jeanne Trippeer and Marion Miller Adams that took place on September 11, 1920. The irony of it all is that while Iris was getting married on Sunday September 11, Gipp, thinking he still had a fiance, arrived in South Bend on the same day to begin football practice on the following day.

The wedding in Shelby County was a secret that the couple kept from their parents. Iris apparently returned home to live with her parents and to continue working for the Indiana Public Service Commission while her new husband also stayed with his parents until he could establish a home for his bride. Gipp in the meantime had left South Bend after being expelled again, and returned to Laurium.

Rockne, sensing a victory in his efforts to get Gipp re-instated, telegraphed Gipp to return and George, on his way to South Bend, decided to stop in Indianapolis first and surprise Iris. This was on September 23. Her father apparently was home and the next day Gipp wrote an apologetic note saying he was sorry he acted as if he did not know that he was a persona non grata as far as her father was concerned. To get rid of Gipp, Iris feigned being sick and Gipp departed, going directly to the Claypool Hotel. At that meeting, because of the presence of her father, it would have been difficult for Iris to tell Gipp she was married.

Iris, now married less than two months, met with Gipp again on November 6, during Notre Dame's homecoming week. Perhaps she was going to tell him about her marriage at that time, but for some unknown reason, she didn't.

Instead, she told him to stop phoning her at work. She waited until the following week, during the Indiana game of November 13, to tell Gipp that she was a married woman, which, indeed, she was. Where her new husband, Marion Miller Adams, was at this time or if he knew what Iris was up to is and probably will remain unknown forever.

The failure of Iris to answer Gipp's letters from March through August could have been a warning signal that Iris was seeing someone else. Yet, when Gipp went to visit Iris in early August to find out why his letters weren't answered, instead of leveling with him, she continued her perfidy and failed to mention she was dating someone else, namely Marion Adams. She also could have told him of her marriage when Gipp made those disruptive phone calls, but she didn't.

With this new information in hand, Iris does not come off as a truly honest person but, in her defense, it is difficult to condemn someone when it comes to affairs of the heart. It is interesting that her granddaughter, Victoria, and niece, Gloria, always refer to Iris by her maiden name of Trippeer. When mentioned in the Ostler article Victoria's last name was given as Adams, which we now know to have been Iris' married name. What eventually happened to the Iris-Marion Adams marriage is unknown. The 1930 census reports that Marion, now called "Jack," and Iris, had two sons. He is listed as the manager of a merchandise dry goods store, she as a housewife. Other records reveal that Iris died in Arizona in 1974.

Whatever the true story is, the Gipp-Iris-Adams triangle is certainly more grist for the Gipper legend, where fact is often more intriguing than fiction.

With Iris out of the picture, it seems as if the lady named Irene quite likely would have been Gipp's wife had he lived and it is my belief that if there actually was an Irene, that she very well could have been the cute, blond manicurist at the Oliver Hotel.

# 7

# 1919 —
# WESTERN CHAMPIONS

In 1919, the return of Notre Dame student-athletes who were in the armed services during World War I helped Knute Rockne parlay their talents into his first undefeated season as head coach. This was also the first full season Gipp was able to display his talents to the fullest inasmuch as a broken leg in 1917 and a shortened 1918 schedule had previously denied him that opportunity.

The season's first game against Kalamazoo turned out to be a tough battle and Notre Dame didn't score until the third period, although two long runs for touchdowns by Gipp in the second quarter were called back for infractions. Notre Dame won 14-0. Gipp gained 148 yards on 11 carries, and left the game with an injury that turned out not to be serious. Mount Union was the next game and Notre Dame clobbered the Ohioans 60-7. Gipp scored the first touchdown and left

the contest after Notre Dame had piled up an early 27 to 7
lead. Gipp, in his abbreviated appearance, ran for 123 yards
in 10 carries and passed for 50 more on three attempts.

The third game, on October 18, was with the big and
formidable Nebraska team. Notre Dame scored on the opening kickoff on a Rockne trick play — a reverse where the halfback who got the kickoff was to hand off the ball to the other
back from the opposite side. Gipp got the ball but Bergman
didn't get close enough for the handoff, so Gipp then lateraled
the ball to him because the potential tacklers were almost
upon him. Nebraska used the kicker as a primary tackler to
avail themselves of his accelerated speed as he kicked the ball
while the fastest man on the team, the end Swanson, was to
be the conservative safety. With the entire Nebraska team
converging on Gipp, Swanson was the only man left who
could have tackled Bergman. Hunk Anderson, after making
one block, saw Swanson maneuvering to tackle Bergman and
hustled to get in front of Dutch, who slowed down a little for
Anderson to get a position on Swanson. Hunk barreled in
with a vicious cross-body block and knocked Swanson off his
feet and flying backward to the turf, clearing the path for
Bergman to score on what was a 90-yard play.

The Cornhuskers keyed on Gipp in the game, but he
still managed to run for a respectable 70 yards by one report
or 72 by another, while passing for 145 yards. George completed five passes in eight attempts, one of which set up the
other Notre Dame score that won the game when Bahan
sneaked in for the touchdown. It was a tough battle in the
trenches but the Benders won by a 14 to 9 score. While
Bergman made some good gains, it was the trick play and

Gipp's passing that were largely responsible for the victory.

Next came Western State Normal, a Michigan team with a two and one record. The Normalites were no match for Notre Dame's high octane offense and stingy defense and Notre Dame won easily by a 53-0 score. Gipp scored two touchdowns and chewed up a lot of yardage in the first quarter and then was replaced first by Grover Malone and ultimately by Norm Barry. Almost everyone on the team got in the game, even if only for a few plays.

Indiana, at home, proved to be a much tougher opponent than Western State. It had help from an uninterrupted rain that slackened into a drizzle at game time. Washington Park was one vast mud puddle which slowed down Notre Dame's speedy backs, but Notre Dame still managed to win by a score of 16 to 3. Anderson's blocked punt set up a Slackford touchdown and then a field goal by Gipp and, later in the third quarter, an eight-yard Gipp run into paydirt ended the scoring for the Gold and Blue. In spite of the mud and drizzle, Gipp managed to average six yards per carry.

Rockne now was sensing an undefeated season if Notre Dame could dispose of a fine Army team that had lost only one game, to a then undefeated Syracuse team by a score of 7-3. The 1919 Army squad was a better club than the 1920 team that sparkled on offense with the addition of Walter French from Rutgers. Lacking offensive punch, this same 1919 Army team's personnel, when playing defense, was considered the strongest defensive team in Army's history. Earl Blaik, Briedster, Vogel and Captain A. L. George were in the line with bone crunching tacklers, Schabacher and Lysted, in the secondary. Defensively adept as they were, the determined Cadets found some solid offense and were leading Notre Dame by a 9-0 score as the end of the first half approached. Gipp was pretty well bottled up but with the first half's end approaching he started a drive for a score with a passing game after making a run for 10 yards, his longest of the game. Two short completed passes went for good gains, then a long pass to Pete Bahan brought the ball to the Army one yard line as the Catholics were hustling to line up before the gun went off to signal the end of the half.

A few years before this game, in 1915, the College Football Rules Committee had added an official called the Field Judge and placed him behind the defense to watch for infractions. It also took away the timing chores that the Head Linesman had on the sideline and gave the job to the Field Judge. There were no stadium clocks in those days but both teams knew the half was coming to a close and as Notre Dame lined up, Gipp noticed the Field Judge looking at his stop watch as he began walking toward the line of scrimmage to pick the ball up. Pete Bahan, who caught a pass from Gipp on the Army one yard line, was slow getting up, having been hit hard by safety back Schabacher. Gipp saw the Field Judge pull a pistol from his pocket and didn't wait for Bahan to get set before he called the signals. Instead, he shouted at Slip Madigan to snap the ball and the alert Slip did just that. Both teams were frozen by surprise when Gipp sauntered into the end zone as the official ended the half with his pistol shot.

There is another version of this, stating that a horn was blown to end the half. Hunk Anderson told me that the horn was still used in some games, but the method of denoting the end of the half and the game was in transition and he distinctly remembered a pistol being used in all the Army games in which he played. Another point in error in the other version was that Gipp was looking toward the sidelines where the timekeeper stood. In 1919 the timekeeper was the Field Judge and he was positioned behind Army's line and not on the sideline. A third error was that Gipp yelled to Ojay Larson to snap the ball. That would have been hard for Larson to do because, like Chet Grant, he did not attend Notre Dame in 1919 but waited until 1920 to reenter school.

Army was leading 9-6 at halftime and came out determined to win. But it was somewhat of a stalemate, with defenses dominating the game until the fourth quarter, when Gipp began moving the team with a mix of runs and a long pass which enabled Notre Dame to reach the Cadet four-yard-line. From there Walt Miller plunged in for the score that won the game, 12-9. This is the Army game in which both teams were betting on themselves to win and Hunk Anderson, with an Army team member, had a town shoemaker hold the bets in his safe.

Although Gipp was held to 70 yards for an average of almost five yards per carry (15 attempts), he made some key first downs in the two scoring drives with his runs and he completed seven passes, most of them in those aforementioned two scoring drives.

In every game Gipp had played up to this Army game he received praise from his opponents, most of whom ventured to say he was the best football player they had ever played against. The Cadets had the same opinion of Gipp. As one put it, "We thought we had stopped him, but if you stop him on the ground he goes to the air, and when you think he's going to pass, he manages to ram the ball down your gullet with determination that eventually ends in a score. I've never played against anyone as good as he is." And that was no less than the Army team captain, Alexander George, who said it.

No one was more impressed, however, than the scribes who were at the game. As one put it: "Standing head and shoulders above every individual player on the field was George Gipp of Notre Dame."

It was after this Army game that Gipp began missing classes with regularity in anticipation of quitting school when the season, which had only three games remaining, was finished. It was also around this time that Gene Basker said his dad referred Gipp to Dr. Joseph Abel. And it was also around this time that Gipp met Iris Trippeer and began dating her. He did show up for the Michigan A&M (State) game but sat on the bench in the first quarter, which has been reported as a form of Rockne's punishment for George missing practices. If this is true, then why did Rockne also have the rest of the first string on the bench? Rockne many times throughout his coaching career started the second team and allowed it to play the first quarter. The Aggies, as Michigan State was called then, were tough and Rockne, who remembered that it was the only game he lost the year before in the short 1918 season, did not hesitate to put the entire first string — Gipp included — into game in the second quarter. Notre Dame won 13-0 but had to earn it.

Gipp and Slackford brought the ball to the Aggie three yard line in the first Notre Dame deep penetration but failed to score. The second drive of Notre Dame's led by Bahan, Gipp and Slackford, plus a catch by Kirk on a pass from Gipp, got the ball near the goal from where fullback Slackford scored. It was tough on all Notre Damers but the game was iced in the fourth quarter on a Gipp pass to Coughlin. Gipp averaged five yards per carry and completed five passes for 73 yards.

Purdue was next for Notre Dame and Gipp again displayed his superstar qualities. The Boilermakers were a big, rugged team that had three losses to tough Big Ten opponents, but managed to keep those games close while delivering physical punishment to their opponents. Illinois, who won the 1919 Big Ten championship after beating Minnesota, Ohio State, and Iowa and demolishing a good Michigan team by a 29-7 score, had its hands full with Purdue, barely winning 14-7 on a last quarter touchdown by Dutch Sternaman.

Purdue coach A. Scanlon promised that a big effort would be made and the Boilermakers would hand Notre Dame its first loss. That turned out to be a pipe dream. Hunk Anderson started the scoring by intercepting a Boilermaker pass and taking it in for 32 yards and a touchdown. Gipp riddled the Purdue defense with passes throughout the game, completing 11 out of 15 attempts for 217 yards. One pass to Kirk was good for a touchdown and two other passes set up scores. The tough Purdue line limited Gipp to only 52 yards running but Gipp had only 10 carries. The final score was Notre Dame 33 and Purdue 13.

As the team arrived in South Bend late that evening or early morning, six Notre Damers with some of their gear took a cab from the Grand Trunk Line to the New York Central in order to catch a train to Rockford, Illinois, via Chicago. Slip Madigan had arranged for them to play in a Rockford city championship game. This event was treated in a previous chapter.

The ninth and last game of the season was against Morningside on a cold Thanksgiving Day in Sioux City, Iowa. It snowed, the temperature hovered around 10-degrees and a cold, blistering wind penetrated to the bone, yet the attendance at the game was 10,000 diehard football fans. This Morningside crowd tied the Nebraska game's attendance figure of 10,000, as the largest crowd to see Notre Dame play in 1919.

On the football field, the cold weather hampered both teams, but a fighting Morningside team took the lead on a first quarter score. Early in the game the Notre Dame team seemed to be mesmerized or fossilized by the cold, but Gipp managed to display his ability in spite of the severe weather and the slippery field. George got enough traction on the icy turf to gain 94 yards and his frigid fingers still managed to toss the ball for 66 yards. A Gipp pass set up the first score. Bergman, on a short plunge, went into the end zone and Gipp kicked the extra point to put Notre Dame ahead, 7-6. An insurance touchdown also came from a long Gipp pass to Bernie Kirk. The final score was 14-6.

Notre Dame won the Western Championship which was bestowed upon them by the midwest sports writers. Illinois, with one loss to Wisconsin, disputed the award. Rationalizing that as Big Ten champions they deserved to also be named Western Champions and as Illinois coach Bob Zuppke reasoned, it was a common practice to select the Big Ten champion for that regional honor. But there was no recount or reconsideration. Notre Dame was the only undefeated team in the region and there never was an obligation on the sportswriting fraternity to choose a Big Ten team as champion. Notre Dame met and beat teams from the Big Ten as well as non-Big Ten teams such as Nebraska and a powerful eastern football squad, Army. Notre Dame deserved the honor.

While the Western Championship was a big bone of contention for the Illini, there was some satisfaction for Coach Zuppke to know that Parke Davis of The Official Football Guide named Illinois and Notre Dame co-national champions for 1919.

# GIPP'S EXPULSION
# AND REINSTATEMENT

The Notre Dame school year of 1919/1920 was to be as hectic as the post-World War I decade that followed. Father John W. Cavanaugh was replaced by Father James A. Burns as president of Notre Dame and Burns inherited many problems that only money could solve. Putting his woes into historical perspective, it must be noted that with the signing of the Armistice on November 11, 1918, our troops began returning from Europe and were being discharged, only to find that not many jobs were available. The manufacturing base of our country was retooling from armaments and other war supplies to products for civilian use. Thus the first part of 1919 saw our country in an economic recession.

By the time the school year began in September of 1919, the economy began perking up and the products manufactured were being gobbled up as quickly as they hit the market. There were shortages and shortages cause inflation, so 1920 found prices escalating but wages in all industries remained the same and that created a strain on the family pocketbook.

Perhaps the greatest advancement in women's basic rights occurred when in 1919 Congress passed the 19th Amendment to the Constitution which provided that "the right of citizens of the United States to vote shall not be denied or abridged by the United States or any state on account of sex..." It was ratified rapidly and became law in August of 1920. Also, August of 1920 saw a women's march on Washington protesting the high cost of living. Inflation was a factor that Notre Dame's President Burns had to deal with while trying to solve his problems.

In the postwar period many ex-soldiers decided that an education was what they needed in a new era and that September of 1919 Notre Dame found itself over-enrolled and bursting at the seams. Classrooms, office space and residence halls were crowded. Notre Dame advertised in the South Bend papers for local citizens who had spare rooms to rent them to the students. Athletes who were in school on a BT scholarship (bed and table) were assured of having a room. Gipp, however, preferred the room at the Oliver Hotel which he got without cost in trade for being the house player for billiards.

George was to make himself available specifically on Mondays, especially during the early evening hours, because that was three cushion billiards night. That was the "white collar" night and prominent South Bend executives, businessmen and professionals, such as lawyers and doctors, would assemble for competition as well as instructions and advice from the "house player." Gipp had learned the three cushion game so well that he met and beat his own mentor, Elwyn Moore, for the 1920 South Bend billiards championship after both men eliminated all challengers to reach the finals.

Gipp had no problem with his Monday billiards schedule at the Oliver. Under Rockne, the regulars usually got Mondays off after a Saturday game. That was sort of a reward and also it was used as an opportunity for extra time to heal bumps and bruises. Even though the regulars weren't involved in field workouts as the subs had to be on Monday, Rockne still expected the first stringers to observe on the sidelines or from the stands. Using the Monday off for studies was also encouraged by Rockne.

Gipp also took a lot of Tuesdays off. Hunk Anderson vouched that it was his leg that bothered Gipp, causing his absence. George had that Spartanesque attitude of bearing pain without revealing it to Rockne or his teammates. Only Hunk, his closest friend, would usually be in on Gipp's personal problems.

In the Morningside College game of 1917, Gipp broke his leg when he was tackled in a way that his flailing leg hit an iron light post only a few feet from the sideline. The break never healed properly and at different times it gave him different degrees of pain.

What Hunk said was true about Gipp's leg bothering him. My uncle, Frank Koszewski, was a podiatrist, physiotherapist and had chiropractic training. He took over the Turkish baths at the Oliver Hotel in 1905 and stayed on until early 1921.

In 1920, new Oliver Hotel owner Andy Weisberg decided to build an addition to the hotel, which would also be six stories high with 200 rooms and would be fronting Washington Street. Simultaneously, the interior of the main building would be remodeled and respaced. The work began in early 1921.

The basement space was needed more urgently for storage than were some of the amenities in it. The pool tables were moved up to main floor, but to the far side of the lobby. The popularity of the Turkish baths began to diminish prior to the war, so Weisberg labeled that feature as dispensable.

The last months at the Oliver for Gipp were also the last months for my Uncle Frank. It was Frank -- called "Doc" by Gipp -- who treated Gipp's bad leg. He first put hot towels on the area of the leg that had been broken, then he manipulated and rubbed it down. Gipp felt that it helped him because he was Frank's steady customer. Uncle Frank never charged him.

Gipp would give him some game tickets, but more than that, Gipp would come in a few days later and give Frank a wad of bills, a far greater amount than what Frank would have gotten if he charged him.

All this about my Uncle Frank, Gipp and Dr. Abel, was told to me in October, 1986. My cousin, Gene Basker, Frank's second youngest son, had been the St. Joseph County Treasurer for several terms. Gene and I were discussing football in general and Gipp in particular at the wake of my sister-in-law who died of breast cancer at a very young age.

We continued talking about Gipp the next day at a

luncheon for the mourners after the funeral. Gene said that when his Dad got real sick, weeks before he died, Gene would visit him and his Dad would reminisce. Gene remembered the stories his father told about the prominent people he attended at the Oliver Hotel Turkish baths. His favorite was the Gipper. He said that Gipp was a likable "chap" with a sense of humor and "full of generosity when dealing with the employees of the hotel." Of course, Gipp was also an employee by bartering his services for a room, but he did have celebrity status and respect from all who knew him at the hotel.

Gipp had three sayings he used at times. One was "That's jake with me," which was another way of saying okay. The second favorite saying was "There's always tomorrow," a variation of his own of the commonly used "Tomorrow is another day." It was Gipp's way of sympathizing with a loser that he might have better luck next time.

The final saying was one he always followed. It was "When in Rome, do as the Romans do." Gipp adjusted his demeanor accordingly, be it the pool hall, corporate executive's home (and he had invitations) or an elite society bash. His Oliver Hotel residence and house player job brought him in contact with many prominent citizens.

Gene said that besides treating Gipp's leg, his father did prepare Gipp to play in home games. Gipp would play poker on Friday, all night...and he did some imbibing, too. Then, on Saturday morning, he'd walk down to see Frank to get "refreshed" and have his leg rubbed. Yes, as always, *he walked* -- although I'll bet the next book out on Gipp will have him "staggering" to the Turkish baths and in the book after that one, the author will say that the hotel bellhops carried a drunken Gipp downstairs for resuscitation and detoxification. Gipp's actions and image seemed to have gotten "blacker" as his old friends and teammates died off. The fairest and most complete book on Gipp was "One for the Gipper" written by Pat Chelland in 1976. Some of the other books of recent years not only contain exaggerations, but also downright fabrications.

It's true that Gipp, while playing brilliant football on the field which led to Rockne's first undefeated team and a Western Championship for Notre Dame in 1919, did not attend classes regularly and missed enough of them to be far over the allotted absences per term. But football players were given a perk by the pro-athletics president, Father John Cavanaugh, that allowed them an opportunity to recapture the lost school time if an injured player kept up with his school work during absence from class and passed the required exams. Sometimes a hospitalized injured player or one who was ill and had a prolonged absence, could get an opportunity to preserve the work and time of his attended semester classes by getting a doctor's statement saying that he had been in the doctor's care. The makeup class work and exams were still required. Some Big Ten schools had a similar policy, so it wasn't unique with Notre Dame.

As 1919 passed on and the New Year began, Gipp's absences from class attendance had been brought to the attention of Dean Francis J. Vurpillat. He was appointed dean by Father Burns in July of 1919 and had been a law professor at Notre Dame since 1915. He believed in abiding by the rules and was adamant that Gipp's days at Notre Dame would soon be over. He was aware of Gipp's scholastic record and felt no sympathy for him.

On March 8, 1920, Gipp was expelled from school. That news traveled fast and there were at least five universities, including the University of Michigan, who contacted Gipp, trying to lure him their way. Even the U. S. Military Academy — Army — contacted Gipp at the insistence of its superintendent, General Douglas MacArthur.

Vurpillat's action was applauded by many members of the faculty. Hunk Anderson told me that he felt that the professors discriminated against football players. Hunk said he and professor Marty McCue of Hunk's engineering class got along fine until McCue learned that Hunk was a football player. While other schools gave class assignments to the football players ahead of time for study whenever there was a football trip involved, the Notre Dame faculty did not adopt that policy. Hunk said he had Skidder Mahoney give him assignments upon arrival from a game trip and Hunk, without breakfast, had to hurriedly prepare them for class. The train would arrive early Monday morning from the East and the team had to hustle to make the 8 o'clock classes.

When Hunk was called to the blackboard and gave the correct answer and formula, McCue was very surprised, but undaunted, and commented with a barb. "You know, Mr. Anderson, that there has not been one football player who graduated from my Civil Engineering class."

"You're looking at one who is going to," answered Hunk. "You can flunk me if I didn't do my work, but don't flunk me because you don't like football players. If it wasn't for football and the scholarship I got to play, I wouldn't be able to afford to go to school." With that encounter Hunk believed he made a convert because Hunk and Professor McCue got along fine after that.

When Gipp's dismissal was made public, almost immediately all of South Bend began besieging Father Burns with phone calls and letters. Important South Bend businessmen made calls urging Gipp's reinstatement while other important local people tried to arrange a meeting with the very busy Father Burns, thinking that in a face to face meeting they could be persuasive. There were petitions as well but Burns supported Vurpillat completely and did not back down.

Just about every book written on this episode of Gipp's expulsion states that Father Burns caved in to the pressure because on April 29, 1920, Gipp was reinstated. They wrote that Burns needed the cooperation of the community because of the fund drives that were in progress at that time. Yes, that was true, but also it was true that Gipp took his oral exam and passed it. All of the writers who mention this incident in their books have a doubt there was an exam or just state that no exam was given to Gipp, and that the exam was a flat out lie.

In his autobiography, which was made up basically of Rockne's Collier's Magazine articles and diary, Rockne summed up Gipp's oral exam this way: "...townsmen of South Bend even appealed to the school authorities to give Gipp another chance. Gipp claimed to have been ill and he got it on that account.

"Gipp went into that examination room with the whole school and whole city waiting on that outcome," Rockne continued in his autobiography. "Some of his inquisitors were no fans. They were prepared to stop his scholastic run with tough questions and blocking from the books. His professors knew that Gipp was no diligent student. But he astonished everybody with what he knew when it came to cross-examination. He passed back into school and there was general rejoicing."

Gipp's "inquisitors" were Dean Vurpillat and law professors John Tiernan and Joseph O. Plante. They were tough because the faculty had no love for the policies existing under university president Father Cavanaugh and Gipp's special exam was one. They had confidence there would be changes during Father Burns' tenure. Father Burns had toughened up the curriculum and had plans to make Notre Dame, academically, the Harvard or Yale among Catholic universities. Accreditation and endowments were needed to attain this goal.

After his expulsion notice, Gipp moved whatever clothing he had from his campus room to his room at the Oliver. When he was expelled, he told hotel owner Andy Weisberg that he was quitting his job as house player and probably would leave South Bend after he heard from Rockne. Rockne was trying to work behind the scenes, hoping to get some concession and at the same time, keeping the protest alive in South Bend. When the situation remained in status quo for several days after his expulsion, Gipp wanted to ask Weisberg if he could get his job back, but he never did because he found out that John Vermande, a good local area pool player had been hired.

Gipp went to Hullie and Mike's to try to get the house player job there, but both owners were out of town on business. What they went to get was some whiskey that was still available for a bootleg price. He didn't bother going to Jimmie and Goat's because they both were their own house players. He ambled over to the Elks Club and did get the day job which was only a few hours a day. When Hull and Mike returned, the next day, Gipp was hired by them and a few days later he quit the Elks job so that he could be free to go to the campus. While waiting for the finalization of his fate Gipp umpired a game and played in a game on the Notre Dame campus. Goat Anderson scheduled a game with the spring training Pittsburgh Pirates at Cartier Field. It was Jimmie and Goat's South Bend All Stars with four Notre Damers in the lineup in the exhibition game against the Pirates. Bahan was on first base, Mohardt at third base, Barry, catcher, and Gipp in the outfield. The Pirates won while Gipp had two hits out of three at bats and a walk, which wasn't bad going against big league pitching.

After his reinstatement, Gipp played in two baseball games in May for Notre Dame. He did not appear for the last game on Notre Dame's schedule and undoubtedly the condition Vurpillat imposed on Gipp if he passed the exam had something to do with it. If Gipp passed, he had to also submit a term paper on case studies. He had to research the list of cases he was given and determine if the decision in each case was based on statutory law, constitutional law or common law; whether or not it set a precedent; were there grounds for appeal and so forth. That was a lot of work for Gipp and he obviously thought that by next school year all would be forgotten if he didn't turn the paper in.

A few years before he died, I received a folder from Chet Grant, who had been a South Bend resident since his pre-high school days when his parents moved to the city from Defiance, Ohio. In the folder were crudely typed summaries of Grant's recollections of many Notre Dame games in which he played or watched as a sub sitting on the bench. He had typed these in 1931 according to the date on the crumbling sheets of paper. I also found a small note on which had been written some sort of a reminder. It said: "Wm. McIner-ney/Gipp." Chet said it was a reminder that McInerney once told him — around the time he typed the summaries of games — that McInerney helped Gipp study for the exam that would determine if Gipp was to remain expelled or to again become a student. It must be pointed out that no one doubted that the exam took place until recent books began to say it was all a lie. Well, Chet was going to correct that.

McInerney graduated from Notre Dame law school in 1901. In 1906, he formed a law partnership with his brother, Walter, who also was a juvenile judge. Notre Dame records have William on the law department's faculty staff in 1917. He was a highly regarded criminal lawyer locally. In 1912 he became an attorney for the utility companies and gained national exposure and fame by winning a favorable decision in the United States Supreme Court for an Indianapolis water utility company. He also headed the local Democrat Party. His office was across the street from the courthouse on Washington Street, near the Oliver Hotel. It was Gipp who gave the attorney lessons in playing billiards and the two were friends as evidenced by McInerney's helping Gipp prepare for that special exam. McInerney claimed that it was he who gave Gipp the idea of changing his major from arts and letters to law.

Grant's story, most of which was told to him by McInerney, starts out with the April exam. When Gipp handed Father Burns a statement from Dr. Abel that Gipp had been under his care for a three month period, Burns then decided that Gipp was to be given an exam. Father Burns notified Dean Vurpillat, who vehemently objected, but was reminded by Burns that it was the policy at Notre Dame in such cases as Gipp's.

The Dean then agreed, but it had to be given on his terms: it was to be an oral exam to assure there were no crib notes and, if he passed, Gipp would still have to turn in a required term paper. McInerney spent a couple of hours with Gipp in his Oliver Hotel room, boning him up for the exam. Gipp had a good memory and it served him well in this case, as he astounded the examiners with correct answers. Rockne wrote in his autobiography that Gipp would have been a good lawyer if he only applied himself to his studies. Father Frank Cavanaugh, who was the liaison agent for Notre Dame in negotiating Frank Leahy's departure from Boston College to Notre Dame, was a classmate of Gipp's when they both were in Arts and Letters.

Father Frank said this of Gipp: "George was no ordinary student. He had his social lapses, but he was older than most students when he entered Notre Dame. He was also brilliant and didn't have to spend much time studying. If they could have convinced him to come to class regularly, George could have been an honor student."

As for the man who made it possible for Gipp to get that exam, it was a then-young doctor from Chicago who came to South Bend as a possible place for him to practice medicine. And it was my Uncle Frank who introduced Gipp to Dr. Joseph Abel when he was visiting Frank at the Oliver Turkish baths.

Dr. Abel received his medical degree from Northwestern University in June of 1917 and immediately joined the army. Upon discharge from the army in 1919, he returned to his native Chicago, thinking of setting up an office. For some reason he became disenchanted with the idea of a practice in Chicago. He decided to check out a smaller but growing city and South Bend filled the bill.

Gene Basker knew Dr. Abel did some doctoring while looking at local areas for an ideal office site. In those days, doctors made house calls and hospitals needed doctors, so Abel had no problem finding work.

Dr. Abel married his college sweetheart, Theresa O'Donnell, in early 1920 and later returned to South Bend. He eventually opened his office in the People's State Bank Building on West Division Street. In 1927, he was named South Bend's Dynamic Man of the Year. Dr. Abel also served as president of the Western State Bank.

As for Gipp, he failed to submit the required paper by whatever deadline Dean Vurpillat set for it. When school was out for the summer, Gipp and Pete Bahan went to work for General Motors in Flint, Michigan, and played baseball in the factory league.

Gipp, being busy, had time only for sporadic letters to his Indianapolis girl friend, Iris Trippeer, who failed to answer them.

From September 9 through 11, 1920, the time Rockne set, Notre Dame players began arriving in town. It was Gipp,

Dooley, Kirk and Prokop, as reported by the South Bend Tribune, who were the first ones.

On September 14, the Tribune's sports page headlined, "Notre Dame Practice Begins" in reference to the previous day, the 13th. Reporting on the practice session of the 14th on the next day, the paper stated that Rockne was pleased with the first practice session. Wrote the Tribune, "Gipp was very impressive and was rewarded by Rockne with permission for an early departure."

This early departure was not only a reward for "impressive" play, but, according to Hunk Anderson, when Vurpillat read of Gipp's arrival, Gipp was summoned to the Dean's office and told that he was expelled again for not completing his scholastic obligation.

So his "off time" granted by Rockne served a dual purpose. On the 16th, Rockne held a scrimmage and the South Bend Tribune, reporting on the next day, ran a headline that read, "Rockne Holds Full Scrimmage" with the subhead, "Stars Missing...Gipp and Mohardt." Mohardt had a personal problem while Bahan was not yet notified that he too would be ineligible because of scholastic reasons.

Obviously Rockne was not told in advance of Gipp's and Bahan's status, either by inadvertence or by design. He learned of it from Gipp that evening. Gipp was staying at Rockne's new house in Marquette Park because when he arrived in South Bend, he was broke. Rockne talked to Father Burns, who at that time suggested that he meet with Faculty Athletic Board, that it was out of his hands. In a lunchtime meeting on September 17 with the Board, Rockne could not get the members to reverse the decision.

While the Studebaker family lost control of the company when Albert R. Erskine became president and board chairman in 1915, John Studebaker, a board member and a former Notre Dame fullback who played in 1893-94, became Rockne's ally in the cause to get Gipp made eligible again. Studebaker still had a lot of clout locally among businessmen and arranged for a South Bend Chamber of Commerce meeting on September 20. Notre Dame tried to keep Gipp's dismissal under wraps, remembering the furor that it caused in the spring when Gipp's first expulsion was announced. There were no reporters at the hurriedly scheduled meeting of the chamber. Rockne was to address the meeting but Rockne and Studebaker came early to buttonhole each member at the door to sign a petition to present to Father James Burns. That very evening, after the meeting ended, Father Burns, working late in his office, began receiving phone calls. With no publicity at this point the news still managed to spread fast in South Bend. After all, this was the football season and everybody counted on the Gipper to keep the Irish undefeated. And this was the year the Hoosiers, the Ramblers, the Catholics, the Rockmen, the Benders — all Notre Dame nicknames — were to become the "Irish."

On September 22, the South Bend Tribune, in a column by student reporter Arch Ward, headlined the sports page this way: "Gipp and Bahan Ineligible for ND Eleven." Now, the rest of South Bend was going to contact Notre Dame with anger and fury.

A Chamber of Commerce committee headed by John Studebaker met with Father Burns on Saturday, September 25 and presented the petition urging reinstatement of Gipp "for the good of Notre Dame and South Bend." This petition was served with an ultimatum: Reinstate Gipp or the business community will not support any fund-raising drives underway or of the near future and will urge the city and citizens of South Bend not to cooperate with Notre Dame. Newspaper ads were to be placed in local papers to that effect.

Ordinarily, Father Burns might have told the committee to go fly a kite or shinny up a tree, but he was over a barrel. While Notre Dame's residence halls were full in the 1919-20 school year, another record breaking enrollment far greater than the last one definitely required no less than 500 rooms in South Bend to accommodate new students. Notre Dame had already placed an ad in the South Bend papers on the 21st urging the citizens to make spare rooms available to Notre Dame students.

At the time that Gipp's expulsion problem came up, Father Burns was working on a plan for the formation of a board of lay trustees to be patterned after Harvard's board. The petition he was given with an ultimatum for Gipp's reinstatement was signed by some of the prominent people he was considering to place on his "Associate Board of Lay Trustees." Beside the reality of 500 homeless students if South Bend citizens refused to rent their spare rooms, he also had to think about refusals to serve on his board by those he was considering for it.

The remodeling of Cartier Field to seat 20,000 fans was yet to be paid for and Burns counted on South Bend to help. But greater plans were underway. Accreditation was now a big item in academic institutions. Foundation grants were based on several factors, but definitely accreditation was foremost. Burns had been in contact with the Carnegie Foundation and Rockefeller Foundation and was challenged by both to raise a certain amount plus a few other stipulations included and if that was met, grants would be given.

When colleges need funds the presidents turn to their Board of Trustees, who are generally men from corporate and business enterprises and financial institutions who are capable of raising the required funds and also investing funds for growth. Notre Dame's Board of Trustees was composed exclusively of Holy Cross priests — wonderful men, but with no money, and their vow of poverty kept them that way. Father Burns was in the midst of planning a board that was to be patterned after Harvard's and many of the men he intended to ask to serve on the Board of Lay Trustees were the very ones on the chamber committee who signed the petition and the ultimatum. Thus, Father Burns had no alternative but to overrule the Faculty Athletics Board's decision on Gipp if his plans for a modern, financially healthy Notre Dame were to succeed.

Father Burns told the committee representing the South Bend Chamber of Commerce that he would have to discuss it with the Faculty Board that very weekend and would give them an answer on Monday, September 27.

On Monday, Father Burns told John Studebaker to let his committee know that as soon as a suitable statement was drafted, the announcement of Gipp's reinstatement would be made public. Francis Wallace wrote in one of his books that he was waiting to see Father Burns when Rockne and Gipp went right in to see the prelate. Wallace said that it was then that Gipp had his oral exam, given by Father Burns.

Father Burns knew nothing about law to give such an exam. Francis said that Rockne and Gipp were in Burns' office a long time. The subsequent announcement of Gipp becoming eligible again made Wallace assume that Gipp was taking an exam at that time. Father Burns tried to impress upon Gipp and Rockne that this was Gipp's last chance. Contrary to what other books contend, that Gipp after that latest jam and victory continued to skip classes, carouse and remained the same old Gipp, this book will prove otherwise. Gipp took this warning seriously and "straightened out his act."

Gipp could bring a situation to a boiling point with his indifference, but when indifference made a difference, he'd rally and pull it out as he did on the gridiron, in pool or poker.

It should be reported that the Faculty Athletics Board was against a reprieve for Gipp. Father Burns' pragmatism prevailed and on Wednesday, September 29, 1920, The Tribune announced in print that Gipp had been reinstated. The Board stated that it was brought to its attention that Gipp passed an exam in "June." The exam was given in April, so the Board was wrong on that point. There was no term paper mentioned, which was the reason Gipp was dropped from school in June.

As for Gipp, he practiced with the team the next day -- Tuesday the 28th -- getting ready for Saturday's opener against Kalamazoo.

# 1920 —
# GIPP'S FINAL SEASON

During the 1919 football season, Gipp led Notre Dame to an undefeated, untied record in nine games and established himself as a superstar of the gridiron.

Playing in the East, where college football was supreme according to Eastern sportswriters, and against an Eastern powerhouse, Army, Gipp's heroics against the Cadets received rave reviews and national attention. Gipp earned All-Western (Notre Dame was considered a "Western" team in those days) honors for his stellar play, but Walter Camp, the Eastern football-biased All-America team selector, did not see fit to place Gipp even on his third team, a position relegated to non-Eastern gridiron standouts.

Lou Salmon was the first Notre Dame man to be placed on a Camp team, being selected as his third-string fullback in 1903. The 1913 shock of Notre Dame not only beating mighty Army but by a whopping 35-13 score forced Camp to place Ray Eichenlaub on the second team at fullback and Knute Rockne made Camp's third string at end. However, other selectors in the pre-Gipp era were not reluctant to select Notre Damers. International News Service picked Gus Dorais first team in 1913 and center Frank Rydzewski made first team INS and Newspaper Enterprise Association (NEA) in 1917 while Camp did place him on his second team that year.

Gipp was elected captain for the 1920 season at the annual banquet honoring the Notre Dame team held at the Oliver Hotel. But Gipp had begun skipping classes not only for medical treatment by Dr. Abel, but also for extracurricular activities which included social and recreational pursuits.

Gipp told Hunk Anderson that he made up his mind to quit school after the 1919 season was over, as he had said he'd do in 1917 and 1918 only to change his mind about abandoning Notre Dame for good. This time it could have been the meeting of Iris Trippeer, to whom he was introduced at a post Notre Dame game dance, that changed his mind.

Gipp lost the captaincy upon his first expulsion in March of 1920 during a vote conducted by Rockne at a spring practice session. The popular Frank Coughlin, a tackle, was picked to replace Gipp. When the 1920 season began with Gipp's reinstatement, George expected Frank to relinquish the captaincy back to him and was very disturbed that Frank did not do that.

Gipp contacted Rockne upon his arrival in South Bend on September 9, 1920. Gipp was broke and Rockne put him up at his house on St. Vincent Street. Both Gipp and Rockne knew that George might be in trouble with the Faculty Athletics Board. Gipp had no money for a room elsewhere, but he made no attempt to claim a room at Sorin Hall. Rockne made arrangements for the other football team members to get their rooms upon their arrival prior to registration, yet Gipp was not included. When Gipp learned from Dean Vurpillat that the Board had expelled him, he waited until that evening at Rockne's house to tell him.

On September 16, Hunk Anderson got permission from Rockne to miss the afternoon practice so he could see Manager Joe Benko of the South Bend Arrows pro football team about a coaching job. They met on the Main Street-side steps of the County Courthouse. Hunk was recommended for the coaching job by Rockne and actually it was Rockne who arranged for the meeting at the courthouse and set the time at one o'clock for Benko's convenience. After the Arrows deal was made, Hunk was to meet Gipp right across the street in the Oliver Hotel lobby, but Gipp was waiting for Hunk outside the hotel.

Gipp told Hunk that he had packed his suitcase and left a note for Rockne telling him where he could be contacted. Gipp left his suitcase with bellhop Eddie Borkowski, or "Jinks," as George preferred to call him, while he waited outside for Hunk to show up. Jinks put it temporarily under the registration desk. Hunk had just agreed to coach the Arrows three nights a week for $25 a week and received an advance to seal the deal. Hunk suggested they see a movie because there were cowboy films featured in two of the theaters. Research shows that playing at that time at the Auditorium Theater was Gipp's favorite cowboy, Tom Mix, in "Three Gold

Coins." At the LaSalle Theater, William S. Hart, another Gipp favorite, was featured in a film titled "Toll Gate."

Heading toward the movie houses, Gipp told Hunk that he was broke except for a dollar he had in his pocket. "Hunk, I'm going to ask you to lend me $20 if you can spare it. I need the money for train fare."

"Here's the money George," said Hunk as he gave him the $20. "But for chrissake, don't use that word borrow or lend again or I'll kick your ass. As many times as you treated me, goldammit, it's time I treated you. And if you need more, George, say so. I've got some money in my room." (Hunk had a vocabulary interspersed with profanity from boyhood which he could never shed. I've never come across anyone who could match him in a cuss-off. When Marie asked if I could tone down that kind of language in Hunk's book, Hunk agreed to a "cleansing" though he insisted, "never change the meaning of what I said.")

Hunk had worked that summer for the trolley company in Calumet, putting his earnings in a bank and when the time for school came, he withdrew enough to cover expenses although 1920 was the first year that the football scholarship at Notre Dame included tuition and books along with the usual bed and table.

While Rockne battled for Gipp's reinstatement, Gipp was going back home to Calumet. He told Hunk that he would also check with Pete Bahan at the University of Detroit, where Bahan was going to enroll, about possibly enrolling there. When Gipp was suspended in March, he had offers from many universities but only considered in-state Michigan schools as alternatives to Notre Dame if his expulsion became final.

Gipp was in limbo during the period from September 16, when he received official notification from the Faculty Athletics Board that he had been expelled, until the Monday of the 27th when he and Rockne walked into Father Burns' office to learn that Gipp was reinstated. What transpired during this period of time and his return has been incorrectly reported in some books on Gipp. The version that Coach Gus Dorais was sent by Rockne on the 25th of September to bring Gipp back from the University of Detroit doesn't agree with the facts.

By the 25th of September, 1920, Walter Halas was Rockne's new assistant coach, having replaced Dorais. To make sure that Gus didn't quit after that above date and the hiring of Walter Halas was correct, I checked with Bob Dorais, Gus' grandson. Bob was almost finished writing the biography of his grandpa Gus at the time of my contact with him.

This is part of the reply I got from Bob Dorais: "Gus returned to Notre Dame in January of 1919, after serving a year at Fort MacArthur in Texas, Rockne having had him appointed Head Basketball Coach (for the remainder of the season) and Head Baseball Coach that spring. In the fall of 1919 he was Rockne's only assistant, responsible for coaching the backfield, which, of course, included Gipp.

"Gus stayed on into the spring of 1920 and again coached the basketball and baseball teams. By the summer of 1920, Gus had found a position as Athletic Director and Head Football Coach at Gonzaga University in Spokane, Washington. There he coached for five years, including one undefeated season."

Thus on the 25th of September, 1920, Gus was 2500 miles from Notre Dame, a time when some say Dorais was bringing Gipp back to Notre Dame. Gus was actually preparing Gonzaga footballers to play their first game that very next Saturday in Spokane.

His five years at Gonzaga were successful and Dorais' desire to return to the Midwest saw him accept the coaching job at the University of Detroit, where he coached for 18 years. Bob Dorais indicated that grandpa Gus won a co-national championship at Detroit in 1928 with an undefeated season.

Father Burns, in his meeting with Rockne and Gipp, warned both men that it was the last chance for Gipp. Contrary to other versions about Gipp returning to his old habits, Hunk Anderson said that George did straighten out. He said that he saw Gipp going to class and his attitude was different. Gipp's change of attitude was also noted and mentioned by Joe Donaldson, the student football manager in Gipp's time. Joe told I. I. Probst in 1997 that during Gipp's junior year he thought Gipp was disrespectful. When Rockne called on Gipp to run some plays, Gipp would say, "Wait a minute Rock, I got to finish this story," and continued talking to the guys while Rockne and the team waited. But in 1920, Joe said that whenever Rockne called on Gipp, he'd stop his conversation, pick up his helmet and trot toward the huddle yelling, "Coming, Rock."

There was a reason for Gipp to change so drastically and I believe it was because of Gipp's love affair with Iris Trippeer. Whatever Iris' true feelings about Gipp were, she insisted that she would not accept his words alone that he had changed as he had written in his letter of August 27. She told him he must also prove it by his actions and that is obviously what he was trying to do by his 180-degree turnaround.

It was a "new" Gipp that Hunk and others on campus had seen when Gipp returned from his suspension. Father Burns' lecture to him with the "last chance" warning in front of Rockne made a deep impression on Gipp as did his attempts to impress upon Iris the fact that he had mended his ways. That's why he stayed on campus at Sorin upon reinstatement although he gambled on weekends to replenish his depleted funds.

There was a problem for Gipp if he continued his South Bend gambling rounds during the weekdays. Besides the senior student's privilege of downtown visits during the week, there were also an additional 500 off-campus students who might be roaming the same streets after hours. The Prefect of Discipline, Father Donoghue, had a virtual nightmare on his hands. He increased his range of operation, vigilance, and his hours of patrolling the downtown area streets. As the Rev. Arthur Hope wrote in his book, "These off-campus students naturally enjoyed their comparative freedom. At the same time the more careless of them created a disciplinary problem that was, at times, very malodorous. Some priests, particularly Father Walsh and Father Joseph Burke, urged Father Burns to start building some residence halls and a dining hall immediately, to do away with the disciplinary problems created by the off-campus students."

Gipp, having been told by Father Burns of his reinstatement, began practicing on September 28, the day before the announcement of his reinstatement was made. He was ready for the October 2 game against Kalamazoo. In his pre-game rhetoric, Kalamazoo Coach Potsy Clark promised that Notre Dame would have to play its best football because his team was ready and determined to battle to the end in spite of being the underdog.

Although a crowd of 5000 was said to be the largest opening day home crowd on record for Notre Dame up to that time, it was a disappointment because Cartier Field had been enlarged to seat 25,000 fans. Notre Dame won easily by a 39-0 score and Gipp, while playing what amounted to a half game, was easily the star among stars, because everyone played well. He scored a touchdown and set up others with his runs and passes. With the score 18-0 in the early part of the third quarter, Gipp and a few other first stringers were substituted for by Rockne and all the Notre Dame subs got to play before the game ended. After Gipp and Barry left the game, Mohardt continued the offensive show, helped by young quarterback Mickey Kane and halfback Cy Kaspers, who looked good as replacements, each making good gains and scoring a touchdown apiece. Gipp's part time effort netted him 183 yards on 16 carries and one touchdown.

Hunk said that during the week before the next game, practice was "fireproof"...there was no intensity preparing for Western State Normal. Rockne was trying to warn the team of complacency and not to take the Normals lightly. But he worked the first string softly and sparingly, giving more attention to the reserve units. Gipp was in his classes all week and Hunk, Gipp and others were allowed to leave the field earlier than usual, which gave Hunk and Gipp time to go into town early. Manager Joe Benko of the Arrows pro team would pick Hunk up after practices to drive him to the J. D. Oliver field where he coached the team three nights a week and Tuesday was one of those nights. Hunk called Benko to tell him he'd be in front of the Oliver Hotel and to pick him up there instead of at Notre Dame. Gipp was going to play pool after he and Hunk had a sandwich at Jimmie and Goat's place.

Gipp asked Hunk if he was going to the dance at the Oliver on Saturday night after the game. Hunk said he had a supper date with his girl friend Marie at her house and they were planning to stay home and play records. An advertisement in the paper stated that a post game dance would be held in the Cafeteria Room of the Oliver and that Jules Stein's orchestra would be playing. Admission was $1.50, war tax included. (War tax in 1920? The war was over — but taxes do not die easily, which is still typical to this day.)

Digression is in order regarding Jules Stein, who played George Gipp's favorite music. Jules Stein or, more formally, Julius Caesar Stein, was born in South Bend, Indiana, in 1896, which made him a year younger than Gipp. His father had a dry goods and household items store on West Washington Street at the corner of Walnut, and the family lived in a house next door. It was a normal South Bend neighborhood, just a notch above being a poor one only because most people did not rent the homes they lived in, but owned them with mortgage liens attached.

About five blocks east of Walnut Street on Washington near downtown began a parade of palatial homes which included the mansions of South Bend's richest families — the Studebaker and the Oliver clans. Living so close to opulence and splendor, Stein set his goal as a youngster to become wealthy. Through hard work and astute business dealings, Stein became one of America's richest men. He was the co-founder of MCA, Music Corporation of America, the talent agency and entertainment conglomerate that eventually became MCA/Universal, owner of Universal Studios in Hollywood. Stein attended medical school in Chicago during the week and was home on weekends and holidays to play at the Oliver on Saturday and other gigs on Sundays, holidays and special days which included bar mitzvah and christening parties. Stein received his medical degree and became an ophthalmologist but his love for music won out over medicine. However, he did establish the prestigious Jules Stein Eye Institute at the University of California at Los Angeles and always preferred being addressed as Dr. Stein.

Gipp and Stein were acquaintances from the Oliver Hotel venue and it was the orchestra leader, Stein, who presented the gold watch prize to Gipp when dance expert Charlie Gates announced that George and his partner had won the dance contest held that evening. It is fascinating that Stein crossed paths with Gipp and that later Stein would have a close friendship with Ronald Reagan who was contractually associated with Stein through the MCA agency, and later socially as friends. Reagan then completed the round robin connection by playing the role of Gipp in the "Knute Rockne All-American" movie in 1940 through which he acquired Gipp's nickname, "Gipper."

October 9 was game day for Notre Dame and Gipp

against Western State Normal, a Michigan team. It was another romp, 41 to 0. Everybody got a chance to play and everybody played well. Gipp gained 125 yards on only 14 carries in the short span of time he was on the field. Gipp had two touchdowns called back for offsides. The crowd of 3500 was a disappointment to Rockne and Notre Dame officials.

Next day, the Sunday crowd at Springbrook Park, watching the Hunk Anderson-coached South Bend Arrows independent team play the Goshen Delts, surpassed Notre Dame's turnstile count by selling more than 5000 tickets to the game. The game was hyped on billboards, telephone poles and in saloons as a game against Purdue, Indiana and Valparaiso as the Delts boasted of having former players from those schools. The Anderson-coached Arrows slaughtered the Delts, 71 to 0, and Hunk Anderson got an extra $25 as per his agreement, because he was able to be on the sidelines to coach in that game. Incidentally, the Arrows were named Indiana State Champions that year by the Indianapolis Star, both the South Bend News Times and Tribune, the Fort Wayne Journal-Gazette, and other Indiana newspapers, winning 10 games without a loss. A new pro football league came into being in 1920 (later becoming the NFL) and the Arrows challenged that league's undefeated, but tied Chicago Staleys (later to become the Bears) to a game, but George Halas was trying to get a game with either of the other co-champions of that loose league, the Akron Pros or the Buffalo All Americans, and declined.

Gipp had been receiving offers from the pro ranks as well and they started coming after he had been expelled from school. It was during that summer that he was supposed to have received an offer from the Canton Bulldogs to play for them.

On October 11, while the team was setting its sights on next Saturday's Nebraska game, Notre Dame announced that henceforth, game tickets would be sold off campus by the Oliver Hotel, Spiros, Adlers, (men's haberdasheries), McInerney and Warner Cigar Store, Hullie and Mike's Cigar Store and Jimmie and Goat's Cigar Store. This would make it more convenient for people who wanted to see the games but did not wish to go to the campus to buy tickets. Notre Dame had to do something to fill empty seats.

During the week in preparing for Nebraska, Rockne exuded optimism. Nebraska outweighed Notre Dame and the competition was of high caliber and actually Nebraska was considered a slight favorite. The game in Lincoln drew 9000 fans.

Early in the game, Buck Shaw got two points by tackling Welles who was in the end zone trying to kick out of danger. After a bad Notre Dame punt, Nebraska came right back on a drive from the 50-yard-line. A key pass from Newman to Swanson put the ball on the Gold and Blue three-yard-line and Hubka scored from there on a plunge. Day drop kicked the extra point. With the score 7-2 against Notre Dame, the Ramblers had two good drives but failed to score. Nebraska had equally tough going on its possessions.

In the second quarter, Gipp broke loose on a 55- yard touchdown run that was called back for holding. It was a trick play with a fake injury act by Brandy and a quick snap by Larson. After that failed, Rockne decided to put the ball in the air and with Gipp passing primarily to end Eddie Anderson (no relation to Hunk although they were teammates), Gipp got the ball to the Cornhusker 10- yard-line. Two plays later, quarterback Joe Brandy took it in from the two for a score. Gipp's point after kick made it 9-7 in favor of Notre Dame.

In the fourth quarter, with Gipp taking the airways again hoping to add insurance, he connected with Norm Barry on several key plays. From the Nebraska 20, a Gipp pass to Barry put the ball on the Nebraska seven-yard-line and on the next play, raising his arm as if to pass, Gipp tucked the ball in and went into the end zone for the score. Gipp's kick was good and Notre Dame had the game on ice at 16 to 7, which held as the final score.

The Cornhuskers to a man praised Gipp as the best all around football player they had played against. And in the stands was a group of Nebraska fans from a bankers' club in Omaha who had the same opinion. After a monthly meeting in mid-November they sent an emissary to South Bend to sign Gipp and Bergman to a contract to play pro football in Omaha in 1921. Wrote Gene Kessler in his South Bend Tribune column of November 23:

"Gipp and Bergman have signed contracts to play next year for the pro football club of Omaha, Nebraska. The Aksar-Ben Club of that city made an offer that was too good to turn down."

After the Cornhuskers, Valparaiso was next at home. Monday, October 18, was an off day for most first stringers except center Larson and quarterback Brandy. The rest of the team had to go through a short signal drill.

When he finished his early classes Gipp took the Hill

Street trolley to downtown South Bend. He told Hunk he was going to the Oliver to see someone and to make a long distance phone call. Most likely the call was to Iris. Hunk had one more class, but that evening he had to be at the J. D. Oliver Field to coach his Arrows team.

Both in 1919 and 1920 Rockne and his teams gained national newspaper notice. Notre Dame couldn't schedule the big football powers for its home games because it could not meet the required money guarantee for the visiting team, so Jess Harper and later Rockne were forced to schedule teams whose guarantee demands could be met. Of the first three home opponents, Valparaiso, Notre Dame's next foe on October 23, 1920, was the toughest. That and the fact that Rockne's idea, seconded by Notre Dame officials, to put game tickets in the hands of South Bend businesses downtown, saw a crowd of 8000 fans set a new home game record for attendance.

Valparaiso had won three games in which the opponents did not score, but lost to Harvard 21-0. Harvard's coach Fisher had a strong team led by All-Americans Horween at fullback and Woods in the line. The Crimson had beaten Brown, Yale and Rutgers, but were tied by Princeton 14-14. Rockne did not take Valparaiso lightly, yet he surprised everyone when he started the second team, a strategy that became known under Rockne as "starting the shock troops."

Notre Dame was outweighed per man for the second week in a row and Rockne felt that the second string was good enough to absorb the early pounding without caving in while the bigger Valparaiso team tired, knowing that if the subs got into trouble he had the regulars ready to enter the fray. Another reason, perhaps a more important one, was that Rockne knew Army's coach Daly, in preparation for the following week's game against Notre Dame, had sent two scouts to observe the Notre Dame team for a second consecutive week. One of the scouts was a young assistant named Earl Blaik, who played in 1919 for Army and made Walter Camp's All America third team at end. He graduated in the spring of 1920. Blaik had played for the University of Miami in Ohio previously and he is mentioned because he became one of the all time great coaches in college football and was a formidable rival of Frank Leahy and Notre Dame when he coached Army in the 1940s.

The Army scouts got an eyeful. Rockne's daring move of starting the second unit and then using the mop-up power of the first string caught their attention as did the sensational play of George Gipp. Valparaiso managed to move the ball against the second string, but the second string gave ground only grudgingly and after a drive that sputtered in Notre Dame's territory, Valpo's Echard kicked a field goal giving his team a 3-0 lead.

When Valparaiso marched deep into Notre Dame territory in the second quarter, Rockne rushed his first stringers into the game and they stopped the drive without damage. Valpo led Notre Dame 3-0 when the half ended.

Gipp took over in the second half. As the Notre Dame Scholastic would report tersely: "Gipp Miracle Man." Gipp scored the first touchdown "with four men hanging on," on a 35-yard run. He also scored the second touchdown and converted the extra points after both TDs. On top of that, "his passing had unusual accuracy," as it was reported, "and his punting was superb." The second string then took over and scored two more touchdowns on the tiring Valparaiso team with Chet Wynne and Johnny Mohardt scoring those touchdowns. The final score was Notre Dame 28, Valparaiso 3.

During the week preceding the Valparaiso game, final touches were being put on plans for Notre Dame Homecoming Week which was to be highlighted by the Purdue game. The city of South Bend and its chamber of commerce along with its member businesses were preparing for a gala week of activities beginning on the Sunday after the Army game and lasting up to the Purdue game, the Boilermakers being the designated homecoming victim. One of the events was the heavyweight fight between two respectable and highly regarded contenders, Harry Greb and Gunboat Smith. Greb took on anyone regardless of the weight class and fought heavyweights almost as often as he did the middleweights of his own division. Smith was a legitimate contender for Jack Dempsey's crown, having beaten a former champ, the 260-pound Jess Willard, in 26 rounds. It was an attractive fight. Gipp did his part for the promotion of the fight. Wrote Gene Kessler in his column, "Serving The Punch:" "Gipp is as good a salesman as he is a football player. Gipp has sold 300 tickets on campus for the upcoming Harry Greb and Gunboat Smith bout."

To sell 300 tickets on campus means he had to be on campus to do it, horse-collaring 300 students individually between his classes and theirs. The allegation that Gipp failed to set foot on campus after his reinstatement except for end-of-week practices is further deflated by Kessler's item and a variety of other strong evidence to the contrary. Gipp really did change his attitude and priorities. For once he had become serious on a continuous basis.

# 10

## GIPP'S FANTASTIC PERFORMANCE — NOTRE DAME VS. ARMY

All the preparation in South Bend and on campus for the Purdue game's homecoming week, along with the hoopla accompanying those plans, did not distract Rockne and the team from the Army game ahead of them. The practice for Army consisted of concentration on stopping Walter French, the speedster who could do everything on the gridiron. He played for Rutgers in 1919 and was Menke's second team All-America selection. Coach Daly persuaded French to transfer to West Point where he lettered in three sports and made second string All-America on the Walter Camp teams of 1920 and 1921.

For the trip to West Point, Athletic Director Knute Rockne was limited to a budget not to exceed $4000. Hunk Anderson said that because of the inflation at the time, that amount was hardly enough to pay for the fares and incidental expenses such as meals. The cost for the ride increased when they changed to a Pullman in New York, so two people were assigned to each upper and lower berth. Because Danny Coughlin was injured, he did not make the trip and 23 players were to entrain, but at the last minute Rockne added an extra back named Bob Phelan.

Before the trip, the players were told to take some fruit from their dining room kitchen where the personnel were alerted about the invasion. Hunk said little individual packages were prepared with apples and raisins in them. However, only about half of the players stopped by to pick up the fruit bags, preferring to buy some candy bars at the South Bend depot. When the train made a stop, the fellows would ask the conductor how long would the stop last and if it was for at least 20 minutes, they would find a counter for a quick bite and then hustle back to the train. There was only one full meal for everyone including the support group — student managers, student reporter, two cheer leaders and some priests — and that was when the entourage got off in Buffalo. Hullie and Mike's group of South Benders and a few students who paid their own way were on the same train with the team.

In some books, much has been made about the betting on that 1920 game and Hunk Anderson was the source of the story. Hunk's memory might have failed him about the betting. It was the 1919 game that had both teams betting on themselves as a group and Hunk and the Cadets' student manager collected $2100 from their teammates which made the betting pot $4200. They decided on a neutral party to hold the money and went to a local shoemaker shop where the

owner with a thick accent suggesting he was of German ex-
traction, put the money in his safe until it was claimed by
whomever's team won.

In telling the story about the betting, Hunk happened
to mention that he put $60 and Gipp put $400 into the pot. He
then said, "I remember Pete Bahan gave me $300 bucks be-
cause most of it was in gold coins. Bahan told me he had a
business deal with a guy who had a piggy bank full of gold
coins."

I said, "Whoa there, Hunk. Pete did not play in the
1920 game. After he got kicked out of Notre Dame before the
1920 season began, he went to Detroit University."

"I am as sure about Pete and the gold coins as I am
about it being the 1920 game we bet on," said the puzzled
Hunk. We tried to figure out why Hunk would mix the two
games up.

Actually they were almost identical. Although Army
had lost only one game prior to the Notre Dame contest to a
strong Syracuse eleven by a 7-3 score, Army was still the favorite to win in 1919. And the 1919 game was a much closer
contest. In his autobiography, Hunk used the corrected version, recalling 1919 as the year of the team bets which he collected and handled. The 1920 Army game had involved
different circumstances regarding team bets, although I'm
sure there were individual bets among the players of both
teams.

The baseball scandal in which players of the Chicago
White Sox were accused of being bribed and throwing the
World Series against Cincinnati in 1919 had a lot to do about
what transpired before the Notre Dame-Army game of 1920

in regard to betting. Chicagoans felt that their Sox was the best team of all time with such luminaries as Happy Felsch, Chick Gandil, Fred McMullin, Shoeless Joe Jackson, Eddie Cicotte, Claude Williams, Ray Schalk and Buck Weaver. They knew the games were fixed but the naivete of men in sports and other Americans did not believe that a player could be bribed. Their views were best expressed in an article by John B. Sheridan of The Sporting News who felt that the possibility of fixing any kind of a baseball game was highly unlikely: "For a man to throw a game, he would have to be willing to do terrible things to his friends, admirers, family, employers, fans, the good name of America and the game itself. Such a man would die of his own self-contempt. The emotional price a player would have to pay was beyond monetary compensation."

With that attitude, the interest in the scandal going into the 1920 baseball season had faded. The rigging accusations were sloughed off as a poor loser syndrome or as over-rating a team that wasn't really that talented. But another shock occurred. Charges were made of an attempted fix of a Chicago Cubs-Philadelphia Phillies game during the 1920 regular season. A Cook County Grand Jury convened to investigate the attempted fix and widened the scope to also investigate the 1919 World Series. While the Cook County Grand Jury began calling witnesses, a story broke in Philadelphia through an article by James Isaminger of the Philadelphia North American based on an interview with Bill Maharg, a known Eastern gambler. Maharg told writer Isaminger that he knew two games of the World Series were fixed and those Sox players involved were paid $100,000 for their efforts on behalf of the gamblers. The news of the Maharg revelations spread like wildfire. A few days later, on September 27, Marharg and Rube Benton of the Giants testified about the fix in front of the grand jury. After those revelations, Sox pitcher Eddie Cicotte and Shoeless Joe Jackson, under oath, admitted to the Cook County Grand Jury that four games were fixed and then they named six of their teammates as being involved in the fix with them.

What's that got to do with the Notre Dame-Army game of 1920? Gambler Maharg had told his interviewer that an attempt had been made to fix a college football game between two Eastern football powers but it was nipped in the bud when the players who were approached threatened to get the police involved. The names of the schools were not mentioned and it wasn't relevant to the baseball charges...but it was news. (A fine book on baseball entitled "Baseball - America's Diamond Mind," by Richard C. Crepeau, deals with the Black Sox scandal thoroughly. I served with Professor Crepeau on the University Athletics Committee at the University of Central Florida when the school's president, Trevor Colbourn, decided to inaugurate intercollegiate football at the university.)

Hunk Anderson had mentioned to everyone that when the Notre Dame team was leaving for West Point the players were asked by South Bend gamblers to place bets for them and the players wisely refused. Hunk said that Rockne warned the Notre Dame teams on more than one occasion not to let any gamblers befriend them, no matter how innocent the contact may appear to be.

With all the news about fixes coming out of Chicago

and Philadelphia during September in newspapers all around the country, a directive was issued by Army's superintendent, General Douglas MacArthur, which warned West Point's athletes about gamblers and gambling and the consequences resulting from involvement.

From the first 1913 Army-Notre Dame game, Notre Dame had accepted West Point's hospitality of accommodations and meals on the Cadets' campus and certainly the players of both teams mingled. In spite of warnings, there could have been wagers between individual players...who was to know?

One other item about that 1920 game. There are two versions of a story involving Gipp and an Army player named Russell Reeder. The ending was the same in both versions, but the details differ slightly. "Red" Reeder told how he and Gipp went head to head in a pre-game exhibition drop-kicking duel. Hunk Anderson's version said it wasn't one-on-one. As Reeder made his attempts from various distances, Gipp was watching Red's efforts while warming up with passes to Glen "Judge" Carberry. Reeder quit kicking on about the 30, as the distance became too great and he missed on several tries. Gipp then, with some help, gathered four footballs and laid them down on the 50 yard line. Taking one ball at a time, he proceeded to kick two over the goal post's crossbars in one direction and then turned and kick the two over the other goal post.

Was Gipp, a laid back guy who preferred anonymity to glory, a showoff or a showman? Rockne said that Gipp loved the dramatic. Hunk said that Gipp just tried to prove a point to the pundits. While doing leg stretches, Hunk observed the

Reeder/Gipp pre-game kicking duel. George's entry into it was spontaneous and not prearranged because of a bet. Had there been a challenge by Walter French, who really was Army's kicker, not Reeder, Gipp would have accepted under any given conditions. In 1920, there were no specialists or special teams — the rules precluded it. A team's best football players had to be on the field because if a player was replaced, he could not reenter the game during the rest of that half. The rule was eased a bit later in the 1920s to not allow player reentry in the same quarter instead of the same half. And Reeder was not a first stringer. Actually he didn't get into the game. Army's only substitutions were Goodman, Mulligan and Dodd. Hunk said that Gipp wanted to prove a point by his kicking exhibition. What he meant was that the consensus among Eastern sportswriters was that Army would win and French would prove to be the better player between Gipp and him.

When the train stopped to add on the Pullman cars for the trip upstate, Gipp got off and bought some New York newspapers. In scanning the sport pages and reading all the pre-game opinions, George became quite irked about the idea that the scribes predicted that French would best him on the gridiron. Both George and Hunk read the sport pages and Hunk was the first to offer an opinion. "They're full of sh--. Those 'experts' couldn't tell a football from a cow's udder."

"You're right, Hunk," agreed Gipp. "I'm going to have to go out there and show them who's better."

Notre Dame won the toss and Army kicked off to Brandy in the deep spot and he brought the ball back to the Notre Dame 25-yard-line. Mixing his plays well, Brandy engineered a drive into Army territory where Wynne, running over center, fumbled as he got hit and Don Storck recovered on the Army 37-yard-line.

It didn't take Army long to get into high gear. After a short gain by Lawrence on the first play, Walter French, led by his pulling guard Briedster who blocked end Roger Kiley effectively, rambled all the way to the Notre Dame 15-yard-line. It has been written that Gipp made no attempt to tackle French. My report doesn't mention this. If true, was Gipp giving Army a head start so that his heroics would be more dramatic or was he just caught flatfooted? On the next play, with Notre Dame in a tight 7-2-2 defense, Lawrence went over the middle on a quick burst and scored for Army. French's extra point kick was good and Army led 7-0.

Gipp took the ensuing kick-off on the goal line and got hit on the 25 but shook off the tackler and made it up to the Gold and Blue 38-yard-line. On the first play, with pulling left guard Anderson in front, Gipp cut back over tackle for 8 yards. Hunk, under the pile had gotten kneed and got up swinging. Notre Dame received a 15-yard penalty, but on the next play Gipp picked up the 15 yards circling end. Wynne was stopped cold but on the next play from the Notre Dame 46-yard-line, Gipp swiveled his way and shook tacklers off, reaching the Army 29-yard-line where Lawrence finally brought him down. A short snap to Brandy gained nothing and then on the next play, Gipp passed to Kiley on the Army 5 where he was tackled immediately. The ball was caught near the sideline and according to the rules of the times, the ball was spotted at the point of the tackle. So with all the open field to the left, Brandy called an off tackle play with right halfback Mohardt carrying the ball. The off tackle play as executed under Rockne resembled an end run as the ball carrier ran deep and parallel to the line of scrimmage. The quarterback and pulling guard in tandem knock the end out while the halfback and end high and low the tackle in. (Later in his career Rockne had the end shift along with the backfield which put the end in a position to block the tackle alone, releasing the guard to block downfield.) While the flow of the linebacker and halfback (called cornerback now) is drawn to stop the end run, the right half cuts sharply off tackle with the fullback leading the way. Mohardt scored easily and Gipp converted the extra point making it a tie ball game at 7-7.

Army failed to move the ball for a first down after the kickoff and French was forced to punt. Gipp again amazed the spectators as he brought back the punt 57 yards before being tackled by the kicker French and Captain Willhide on Army's 38-yard-line. Still in the second quarter, Notre Dame went ahead on the next play as Gipp found Kiley alone on the Army 30-yard-line and tossed a short pass to Roger who ran the rest of the way untouched because Gipp faked a run before throwing to Kiley, thus drawing the secondary toward the line of scrimmage. Gipp then kicked the extra point again and the Gold and Blue led Army for the first time in the game.

Army received the kickoff but in the series of plays after, the Notre Dame line toughened up and stopped Richards and French short of a first down. French tried to kick away from Gipp and got a good punt end over end that hugged the sideline and went out of bounds deep in Notre Dame territory. Brandy and Wynne (twice) ran the ball to about the 20 and Gipp then punted to French who gathered the ball on his 40-yard-line and made a brilliant broken field run for a 60-yard touchdown. French added the extra point and the game was tied, 14-14.

The kickoff was a long bouncer that could not be advanced and it was safer for Brandy to fall on the ball. Notre Dame made some gains that were nullified by penalties and with fourth down on the Notre Dame 12-yard-line, Gipp went back into the end zone to punt. Time was running out for the first half. While Notre Dame players were getting up to take their positions after the third down play, Gipp had decided to gamble and whispered to Kiley, who was to cover the punt, to watch for a pass. Gipp, in punt formation, faked the kick and tossed a perfect pass to Kiley who dropped the ball as it went out of bounds.

There must have been some confusion involved among the reporters covering the game. A student reporter for the Tribune wrote that Gipp's poor kick went out of bounds on the 10-yard-line. The West Point facilities were primitive and many people were along the sidelines and behind the end zones prepared to dash to the outhouse as the half was about to end. Because the ends are widely poised to cover a punt, the pass to Kiley was of low trajectory and was assumed to be a bad punt since Gipp did get his leg high up in faking the kick. With the ball on the Notre Dame 12-yard-line, French drop-kicked a field goal and Army was ahead 17 to 14 as the half ended.

The second half was all Notre Dame, with Gipp propelling the offense and the entire team playing an exceptionally tight defense. The defense kept French bottled up and his teammate Lawrence was also ineffective. There was no scoring in the third quarter with Army still in the lead, but toward its end, Notre Dame began moving and Gipp, on some sizable gains, brought the ball to the Army 20-yard-line.

As the fourth quarter began, Gipp carried twice, bringing the ball to the Cadet 10-yard-line. Again field position was favorable for a shift to the left with Mohardt in the tailback spot of the Notre Dame box formation. Brandy could have called an end run, which in this case would have had Mohardt moving toward the line of scrimmage as if going off tackle and then cutting back sharply and arcing to circle the end. This would draw the defense in to stop an off-tackle thrust. Heisman Trophy winner Mike Garrett at Southern California used this type of maneuver quite successfully to skirt the ends although he did it in Coach John McKay's I-formation. But the off-tackle play was executed successfully the first time Mohardt scored and it worked again for Brandy, as Mohardt found a huge hole outside the Army tackle and went in for the score. Gipp again made the point after with a drop kick and Notre Dame regained the lead, 21-17. Having seen Notre Dame surge back into the lead and the Army stars being held in check, the Cadets in the stands began to worry.

After Mohardt scored, Notre Dame had a four-point lead with still a lot of time left in the fourth quarter for Army to come back. On the ensuing kickoff, Army had a good return of a short Notre Dame kick that was carried to the Army 45. In three plays, the Cadets gained very little and French booted the ball to Gipp on the Notre Dame 7-yard-line. Gipp probably should have let the ball go into the end zone with both Army ends converging on him. But Gipp's great starting speed got him past them as they rammed into each other. Gipp was finally brought down on the Notre Dame 45. A couple of Gipp passes to Kiley and Captain Coughlin brought the ball to the Army 8-yard-line. Coughlin was a tackle eligible receiver and according to South Bend pros who were moonlight-coached by Rockne when he was a player and later an assistant coach to Harper, it was a Rockne invention. Rockne introduced it to the Meussel Brewers team and some of the same personnel, playing for the 1915 South Bend Athletics, reprised the play which was successful each time it was tried.

The ball was directly in front of the goal post as Brandy called a shift to the left again to make it look like the same play would be run in which Mohardt had scored two touchdowns. But it wasn't — the ball was snapped to fullback Wynne, who, on a full spinner fake to Mohardt, tucked the ball in his belly and with head down, rammed into the middle of the line and was tackled only after he crossed the goal line. Wynne had gotten his wind knocked out and as he was being treated on the ground, Rockne took Gipp out of the game to the thundering ovation of an appreciative crowd. Shortly after that, Wynne got his air back and as he got up Rockne substituted Paul Castner for him. With Gipp out, sophomore Castner, a bit excited about being in the big game, tried the extra point but it went wide and Notre Dame led 27 to 17 with only a few minutes left to play.

Gipp's brilliant play deserved the accolades he received. There was no denying him All-America honors from Walter Camp on Camp's mythical team. Gipp rushed for 150 yards on 20 carries; completed five important passes in nine attempts for 123 yards, scoring with one to Kiley while the others put Notre Dame in scoring position. Gipp also amassed 112 yards on kickoff and punt returns.

The New York and other big Eastern cities newspapers, plus several Chicago papers, covered the game. The press-wire services had their own writers covering the game. The readers of Sunday papers in every nook and corner of the United States read about this game and George Gipp and digested all the superlatives used to describe South Bend's gridiron marvel's display of football talent and heroics.

There were also other poignant observations made about Gipp. The Chicago American commented: "As Gipp was taken out of the game, the Cadets gazed at the wonder man with sorrow and admiration as he staggered off the field." Father Charles O'Donnell, sitting on the Notre Dame bench, noticed that Gipp "...was pale and silent."

Gipp's exhaustion in the Army game brings to mind what Dutch Bergman told me about an incident after the 1919 pro game that Bergman, Gipp and other Notre Dame men played in Rockford the day after the Purdue game. Gipp exerted a lot of energy in that game and well earned the $400 he got for playing. However, the question of his health comes into focus. The Notre Damers were physically beaten up in two days of hard football, especially the backs. In those days, by rule, a player wasn't down by merely being tackled. He had to be held down in the tackler's grasp and contained or else he could get up and run for more yardage. The whistle was a slow one, but it did prevail when blown. So a player knocked off his feet usually found two or more guys dive on top of him and Gipp, when tackled, had a pile of beef crushing him.

After the Rockford game, Gipp was slow going into the

locker room and while others showered, he dallied quite a bit in taking his uniform off. Madigan wondered out loud why Gipp was in the shower so long after almost everyone had left. Just then, one of the Rockford men who played guard, came out and told Madigan that he better check on Gipp — that Gipp passed out and fell to the floor, but had gotten up a few seconds later with his help. Just then, Gipp emerged from the shower and Slip asked him "Are you okay, George?" Gipp replied, "Yeah Slip, everything is jake. I just got dizzy."

Then returning to South Bend on a New York Central train that was only half full, Gipp and Kirk settled into two empty seats in back of the car and sprawled to get a bit of sleep. About 10 miles from South Bend, Kirk thought he'd wake Gipp up but couldn't awaken him. He then ran to the front of the car to get Madigan and Bergman.

"I can't get George up. He looks like he's dead."

"Cut that crap out, Bernie. Hell, if you're so damned worried, check his pulse," replied Madigan.

Bergman said both he and Madigan shook Gipp vigorously. Gipp's face was ashen and a bit eerie. Then when they sat him upright in his seat, he suddenly opened his eyes. Madigan then asked, "George ...are you okay? We're almost in South Bend."

"Now I am, I guess," answered the still unsteady Gipp. "Don't worry guys...I'll get off the train when it stops." Gipp, rubbing his forehead with one hand while reaching in his pocket with the other, asked, "Gimme a light."

Was Gipp's condition in these incidents one caused by exhaustion or an underlying health problem?

Gipp was six feet tall and weighed 180 pounds, which was good size for backs of his era. Not only could he run and pass, he was an excellent kicker as well.

Knute Rockne, the legendarly Notre Dame coach, convinced Gipp to go out for football.

Hunk Anderson was not only Gipp's teammate, but his best friend as well.

The Oliver Hotel in South Bend was Gipp's unofficial off-campus home.

The 1920 team photo included Gipp, top center, but he was too ill to attend the photo session and his picture from the 1919 team photo was inserted into this one.

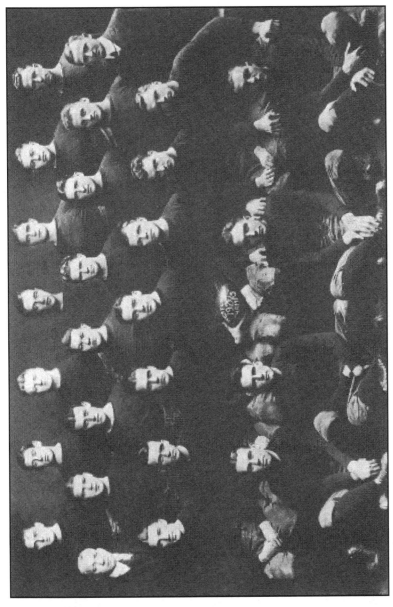

Chet Grant, here in his 90s, was quarterback on the 1920 Gipp team. He became a Notre Dame historian.

Jim Beach was a veteran author, commentator and chronicler of Notre Dame history

John Klosinski, the author's father, was a friend of Gipp's and played on a pre-NFL pro team with him.

Frank Koszewski (Basker), the author's uncle, treated Gipp's sore leg prior to home games.

Gipp is greeted by an admiring fan after a home game.

Dr. Jules Stein, later to become the co-founder of Music Corporation of America (MCA) and president of Universal Pictures, led the band that Gipp danced to at the Oliver Hotel.

# 11

# HOW NOTRE DAME BECAME "THE IRISH"

In addition to perhaps Gipp's greatest all-around performance at Notre Dame, another development of major significance emerged from the 1920 Army game. There was a small group of Notre Dame fans among the 10,000 in the bleacher stands sitting close to the area where Notre Dame student-cub reporter for the South Bend Tribune, Arch Ward, covered the action on the field with written words. Small in number but "big" in voice, it appeared that this group just might "shake down the thunder" and perhaps wake up not only the echoes, but the dead as well. Ward was very impressed, thinking these were South Benders who were buoyed by the Notre Dame spirit as well as spirits that came in a bottle. He was to discover later that this group was from New York City, perhaps Notre Dame's charter-member class of the now omnipresent "subway alumni."

There's more. When Notre Dame fell behind early in the game and then throughout the game, these rabid fans shouted in unison and with foghorn volume: "Let's go Irish! Let's score Irish! Come on Irish!" The team in previous years had been called Irish at times, but on campus only. Legend has it that Pete Vaughan used the term Irish first in the 1909 Notre Dame-Michigan game. In a huddle before the kickoff against Michigan, Vaughan, the Notre Dame fullback, spoke after Captain Howard Edwards finished.

"Look fellows, you're Irish, so let's show them how tough you can be. Go get 'em!" Only two players were non-Irish on that 1909 squad: Ralph Dimmick and Bill Schmitt. Fielding Yost's "Point a Minute" team lost the game to the "Irish" by an 11 to 3 score and after that Michigan avoided playing Notre Dame until the 1940s. This victory established Notre Dame as a midwestern football power, having defeated a school that was considered a football factory by many of its fellow Big Ten members.

It took quite a while for "Irish" to officially catch on. Archie Ward, as his name was by-lined in his reports for the South Bend Tribune in 1920, only mentioned "Irish" once in his Army game article. In fact, what he actually wrote was "Fighting as only a bunch of Irishmen can fight...," might have been the first seed for the growth of the nickname, Irish, because it was the first time that term was used in print off campus. The Tribune, a local paper, was requested to feed the press wire services its reports on Notre Dame practices. The 1920 Army game and Gipp's spectacular performance in it had newspaper coverage from coast to coast and all football fandom wanted to read more about Notre Dame and the spectacular George Gipp. In his practice reports, Ward used the sobriquet "Irish" often instead of the other nicknames Notre

Dame had unofficially acquired. The country was now exposed to the Notre Dame Irish. Sportswriters for various newspapers and magazines were also calling Notre Dame the Irish and it was deeply ingrained in the minds of America's sports followers until 1922.

In 1922 the fund raising campaign set to meet the challenge of the Rockefeller and Carnegie Foundations was far short of raising the required goal of $750,000 and the grants would be lost if Notre Dame failed. Father Burns gave up his presidency at the beginning of 1922 to intensify his fund raising activity and Father Matthew Walsh became Notre Dame's new president.

The deadline was fast approaching for Notre Dame to meet its fund raising quota. Father Walsh had been quoted by the South Bend News-Times as saying that those of whom he had counted on to contribute had failed to do so. He said he was very disturbed by the hundreds of letters he had been receiving daily — and for a long time — from Catholics of all nationalities who protested the "Irish" nickname for Notre Dame. The paper quoted Father Walsh as saying, "...the writers insisted that a Catholic university must represent and serve all Catholics and not be identified with one ethnic group."

A few days later, a story appeared in the Tribune stating that the bishop of the Fort Wayne Catholic Diocese indicated displeasure and grave concern because he too had received a volume of mail from angry Catholics voicing the same protest.

No one saw the situation in its proper perspective better than Father Walsh. If Notre Dame was to succeed in the university's fund drive, it must not alienate the very people from whom the money was expected to come.

A subsequent article in the Tribune indicated Father Walsh had stated that Notre Dame never adopted a nickname and now was seeking a new and appropriate one. Suggestions were welcome, and they came in volume — ranging from the names of predatory animals like Lions, Tigers and Bears, to nature's devastators such as Cyclones, Avalanches, Golden Tornados and Blizzards. Then there were the Warriors, Knights, Tillers, etc. The previously used "Ramblers," descriptive of the Notre Dame teams traveling to all parts of the country to play a worthy opponent, was selected as the nickname. Because of the Notre Dame team's many journeys, it had also had been called "Nomads," "Rovers" and "Roads' Scholars," but "Ramblers" won out.

In 1923, Francis Wallace, who had been a student sports reporter for South Bend's other paper, the News-Times, went to work for the Associated Press in New York upon being graduated. In writing a report on Notre Dame, Wallace used "Irish," but his copy was returned to him with a note from the editor that because of Notre Dame's request, this name was not to be used in referring to Notre Dame. Later, Wallace became a writer for the Evening Post, a small newspaper, and used "Irish" frequently and got away with it because the paper was unaware of the requested ban and too small to learn about it. Father Walsh had notified the big newspapers of New York and Chicago and the news wire services and syndicates but apparently missed some of the smaller publications.

In his book, "The Notre Dame Story," Wallace discussed the ban. Apparently he wasn't aware of the financial reasons given by Father Walsh to the Tribune and News-Times, because he thought the reason was that Notre Dame tried to lessen the derogatory sniping that Notre Dame had been receiving. He cited a Lincoln, Nebraska, newspaper headlining Notre Dame's game with the Cornhusker's thusly: "Horrible Hibernians Come to Town Today."

South Bend itself was no stranger to ethnic tensions and bigotry. An incident that took place just two years after the "Irish" name brouhaha, while having nothing to do with Father Walsh's decision to ban the use of the Irish nickname, nonetheless indicates the temper of the times. Indiana became a Ku Klux Klan hotbed when D. C. Stephenson of Indianapolis became the Grand Dragon or head of that malicious organization. South Bend, because its growing manufacturing economy was creating numerous jobs, had a tremendous influx of immigrants, mostly Eastern European Catholics and blacks from the South. It was a fertile ground for hate groups like the Klan to terrorize, persecute, spew malice and attempt to recruit WASPs (White, Anglo Saxon, Protestants) into its group.

Stephenson and many of his Indianapolis Klansmen arrived in South Bend in the early morning of May 18, 1924 for a planned big Klan picnic and a nighttime parade. But God and Notre Dame students intervened. A torrential rainstorm cancelled the picnic and when the rainstorm lessened a bit toward evening the Klan decided to go through with the parade. They assembled in two groups, one at the intersection of Michigan and Washington Streets and the other at the intersection of Michigan and Jefferson. As the parade was

GIPP AT NOTRE DAME — The Untold Story

about to begin the Klan was greeted by a huge downpour and gangs of Notre Dame students who ripped off the Klansmen's hoods and dunce caps that were worn by some and shredded their robes. The students roughed up some of the Klansmen who were reluctant to have their symbol of superior bigotry shredded. Most of the Klansmen fled to the safety of the train station and left as soon as a train going to Indianapolis arrived.

Wallace insisted on restoring the Irish nickname for Notre Dame. His national name recognition and Notre Dame allegiance can be compared to modern-day alums like Regis Philbin. Wallace had been writing books of sports fiction and his first book, "O'Reilly of Notre Dame," caught the eye of Hollywood and was made into a movie in 1929 with a new title, "The Spirit of Notre Dame," which starred Lew Ayres, Sally Blane, J. Farrell MacDonald as the coach and several Notre Dame players including the famous "Four Horsemen." During his career as a writer, Wallace wrote 17 books and five were made into movies. Because of his columns, books and movies, Wallace gained national name recognition and was very influential among his colleagues and at Notre Dame. His syndicated column in New York's largest paper, the Daily News, gave him freedom of content and on every writing opportunity he'd use "Irish" in connection with Notre Dame with the added descriptive adjective, "fighting," thus "Fighting Irish" was born. Some sportswriters who were Irish followed Wallace's example and also used Irish for Notre Dame in writing about the school's teams. This, however, was sporadic and the nickname Ramblers was still predominant and in use.

It seems that there had been some rumbling at Notre

Dame caused by Wallace's one-man campaign for the restoration of the "Irish" nickname to Notre Dame's teams. It had been reported that in a 1927 Scholastic publication, Father Walsh reversed himself and said that Notre Dame's official nickname was "Irish." This apparently was for campus consumption because he neglected to notify the local and national media as he did in 1922 when he said that Ramblers was the official Notre Dame alias.

In 1928, Notre Dame planned to embark on a building program of some much needed buildings and a new stadium for Rockne's team and I'm sure Father Walsh did not want to antagonize the non-Irish Catholics, although some of those 1922 protestors were dying off. And when the building of the stadium began, Notre Dame played its entire 1929 schedule away from home, temporarily blunting the inroads of Wallace's campaign and solidifying the Ramblers nickname. Father Walsh was to be replaced by Father Charles L. O'Donnell in 1928 by operation of cannon law. If there was to be a controversy between the other ethnic Catholics and Francis Wallace and his followers over a nickname, it would be in the hands of the new president to settle.

The 1935 "Game of the Century" against the Ohio State Buckeyes heralded the "Ramblers" in headlines such as the one that appeared in the Columbus Sunday Dispatch: "Ramblers Rally to Beat Fumbling Ohio 18-13." A New York newspaper headlined, "Layden's Ramblers upset Ohio State."

Perhaps Notre Dame's best basketball team of all time, the 1935-36 Helm's Foundation National Champion (the NCAA wasn't in the declaring champions or the annual championship tournament business at that time) was known

174

nationally as the Ramblers. Coach George Keogan's potent team had Johnny Moir and Johnny Ford augmented by Ray Myer at forwards. Paul "Giz" Nowak was at center, George Ireland, Frank Wade and Tommy Wukovits were the guards, with two other good young subs filling in, namely Earl Brown and Ed Sadowski, so the team was getting national publicity for the "Ramblers" nickname.

Wallace, in continuing his campaign to restore "Irish," did manage around 1937-38 to get Ted Husing and other radio announcers to use Irish in their play-by-play broadcasts of Notre Dame games. On the airwaves, the football team was the Irish, although Ramblers wasn't completely eliminated because of its use by the press. Toward the end of Elmer Layden's tenure as Notre Dame coach, an Irish Terrier mascot named Clashmore Mike was introduced. (In later years, a succession of Clashmore Mikes was replaced by a new mascot, a student dressed as a Leprechaun.) Wallace was on his way to victory, which was finalized and sealed when Frank Leahy replaced Elmer Layden as coach.

I had contact with Wallace when he lived in Bellaire, Ohio, but got to know him better when he moved to Cocoa Beach in Florida. Wallace had suffered a heart attack and appreciated Florida's warm winter weather. I visited with him on several occasions and we would discuss Notre Dame, past and present, almost exclusively. He was a fine gentleman and very gracious. He even allowed me to bring my son Marc to visit with him although most convalescing men wouldn't relish third graders as company. Marc had seen a movie on television titled, "Kid Galahad," based on Frank's book by the same name, and was impressed. I had the book on my book shelf and promised to give it to Marc if he got it autographed by Wallace, which he did during that visit.

During one of our conversations, Wallace told me how long it took him to get the "Irish" name back for the Notre Dame teams. He admitted that he wasn't sure it would stick until Frank Leahy became coach. There were younger sports editors on the scene however, and the old ones who may have used Ramblers at one time switched over to using Irish when they saw the Notre Dame teams outfitted in green jerseys.

Frank Leahy not only replaced the traditional blue jerseys with green, but he also scrapped the famous Notre Dame shift, which had been used with such great success by Rockne, and adopted the Chicago Bears modernized T-formation. And if those two major changes didn't bring enough screams of protests from rabid Notre Dame followers, his first use of the T-formation (1942) ended up with only a 7-2-2 record after his initial 1941 season, when he used Rockne's system, was an undefeated one, marred only by a 0-0 tie with Army. Unfazed by criticism, Leahy went on to win ball games and championships and everybody (at least the Notre Dame partisans) was Irish and is Irish on game day just like they are on St. Patrick's Day. And even if the jerseys now are blue, rest assured that in the stands there'll be a lot of green. Go Irish!

# 12

# THE BEGINNING
# OF THE END

Notre Dame left West Point immediately after the Army game for New York City and a night on the town, hosted by some New York "Irish" alumni. Leaving New York early Sunday morning, the team arrived in South Bend that evening to be greeted by a large jubilant crowd at the station.

Homecoming week with all its activities was in full swing on Monday. Practice for the first string began Tuesday and fundamentals were stressed by Rockne during the week's preparation for the Purdue Boilermakers. Hunk Anderson's pro team, the South Bend Arrows, was still undefeated, having beaten the Michigan City Nepos 40-0, so he asked Manager Joe Benko for the week off from his moonlight coaching chores and was accommodated readily.

On the personal side for Gipp, it didn't seem to be going too well with Iris Trippeer. As reported previously, he hoped to have her stay the week during Homecoming Week but she came into town for only one day and left the same night for Indianapolis at 11 o'clock. Speculatively, it can be assumed that she came to town to impress Gipp that his telephone calls to her at the Indiana Public Service Commission were disruptive and drawing the ire of her supervisors. Hunk and his future wife Marie Martin were with Gipp and Iris that evening and saw from a distance that Gipp and Iris quarreled as they danced, but there was no break in their relationship at that point. Iris, though, had a week to think about it because she was to meet Gipp the following Friday at the Claypool Hotel in Indianapolis on the eve of the Indiana game.

Kewpie Night for the Purdue game was held in the Oliver Hotel's Tapestry Room. There were two downtown parades during the week, including one with Notre Dame students marching to the Oliver Hotel to serenade the Purdue party. In his book, "One for the Gipper," Pat Chelland quoted Arch Ward's report on that festivity on the game's eve, which stated that there were impromptu speeches by Purdue Coach A. Scanlon and some Purdue players. The call for Gipp to speak, however, went unanswered. Gipp wasn't hiding in the crowd of students nor was he reluctant, as Ward suggested — he was on campus.

What Ward apparently lost in the conglomerate of activities was an "athletic circus" which included a boxing card at Notre Dame in the gym along with wrestling matches, featuring interhall teams. Both Gipp and Hunk Anderson were prevailed upon to serve as judges and Rockne was the referee of the two sports contests. This event was organized and staged for the homecoming by Father Bernard Lange, the physical education director of the school. A pep rally and a snake dance preceded the boxing/wrestling bouts.

Another feature of the week was a dinner for all mono-gram winners, held at the Carroll Hall dining room. Lou Salmon, Notre Dame's first All-American in 1903, was hon-ored.

On game day, the crowd of 12,000 set a new home game attendance record, the third time it had been broken that year. Perhaps that figure should bear an asterisk with a notation that there was a double header at Cartier Field. The Mishawaka-Elkhart high school game started at 12:30 and the Notre Dame-Purdue game followed at 2:30 that after-noon.

Rockne started his shock troops, or second team, and they were more than capable of holding Purdue scoreless. In the second quarter, the first string came in and Notre Dame began to move. Gipp resumed where he left off at West Point. He carried for one touchdown and passed for two more. His run was spectacular. From the Irish 20-yard-line, Gipp daz-zled the home crowd with a sensational 80-yard run in which it seemed he was in the grasp of at least half of the Boiler-maker tacklers, only to dervish out of their hold and continue to ramble for the score. His extra point kick was good. Gipp was in the game for about only two quarters, yet he still man-aged to amass 257 total yards with 129 coming on 10 carries and 128 yards from four out of seven completed passes. Two went for touchdowns — one to Buck Shaw on a tackle-eligible play and the other to Eddie Anderson. While Eddie was neglected in the offensive play calling against Army the previous week, he stood out defensively in throttling the revved-up cylinders of Army's All-America Walter French in the second half of the game.

The last touchdown against the Boilermakers came on a blocked kick by left guard Hunk Anderson, who scooped up the ball and went 30 yards for the score. Paul Castner, who replaced the slightly injured fullback Chet Wynne, converted the extra point.

Notre Dame record books don't have a category for scoring touchdowns by defensive interior linemen, but I'm sure Hunk owns the record because he also scored two others against Purdue after blocking punts in another game. Hunk told me it was in the 1919 game; Notre Dame's media guide, in the section of Notre Dame's all-time All-Americans in the blurb under his photo, credits the two touchdowns to him in the 1921 Purdue game, but doesn't mention the 1920 game.

Hunk's touchdown ended the scoring for Notre Dame and the final score was Notre Dame 28, Purdue 0. The next day, with Hunk Anderson present on the sidelines at Springbrook Park, his South Bend Arrows defeated the powerful Wabash pro team, which had wins over the Jim Thorpe-led Canton Bulldogs, Columbus Panhandles and Cincinnati Celts. The Arrows won by a score of 20 to 7.

At this time during the 1920 season there were talks of a post season game for Notre Dame and several teams were mentioned. A game against Penn State, which had not lost since its fourth contest of 1919, was turned down by the Faculty Athletics Board. Besides, there were three more games left on the schedule and Rockne was hoping that with added victories Notre Dame might get some consideration for the prestigious Rose Bowl.

Indiana was a more formidable hurdle for Notre Dame to overcome than Purdue, but there was no special emphasis in regard to personnel or tactics employed by the Hoosiers during the week's practice. After losing its opener to Iowa, Indiana had beaten DePauw, Minnesota, Northwestern, Purdue and Wisconsin. This team was tough and not one to be taken lightly.

On Friday noon, November 12, the Notre Dame team left South Bend for Indianapolis, a two-hour train ride without other station stops. It was getting cold in Indiana that time of the year and Rockne told the boys to wear appropriate clothing. Gipp and Hunk were prepared. George wore a light aviator jacket with a topcoat folded over his arm. He told Hunk that morning on the train that when he got up and out of bed he had the chills. On Saturday morning, game day, Gipp said nothing to Hunk about how he felt and Hunk, thinking the problem had passed, didn't bother to ask. Hunk also remembered that Gipp had a slight cough, but Hunk thought that it was akin to a throat clearing cough rather than a deep seated persistent cough that usually accompanies a cold. John U. Bacon, in his article on Gipp in the January 5, 1997 Detroit News, wrote that Gipp was coughing on the day of the Indiana game and was not in the best of health.

On game day morning, after a quick breakfast with the team in the Claypool Hotel, Gipp rushed to the depot to greet his youngest sister Dorothy, or Dolly, as friends and family called her, to get her registered at the hotel. Dolly had traveled from Kalamazoo, where she was attending college, to see her brother play. Gipp had fulfilled one appointment on Friday, that of meeting Iris at their familiar rendezvous spot on the mezzanine floor of the Claypool, for what he thought would be a pleasant lovers' encounter. It was a rude awakening for Gipp to learn that Iris was married, since she had said nothing about it the week before when she came to South Bend. Gipp told a friend the following week that by the manner in which she told him the news he knew she made a fool of him and was playing him for a sucker.

Going by the public records, it seems that Iris was a married woman when she met and dated Gipp. If those records for some reason are wrong, then there has to be an assumption that she was an engaged woman with a fiancee in the background during the time she was seeing Gipp. A young woman of that era just didn't marry as suddenly as she told Gipp she had done. It could be assumed that if she was married, she was separated and later reconciled with her husband and dropped Gipp. If she was engaged, she might have had a quarrel with her fiancee that was patched up and then decided to drop Gipp. Her demand that Gipp change his ways before she would date him, was a false excuse.

The Indiana game was played in Washington Park in Indianapolis Saturday afternoon before a crowd of 14,000 fans and Indiana gave Rockne and Notre Dame their biggest scare of the season.

It was a game a journeyman linemen would have loved. Notre Dame could not move the ball throughout the first half and, in the meantime, the Indiana Hoosiers made excellent drives from their territory into Notre Dame's with Kyle and Mathys causing cracks in the Notre Dame defense. Having been stopped on the first drive deep in Notre Dame territory without a score, the Cream and Crimson on the next sustained drive opted to kick a field goal when stopped short of a first down. Elliot Risley stepped back and kicked a 15-yard field goal right through the middle of the crossbars. In the meantime, Gipp had been taken out of the contest after a vicious gang tackle dislocated his shoulder in the second quarter. His pain was agonizing and Rockne, stealing glances, could see Gipp's face contorted from the slightest movement of the upper body.

The Hoosiers scored one more time before Notre Dame showed signs of coming to life. Indiana got into Notre Dame territory again with its running attack, but fooled the Irish when Mathys threw a perfect pass to end Frank Hanny — a big talented sophomore — on the goal line for a score and the extra point by Risley made it Indiana 10 and Notre Dame 0.

Hunk Anderson gave the background on what had happened in that game. Neither the team nor Rockne had taken Indiana lightly, as has been reported. Any team with only one loss in the Big Ten is going to be a tough opponent. Still, they did not expect that Indiana wanted this game so badly that the Irish were going to be exposed to "new wrinkles" never before experienced by them. In fact, the Hoosiers would have sacrificed the Big Ten title just to beat interstate rival Notre Dame and snap the Irish winning streak.

After the game was over, Hunk managed to talk with Hoosier guard John Leonard before leaving the field to return to the hotel with the team. Leonard told Hunk that they had been practicing for the Notre Dame game for two weeks, with Coach E. O. Stiem gambling on beating their opponent, Wisconsin, just prior to playing Notre Dame, without practicing for the game at hand. Coach Stiem was a Wisconsin grad and perhaps he felt that he could handle his alma mater without preparation, which he indeed did. During his practices for Notre Dame he taught the freshman team the Notre Dame shift and plays so the varsity could learn what to do with tactics Stiem was about to install for the game.

Hunk Anderson described the tactics Stiem employed against Notre Dame:

"When we were on offense, Indiana used a stunting defense and that screwed us up. Stiem had three guys (Leonard, Mumbley and Bell) switching positions and darting in and out while our backfield was shifting. When Gipp was in the game, and we shifted right, those guys left one man in front of the two of us and the other stunters acted as linebackers, rushing with the shift to put more men on the side where Gipp usually carried the ball. And the bastards gang tackled and that's how George got hurt. When they were on offense, they didn't try any cute tricks.

"They were like goldamn Kamikaze pilots. They just seemed to pull the two guards in front of some backs and they all exploded toward the spot where the hole was to be made. When they came my way, I just submarined to knock as many blockers down as I could and pile up the interference and Mathys and Kyle didn't make much yardage because of the clutter. I told Clipper (Smith) to do the same thing and with Ojay's (Larson) size at center, we controlled the middle of the line in most of the third and the fourth quarters. And our offense got going when Brandy started calling plays to go over the middle."

In the fourth quarter, Brandy, using Mohardt mostly over the middle with good blocking by Anderson, Larson and Smith, brought the ball to the one-yard-line. This time Mohardt and Wynne found it tough as the Cream and Crimson, taking a cue from Hunk Anderson's tactics, had Leonard, Bell and Mumbley submarine with two linebackers plugging behind them and the Irish backs were stopped cold.

Rockne had watched Gipp along that sideline and it seemed he'd catch Gipp's wince as he'd make an abrupt turn of the head to follow the play. As the Irish called a time out to discuss strategy, Rock turned to Gipp and asked, "George, can you put the ball in the end zone?" Ordinarily, Gipp would have said, "Of course I can" or something such as that. This time he said, "I'd like to try, Rock." George remembered that remark because he repeated it to Hunk later in the hotel, saying his shoulder hurt him so much that he wasn't sure he could hold onto the ball when he got it. (Another version has Gipp pleading with Rockne to let him go in.)

The first call was off tackle. As Gipp got the snap, the pain shot through his shoulder and threw him off stride as he hit the line for no gain. Fourth down and it was do or die. This time the call was for Gipp on what was a direct slant between Hunk Anderson and Captain Frank Coughlin. Gipp, with his head down and plunging like a Bronko Nagurski, scored. He rammed into the goal posts which were on the goal line according to the rules of that time. Hunk said that as Gipp got up, his arm was dangling limply and he was biting his lower lip. He managed to handle the snap for his drop-kick point after touchdown and it was good as the Irish now trailed by only three points, 10 to 7. Gipp stayed in the game because if he was taken out the rules would not allow him to reenter. And Rockne, knowing that Gipp was in pain, but also knowing Gipp's competitive drive in situations such as the one that existed, gambled that he would somehow win the game. And he did.

Indiana got the ball on Gipp's kickoff. The Hoosiers, after having fought so hard, lost some of their zest after the Notre Dame touchdown. A short snap to the upback was juggled and then fumbled when two Irish linemen broke through and hit the runner and Wynne recovered for Notre Dame near the Hoosier 30-yard-line. After a run by Mohardt with good blocking up front put the ball on the Indiana 15-yard-line Gipp lobbed a wobbly pass to Eddie Anderson on the five and Eddie was tackled a yard shy of the goal line. On a quick count from the T-formation, Brandy sneaked it over. But Gipp, in pain, couldn't handle the ball well enough for the point after try and missed. The Hoosiers had one more chance to win or tie as they drove the ball with relentless determination into Irish territory. The battered and bruised Notre Dame line managed to stop the Hoosiers' drive and on a fourth down field goal try, Risley's kick went wide. Notre Dame won 13-10.

Hunk Anderson with his submarine tactics that piled the interference up — many times on top of him — played most of the game injured. The whole squad took a battering from a rough bunch of Hoosiers who were well prepared for the game.

Notre Dame players had dressed for the game at the

hotel and did not shower until they got back. Rockne had reserved rooms that had showers although most of the other rooms in the hotel featured tubs. When Gipp got to his room, Joe Donaldson, the team's student manager and his "Man Friday," was there to assist him. It was Gipp's left shoulder that was injured but any movement of the right side or using the right arm also caused pain in the injured area. Joe had to get Gipp undressed and the jersey presented a big problem. If he had had scissors, Donaldson would have cut it away, but he had to work it off Gipp inch by inch, as Gipp endured terrible pain in the process. Donaldson, who passed away on March 18, 1999, told I. I. Probst quite a bit more about what transpired in Gipp's room.

"After I got him undressed Gipp went into the shower and I adjusted the water to his comfort. I soaped the area where he couldn't get because he couldn't raise his arms. Later when he finished I got some towels and I helped by drying the same upper part that was too painful for Gipp to reach. He managed to slowly get the rest of his body dried. I helped dress him and combed his hair for him."

While Gipp was in the shower and also after Donaldson got him dressed, teammates were dropping by his room to ask him how he felt. Hunk Anderson and Ojay Larson came to see him together. Larson was the first to speak, using George's Laurium nickname. "How you doing, Gipper?"

"Not so hot," replied Gipp.

"Hey, that was a tough sonovabitchen bunch of Hoosiers we played," added Anderson. Hunk himself was quite battered and bruised. Gipp also complained of having a sore throat and he did cough sporadically. Gipp asked if someone would go to the drug store on the corner near the Claypool to get him something with which he could gargle his throat. Fortunately, the other student manager came by to check if Donaldson needed help, so he volunteered to run the errand for Gipp. Rockne also came by to check on Gipp and made a decision that Gipp should have his shoulder examined by a specialist. Rockne suspected a broken collar bone as the cause of Gipp's pain. Rockne was not without credentials for making the diagnosis. Upon graduation from Notre Dame he was going to study medicine at the University of St. Louis and get some much needed income by coaching a local high school team there. The dean of the medical school didn't think Rockne could or should do both chores and Rockne had to make a choice. Rockne needed the money because he had just married Bonnie Skiles on July 15, 1914. So he then accepted a job at Notre Dame teaching chemistry and volunteered to assist head football coach Jess Harper after which Jess managed to make it a permanent job with a little extra compensation added to his pay check.

Gipp's youngest sister Dorothy, or Dolly, told author Jim Beach about Rockne's decision to send Gipp to Chicago. Sunday morning, while the team was at Mass in the hotel's conference room, Gipp came down to her room to lie in a tub full of hot water, hoping to ease the pain in his shoulder and neck...actually, the whole upper body. She wasn't sure who said the Mass. It could have been Father Vincent Mooney, a Rockne friend who later, in 1925, baptized Rockne into the Catholic faith. It also might have been Father Charles O'Donnell or Father Matthew Walsh, who as chaplains during World War I, had experience saying Mass with makeshift altars. After Mass, the team ate breakfast at the hotel while Rockne, knowing that Gipp was in his sister's room, had breakfast for them sent to Dolly's room.

Dolly said Rockne had made reservations for Gipp from the Claypool Hotel to stay at the Chicagoan Hotel. The specialist whom Gipp was to see was a friend from Rockne's high school days in Chicago, whose offices were in a building near the hotel. Dolly didn't remember the doctor's name. She said that Rockne also made train ticket arrangements at the station for Gipp to go straight through to Chicago. When the train stopped in South Bend, George stayed on it to continue the journey to the Windy City. On Monday, he was to stay in his hotel room until he got a call from the physician's office, whom Rockne was to contact.

What Dolly said doesn't agree with what has been written in books concerning the reason for Gipp heading to Chicago. The popular reason given was that George promised former classmate Grover Malone to give his team, Loyola Academy, pointers on kicking. If this was so, Gipp's journey to Chicago was a convenient coincidence inasmuch as he could "kill two birds with one stone." No one mentioned a reconciliation between the two feuders from the 1919 locker room incident. Perhaps during the course of the year there was an apology from Malone for the incident and Gipp graciously accepted and reciprocated with the favor.

But one thing is bothersome about Gipp's trip, which took most of three days for Gipp to complete. No writer has mentioned a word about his visit with the specialist and on top of that, Gipp has been accused of carousing around Chicago with Grover Malone during all that time. Malone is given as the source for such a despicable indictment of a man who probably would have had a terrible time raising a bottle or glass to his lips, given the banged up condition he was suffering. More on this later.

On Monday morning Gipp got a call at the hotel from the orthopaedic specialist's office that he would see Gipp at noon, during the doctor's lunch hour, which the doctor sacrificed. After attending to the shoulder dislocation, the doctor began poking other areas with his fingers that brought some loud "ouches" from Gipp. Gipp then was sent to an X-ray lab in the same building, but there, without an appointment, Gipp had a long wait because all the doctors in nearby buildings sent their patients to the lab since it was the only one in that vicinity. These days, some doctors now have their own diagnostic equipment, but in 1920, X-ray machines weren't that available and weren't as "streamlined" nor as sophisticated and improved as they are in modern medicine.

The doctor tried to make some cancellations of appointments for the next day, Tuesday, so he could see Gipp in the late afternoon when the X-rays would be in his office and he had a chance to study them. Dolly Gipp said that her brother not only had a dislocated shoulder, but a fractured collar bone (as suspected by Rockne) and the doctor wasn't sure if it was a pinched nerve or the swelling along the nerve that was involved in the painful area. Since Gipp's time, the emulsion of today's X-ray film has been improved for better pictures and therefore, better reading, but back then the doctor could not pinpoint the exact cause of Gipp's injury.

Somehow the alumni who were planning to honor Gipp at the coming Saturday's game in Evanston against

Northwestern learned Gipp was in town. Apparently they were in contact with Rockne about their intention to honor Gipp, designating the game day as George Gipp Day. Two members of the Chicago Notre Dame Alumni Association took George out to dinner on Monday. He was given some complimentary game tickets to pass on to friends and relatives. My uncle, Frank Koszewski at the Oliver Turkish baths, received two of them from Gipp upon his return from Chicago.

Dolly Gipp apparently did not mention to Jim Beach anything about Tuesday night or about Wednesday except to say her brother returned to South Bend that day.

Gipp ostensibly could have met Grover Malone perhaps that Tuesday night and the next day he would have gone to Loyola Academy to give pointers on kicking to Malone's team. This is assuming that Gipp did see Malone and that the spat had been forgotten or settled. The kicking clinic was entirely verbal. He certainly was unable to demonstrate because he was trussed up with his left arm in a sling so that its weight would not be pulling down and causing pain to the sore shoulder/neck area.

Gene Basker said that around five o'clock Wednesday, his oldest sibling, brother Ed, bumped into Gipp waiting outside the Oliver Hotel wearing a sling with his topcoat draped over his shoulders. Ed attended South Bend High — later named Central High when more high schools were built — which was located only two blocks from the Oliver. On some days he ran errands for his father in connection with supplies for the Turkish baths.

Ed talked with Gipp for about only a minute as Gipp told him that he had just returned from Chicago and was

191

waiting for someone. Then Gipp gave Ed two tickets to the Northwestern game to give to his father. At that moment, a car driven by a young lady stopped at the entrance and Gipp got in and they drove away.

The identity of the young lady is a mystery. Chet Grant learned who she was but he was saving that information for his proposed book. The young lady was probably the South Bend woman who visited Chet Grant at the basement of the Notre Dame Library in the early 1970s, saying she was Gipp's fiancee when he died. Gipp's date that Wednesday was a short one because Hunk Anderson checked Gipp's room around seven o'clock and Gipp was already in it, slowly getting ready for bed. Perhaps Gipp called the girl to discuss their relationship and to resume dating her after Iris finally told Gipp the shocking truth — that she was married.

Gipp gave Hunk details about his Chicago medical experience saying he felt good and the pain subsided somewhat when the doctor gave him a shot (apparently a low dose narcotic) but the pain returned when the medication wore off. He said his sore throat was still that way...sore, but his cough had abated. Grover Malone was not mentioned.

Gipp thought he'd get some rest going to bed early even if he didn't immediately fall asleep.

"I hope you feel better tomorrow, George...see 'ya then," Hunk said as he was leaving Gipp's room.

"Yeah, Hunk, there's always tomorrow."

# 13

# THE MALIGNING
# OF GEORGE GIPP

We have wondered and pondered how the slanderous exaggerations concerning Gipp's recreational vices got their start. Latter day historians not only borrow the "rot" from each other, but some go on to fabricate some real whoppers about Gipp and always give an anonymous source, such as "a friend said...etc." That isn't good enough to warrant misrepresentation and traducement. Hearsay should be presented with skepticism and not dogmatic fervor, otherwise it's a deliberate pollution of the historical atmosphere and needs fumigation.

First of all, one has to research the era in which Gipp lived and place himself in it to fully understand what life was like at that time for Gipp and his contemporaries. Gambling was commonplace...it was a part of the male culture in the America of the first quarter of the 1900s. What Gipp did was what most of the male population was doing. Other Notre Dame students would be placing bets at Hullie and Mike's and, yes, some played pool there and bet some loose change to back their skills. My dad, John Klosinski, who lived and worked in South Bend, said that when he played football the players were expected to bet on themselves and their team. As for drinking alcoholic beverages, that had been an epidemic since the 1800s and by the early 1900s it was being fought by temperance groups that included the clergy and much of the female population.

In my search for the genesis of the degradation of Gipp with stories of his taking part in extended drinking binges, womanizing and doing other ridiculous things — things that Gipp's friends like Hunk Anderson and my dad said were untrue — I turned to the earliest books and writings of Notre Dame chroniclers of the Gipp era. I started with Knute Rockne and Francis Wallace.

I surmised that Rockne must have known that Gipp was a gambler, although he said he learned that after Gipp died. Rockne said that Gipp got lazy in easy games that were against inferior opponents but played like a tiger against the tough ones and that's true. He knew Gipp didn't care much for schoolwork and gave an account of Gipp's "getting fired" from Notre Dame and of his reinstatement after an oral exam. He called Gipp "brilliant" and that he was. So there wasn't anything in Rock's autobiography that would put a label of ne'er-do-well, unrestrained alcoholic, rebel, or an addicted gambler on Gipp. To me, a gambling addict is one who wins some but loses a lot and continues to do so regardless of the consequences.

Gipp lost only in shooting dice and while he rolled dice on occasions, he basically stayed away from that game. As he once told Hunk Anderson, playing poker and shooting pool required brains and skill; rolling dice required luck. Gipp always bet on and stayed with what he considered to be "the sure thing," games where he could use his considerable skills to assure a favorable outcome.

Francis Wallace's books had about the same revelations that Rockne's autobiography had. Wallace had an opportunity to observe Gipp because besides covering Notre Dame sports for the South Bend News-Times as a student, he also had a part time job behind the registry desk at the Oliver Hotel. Gipp would often stop by and converse with him before playing billiards. Rockne and Wallace mentioned Gipp's faults and predicaments, but neither hit Gipp "below the belt" like the iconoclasts have done since Paul Gallico and Jim Beach started the tarnishing that has smeared Gipp. To his credit, Beach was going to tell the real story in a book which he had started to write but never completed before his death.

In 1958 Jim Beach wrote an article for Saga Magazine in which he told of Gipp, after the 1920 Indiana game, remaining on the train after the team got off in South Bend. According to Beach, Gipp continued on to Chicago to meet with Grover Malone. The essence of the story was that Gipp supposedly went there to give kicking lessons to Grover Malone's team at Loyola Academy, but instead the two went out on a three-day drinking binge. Also to his credit, Beach told me in 1988 and again in 1994 that he made some big mistakes in some of his writings on Gipp, alluding to that 1958 article and others, and that he was going to make amends in his new book. Both times he told me he had talked with Gipp's sister Dorothy (Dolly), who gave him a lot of information on her brother that he did not have.

Beach never specified what the mistakes that he made were. The 1988 phone call I received from him was in lieu of a Christmas card but Jim brought Gipp into the conversation by saying that he had had a lunch meeting with an NBC producer who was interested in making a movie about Notre Dame that would feature George Gipp's career. The purpose of the meeting, he was told, was to find out if Jim would help write the script. The producer was making exploratory contacts to see who and what resources would be available for a Gipp TV movie.

Notre Dame had an undefeated season under Lou Holtz in 1988 and the producer — Jim told me his name but I never cataloged it in my mind — was very impressed with Notre Dame's runner/receiver Raghib "The Rocket" Ismail and that gave him the idea of doing the movie on another great runner, Gipp. In his phone call to me, Beach said that he didn't know how much sayso he would have in what went into the script, but he would try to make sure that "Gipp got a better break than the one I gave him." Jim did not hear any more about the project and figured the idea was abandoned.

It was after I talked Jim into writing a Gipp story as therapy after he had his stroke that Beach again mentioned receiving information he hadn't had in his previous works on Notre Dame and Gipp. He said it was Gipp's sister Dorothy, a retired school teacher, who gave him the inside story on Gipp's injury in the Indiana game and his Chicago journey for treatment. I wasn't sure what was involved until I began writing this book and came across the Grover Malone carousing version.

I had read about the three-day drinking binge in other books but wasn't aware that Beach was the writer who first reported the story. In getting hold of his 1958 Gipp article in Saga Magazine and reading about Gipp and Malone, I realized that Jim had taken liberties with that situation and other Gipp related events probably to beef up the story to get it published. Perhaps the Saga format required a bit of sensationalism and maybe Beach was trying to accommodate that requirement in his Gipp piece.

In the article, Jim attributed the story of the three-day drunken binge to Grover Malone. He didn't say he got it directly from Malone, however. Unless it was Malone's way of getting even with Gipp for the 1919 towel incident in which Grover called Gipp a "slacker" for not having been in the U.S. army or the SATC, the wartime student military training program, that incident then amounted to Beach taking liberties.

Further reading of Beach's Saga story revealed that he changed the time of Gipp's death from 3:31 a.m. on December 14, 1920, to a more convenient time of 7:30 p.m. to fit in a prearranged phone call from St. Joseph's Hospital to the Oliver Hotel. Upon learning of Gipp's death, the hotel would then dim the lights and blink them for one minute to inform Gipp's pool-playing buddies that Gipp had just died. In actuality, the pool tables at the hotel were shut down at midnight on weekdays, so there were no pool buddies around at 3:31 a.m., the actual time of Gipp's death. A phone message did arrive at the Oliver switchboard around 3:35 a.m. and the blinking of lights notified the staff and cleanup crew that their friend was dead.

The first one to throw dirt on Gipp's reputation seems to have been Paul Gallico, who wrote sports for the New York Daily News from 1923 to 1936 and who, after leaving the Daily News, went on to write some very popular fiction. (How appropriate.) In the 2001 book "Rites of Autumn," by Richard Whittingham, there is a section entitled "The Two Sides of the Gipper," which excerpts something written by Gallico in which he calls Gipp a womanizer (no numbers, no explanation, or incidents given) and a pool shark, card shark, gambler and a drunk. Gallico indicates this information had been obtained "privately from a contemporary." He neglects to say whose contemporary...Gallico's or Gipp's? Nor does he mention who the informer was. What stands out is his recital of a Rockne-Gipp confrontation in the locker room at halftime of the 1920 Indiana game.

According to Gallico, Gipp was smoking a cigarette in the back of the room and Rockne spotted it. Interrupting his pep talk, Rock asked Gipp if he was interested in the game and Gipp replied that he had two hundred bucks bet on it and that he certainly wasn't "laying down." But poor Paul had some of the facts wrong. It was in the Army game of 1919 that this happened and not the Indiana game of 1920. Gallico wrote that after the Rockne-Gipp encounter, Gipp went on to beat Indiana in the second half, scoring two touchdowns. Gipp did not score two touchdowns in the second half of either the Indiana or the Army game. So much for Gallico's accuracy.

Gallico's column preceded Jim Beach's story and probably gave impetus for writers such as Beach to paint Gipp as an incorrigible bum. Further down in his story, Gallico comes up with Gipp having "agents" who did the betting for him. Gallico implies that these agents traveled to all the out of town games to place bets. One was the Indiana game in Indianapolis where Gipp's agents were planted in the "betting emporium," wherever that was located. Gipp is supposed to have walked in acting like he had a hangover from heavy drinking. He asks for a Bromo Seltzer and while shivering and with his hands trembling, he finds his lips for the glass of Bromo, then coughing and gagging, he manages to swallow it and then he staggers out. When someone asks, "Who the hell was that wreck?," the agents tell them it was Gipp and that he was that way all week...that he probably wouldn't be able to play the next day. Gallico doesn't mention it but we must assume that the bets poured in on Indiana to win. Other books had Gipp running around town looking for bettors. I wonder if he made those plans to search for bettors before or after learning that his girlfriend, Iris Trippeer, was breaking off their relationship? Would he have taken Iris out to the emporium to see him put on the hangover act? Or would he have taken his sister Dorothy, who had a room in the same hotel?

While we're at it — "debunking the bunk" — it might be worthwhile to mention an incident reported by Indiana University Professor of English Murray Sperber in not one, but two of his books: "Shake Down the Thunder," published in 1993 and "Onward to Victory," published in 1998. Professor Sperber, who has practically made a new career out of critiquing college football in general and Notre Dame and its icons in particular, quotes a fellow named Moe Aranson who was a kid (12, 13...?) hawking newspapers in downtown South Bend in 1920 and who heard a story that Gipp was found drunk in a pile of snow. This should have been taken with much skepticism and reported that way by such a meticulous researcher as Sperber, but it wasn't. Running the item in both his books, Sperber pretty much lets it stand as gospel and in his notes for "Shake Down the Thunder," he says, "Moe Aranson offered his story about Gipp's fatal illness in an interview for this book, 24 June 1991." This is, of course, more than 70 years after the fact.

One thing that makes the whole item questionable is, if Aranson knew about it, doesn't it stand to reason that all of South Bend would have heard about it, also? Keep in mind that by 1920 Gipp was Notre Dame's most famous football player. Not only was he well-known in South Bend, his fame had spread nationwide. If he had been found in a drunken stupor, passed out overnight in the snow on a South Bend street, one would think the story would have made at least one if not all of the local newspapers. But there was no mention of the incident in the media.

And the anonymous "pals" who spread the story quoted by Aranson couldn't really have been pals, could they? Of course, Aranson must have been a paper boy with a medical degree. He knew that's how Gipp got pneumonia, claiming that the incident in the snow caused his fatal illness. (For the record, Gipp died of a streptococcal infection, not pneumonia.) No time or day was given by the rumor nor by Aranson as to when it happened. I'm sure the whole story is nothing more than hogwash, yet it has been perpetuated by a writer of Sperber's standing as if it is a fact.

Finding Gipp dead drunk in a pile of snow is not the Gipp his friends knew. Gipp played pool and poker and you don't win when you can't hold your liquor, to which his friends, including Hunk Anderson, attested Gipp could. And Gipp would have left from the pool hall's doorstep to the inside of a taxi which was the way he traveled when his pal John Jegier wasn't around with a car.

This is what could have happened, if indeed anyone was actually found in a pile of snow. It could have been perhaps Jegier or Ila Schafer, another of Gipp's pals, who was found, and down the line in retelling the incident, when it reached Aranson, it ended up as Gipp instead of his friend. It was Gipp who would drive Jegier home on many occasions because Johnny was too pie-eyed to get behind the wheel of his car. Gipp would take him down to where Johnny's relatives had a soda pop company on Division Street (now Western Avenue) where Johnny worked at times. Gipp would park the car with Jegier in it in the rear and walk down to the South Bend Lunch Room a block away. There he'd get a bite to eat and hail a cab or call for one from the lunchroom which was open all night because of the Singer Sewing Machine Company plant across the street.

(The British Singer Company was doing some wartime work for Great Britain after England's entry into war in 1914 and when our country got into it in 1917 it was for both the United States and allies that Singer manufactured goods.)

Since that story about Gipp in a snowpile appeared, other detractors have used it to add to the existing slime used in the denigration of Gipp. And so the beat goes on.

There is one item for which I have to give Sperber credit and that is his revelation that in the 1920s era, newspaper editors discovered that readers were interested in sports, sex and violence. This sold newspapers and attracted advertisers, thus making newspapers very profitable. According to Sperber, a new breed of sportswriters emerged which was called the "Gee Whiz" writers. Their descriptions of events turned dull contests into exciting battles and ordinary athletes into miracle men. In other words, they exaggerated, and Sperber names Paul Gallico as one of these. In fact, Gallico, when he quit sportswriting, admitted that he indeed was a Gee Whizzer. Sperber mentions that the Gee Whiz writers received better compensation than the dull ones. This, then, reveals Gallico's motive for the sensationalizing and maximizing of Gipp's faults and vices at the expense of accuracy and honesty. Sperber indicates that the highly respected Grantland Rice was the king of the Gee Whizzers, with earnings listed in six figures. I would add that Rice's exaggerations accentuated the positive while Gallico and others of his ilk concentrated on stretching the negative like some of today's tabloids do.

As for my friend Jim Beach introducing Gipp as a binging drunkard in his story in the 1950s, he probably was aware that a Gee Whiz type of writing existed. Actually, if he didn't know, he himself had a background for "fantasy" writing. He told me that while attending UCLA prior to World War II, he also took a course in script writing at a professional cinema arts school. We know that Hollywood-produced biographies more times than not contain some enhancing or spicing fiction. Jim lived on Gower Street at that time, between two major studios, and possibly had gotten first-hand experience in a part-time job.

There have been other incidents reported about Gipp that are too preposterous to mention and giving them space even in presenting a factual denial, perpetuates them.

One final note about the Malone episode to back up Gipp's sister Dorothy's story. In the South Bend Tribune of November 19, 1920, there was an item about Gipp, not in the sport pages but in the city news section. It was a short item which stated that George Gipp arrived from Chicago on Wednesday evening (17th) where he had been undergoing treatment for serious injuries sustained in the previous Saturday's Indiana game.

It makes one wonder if any portion of the Grover Malone story as originally reported by Jim Beach and later by others, was true...even Gipp meeting with Malone at any time to lecture on kicking. Probably much of the maligning exaggerations resulted from the fact that Gipp pursued his vices and showed his worst traits openly. Much of his good side and good deeds he kept private and, because of that fact, any mention of them is labeled a lie while the unfavorable fabrications are treated as the truth.

# 14

# GENEROUS TO A FAULT

T o my knowledge, there have been no more than two or three books written that were devoted solely to the biography of the Gipper; however, there have been several chapters in most books written about Notre Dame or Rockne that capsulized Gipp's life and career. While paying tribute to Gipp's greatness as a football player, the writers seem to amplify his vices and downplay his virtues. If a writer has written about a reported gift or sharing of Gipp's winning with someone or some charity in need, the writer also adds his opinion that the incident of Gipp's generosity he had just revealed was undoubtedly fiction.

A perfect example is in a book published as recently as 1999, "Rockne of Notre Dame," by Ray Robinson. In his book, Robinson writes that an idyllic portrait of Gipp "said that he invariably turned over any winnings at the gambling table to local people who were in need. This sentimental Robin Hood version was unlikely ever to have occurred."

Never mind the fact that the people citing the incident of Gipp's generosity were witnesses to the deeds — writers dating back to Paul Gallico in the 1920s to Robinson and Murray Sperber in the 1990s seem determined to perpetuate the negative side of Gipp. This chapter will cite some incidents and sources and let the reader decide.

Gipp had problems getting up in the morning but there's nothing unusual with that trait. It happens to a lot of people. And what seemed a mite disrespectful was the way he addressed Rockne at times as well as his lighting up a cigarette behind Rock's back. I think he was playing to the younger audience on the team when he did that — not in the prima donna sense but in a sense of having seniority and that rules were for kids, not for an older man.

Gambling proliferated on a large scale in our country during Gipp's lifetime. Where there were laws against it, there seemed to be very little enforcement of the laws, as it was with drinking alcoholic beverages, and both vices complemented each other. Gipp has been called greedy by people who did not know him. It has been fabricated that greed drove him into gambling. It wasn't greed but the challenge and the competition for him to play pool or poker that drove him toward those recreational games of skill and chance. Gipp loved to win and he loved the prize that came with winning. After savoring his victory, Gipp then would give most of his winnings away.

My father, John "Curley" Klosinski, told me about the time he played poker with Gipp and Jegier in Elkhart, Indiana. Johnny Jegier told that story, too, and had a bit more to add. The story indicates a bit of the bad and good in George Gipp.

Dad got off work on a late Friday afternoon flush with his pay envelope and decided to stop in and say hello to his former manager of the Muessel Brewers Independent football team, which Rockne had coached in 1913-14. Frank Witucki owned the saloon on the corner of Dunham and Walnut Streets, and it was there that dad bumped into a teammate, Johnny Jegier. They bought each other a drink and Jegier invited dad to come with him to Goldie Mann's. He was to meet Gipp at Goldie's because Gipp wanted to play poker in Elkhart, where Friday was payday for the railroad workers. Dad, a recent newlywed, was not yet acclimated to the constraints that go with marriage and decided a little outing with the boys wouldn't hurt.

Elkhart was called a railroad town because the biggest industry there was the maintenance and repair roundhouse, as well as a steam engine and car replacement facility for the New York Central Railroad. Elkhart now is the home of the National New York Central Railroad Museum. My friend and researcher in South Bend, John Kovach, once was the director of that Museum, and created a major exhibit in 1994 called: "Golden Rails — The Railroad and Notre Dame Football."

Gipp had just finished a game of pool when my dad and Jegier arrived at Goldie Mann's and after the trio got into the car, it wouldn't start. Gipp then hailed a cab passing by and that got them to a private club in Elkhart where the poker games were held. The large, round poker tables in the club saw players losing their proverbial shirts because of the counter-bidding rounds of raises filling the pot before a call was made.

Dad, a near-novice at poker, didn't last long as he went through most of his pay and dropped out. Gipp offered to stake him so that he could go on playing but dad refused, with "thanks," saying that with his luck it was more prudent for him to watch. Gipp then offered that there are such days and that "There's always tomorrow," meaning better luck next time.

Gipp was a big winner and Jegier said he broke even. Jegier was a clever poker player but no Gipp. Both Johnnies estimated that Gipp took in over $1100 and most likely it was close to $1500. Incidentally, Gipp had his usual rounds of drinks during the course of the evening, but his mind was clear and his demeanor was normal.

Once Gipp checked two hands in a row and dropped out. My dad was watching the game seated in back of George, and after throwing his hand in without a bid or raise, Gipp turned to my dad and said, "You know, Curley, in the long run, sometimes common sense goes farther than a good bluff." Hunk recalled another Gippesque saying concerning Gipp's favorite pastimes. During a breather Rockne had given the first stringers at a practice session, Hunk asked Gipp what was on his schedule for that evening and Gipp replied that he was going to play pool at Goldie's, so Hunk wished him good luck.

"You need luck when you roll dice, Hunk...pool takes skill and poker takes brains," was Gipp's reply, "but thanks anyhow."

George liked to smoke cigars while playing pool or poker. Both Anderson and Jegier said Gipp's favorite brands were El Producto, which is still around and Frank's No.1, a local brand which isn't. Cigars were usually in cigar boxes on shelves in counter cases and when buying cigars, the open box was put on the counter for the buyer to take as many as he wanted to buy. The boxed cigars had no cellophane wrap, just the name band. Gipp would remove the band and stick it in his shirt pocket before lighting the cigar.

When the game broke up way past one in the morning, Jegier and my dad had to go to the bathroom and Gipp volunteered to get their coats. Unlike bustling South Bend, there was nothing in the form of transportation running near downtown Elkhart at that early morning hour and that posed a dilemma for the boys. Dad was now eager to get home, realizing that his indiscretion and shunting of responsibility created a problem and he wasn't sure how he would explain to his wife Mary that he lost most of his pay gambling.

Gipp spotted a horse drawn milkwagon delivering milk and other dairy products to upstairs apartments and in the back of restaurants. Gipp told his buddies to jump in and with a "giddyap horsey" and a pull on the reins, the wagon headed for South Bend. Upon arrival on Michigan Street, Gipp turned the horse and wagon around, slapped the horse on the rump and the horse was off in the direction of Elkhart. The two Johnnies took the same cab home, both living on the west side of South Bend, with my dad being dropped off first.

Dad slept in late Saturday morning after an uneasy sleep caused by the worry of explaining the loss of his wages. Upon waking up, he discovered that my mom, while preparing to hang his coat in the closet, had gone through his pockets and found a tightly rolled wad of bills inside a cigar band in the inside pocket of his coat. When he counted the money, it was more than double the amount with which he had started. He thought that Gipp put the money accidently in the wrong coat and when he told Jegier about it, he found out that it was Gipp's way of sneaking money to someone without a hassle. Jegier said Gipp did it to him on several occasions, especially when Gipp tried to show appreciation for all the rides he got from Jegier in his car and Jegier refused to accept the money.

As for the milkman's inconvenience, Jegier saw Gipp put some big bills inside the milkman's delivery route book. A section of the South Bend News-Times, which published news about the other cities in the area, carried an item about the milkwagon. Jegier saw it in the next day's evening paper. The story said that in the middle of the milkman's delivery route, the horse decided to head back to the dairy's stables with half the milk undelivered. The management said that the horse was old and the company would retire him. So the horse got back to Elkhart safely. The milkman apparently found the money Gipp put in the route book and kept quiet about it.

Although the three culprits — Gipp and the two Johns — could have gotten in trouble for what they did, the fact that Gipp made on the spot restitution for the caused inconvenience eased the gravity of their act. Gipp giving money lost in poker — and more — to Klosinski without my dad's knowledge, was an unselfish act and typical of Gipp's generosity.

Hunk Anderson told about the time he and Gipp de-

GIPP AT NOTRE DAME — The Untold Story

cided to take in the best features of South Bend during Easter vacation. After the tour, they realized it was past curfew time and they had to get back and sneak in. They took a cab and as the cab approached the campus, Gipp, in going through his pockets discovered that he had only a few small coins. Hunk was broke too. Gipp whispered to Hunk, "I don't have the fare Hunk. While I fumble around in my pockets, you run like hell."

And Hunk did run...like a gazelle with hungry lions in pursuit, only to see Gipp passing him up, making Hunk look as if he were standing still. Gipp disappeared into the darkness while Hunk huffed and puffed into Sorin Hall.

The cab driver woke Father Cavanaugh up and Cavanaugh woke Father Doremus and the lights were turned on while the students were called out of their rooms. Hunk did a quick disrobing and donned his pajamas in an eye blink, lined up in the hall with mussed up hair and squinting eyes. The cabbie hesitated when he looked at Hunk but didn't recognize him. The suggestion was made that it could have been someone who didn't reside in Sorin, but used it to throw the cab driver off his trail, ended the search.

A couple of days later, Gipp went to the cab company's operations office and handed the dispatcher an envelope with money in it marked "personal" and told him it was to be given to the night shift driver of cab #18, an easy number for Gipp to remember because his birthday was on the 18th (of February). Having been a cab driver himself, Gipp surely wouldn't have stiffed the cabbie. Anyhow, a bad act was remedied and Hunk was sure that Gipp included a generous tip for causing the cab driver all that trouble.

There were many instances of Gipp's generosity that didn't involve those type of shenanigans. Some of Gipp's philanthropy, if judged by the value of today's dollar compared with the dollar of the 1918-1920 era, would be deemed extremely magnanimous.

Johnny Jegier was with Gipp when he disposed of a couple of Chicago pool sharks at Goldie Mann's. Goldie had two of his four cigar/pool stores on the south side of South Bend's downtown, both near the train depot. The proposed new New York Central Union Depot wasn't built or even on the drawing boards at that time. The Mann establishment frequented by the Chicagoans was Goldie's on Main Street because of its proximity to the New York Central Depot on South Street. Also, it was near the Studebaker auto plant and many of the auto workers would snack and gamble there after work.

Johnny said that Gipp was feeling pretty good — moreso about beating the Chicago "experts" than the money he had won in doing so. He tried to stuff a bunch of twenty dollar bills into Jegier's jacket pocket as they were driving away from Goldie's place. Gipp told him it was in appreciation for the chauffeuring that John had been doing. John took the money out of his pocket and tried to give it back but George refused to take it. Steering with one hand, John threw the money in Gipp's lap and Gipp told him to stop the car, that if Jegier didn't take the money, Gipp would get out and walk. John then reluctantly pocketed the money.

But Gipp wasn't through giving. He asked John to drive down Division Street near Chapin Street where there was a new branch of the Salvation Army that had just opened in what had been an empty store building.

The service had just ended and they were preparing to serve food to the destitute who were there for food and shelter. John stood by the door while Gipp went to the front to talk to the uniformed preacher. John saw Gipp giving him money and they both shook hands and Gipp walked back to where John was standing.

"I saw you give the guy some money. Was he surprised?" asked John.

Gipp replied, "Well, he did ask me if it was mine and I said not quite...I found it. I told him I tried to find the owner but it probably belonged to some bootlegger who didn't want to claim it. If I told him I won it playing pool he might not have taken it. I know my father wouldn't. (Gipp's father was a deacon and a devout Baptist.) Then the 'captain' asked my name. I told him it didn't matter — what mattered was that he had the money to put to good use."

When they got in the car, George had one more comment: "You know John, that's a good outfit, that Salvation Army. They feed your stomach and they feed your soul." And then, still feeling good, Gipp said, "Let's go to my hotel and see what's happening there. I think Jules Stein's orchestra is playing in the Cafeteria Room tonight."

Another example of Gipp giving his winnings away for a good cause was made in John U. Bacon's well-done article on Gipp in the Detroit News. He quoted Gipp's teammate Arthur "Dutch" Bergman: "I've seen Gipp win $500 in a crap game and then spend his winnings buying meals for destitute families. There is no wonder he was idolized by the South Bend townies."

Gipp's sister Dorothy told Jim Beach that George wired her tuition and expense money from the Oliver Hotel when she was attending Kalamazoo College. Writer Bacon mentioned that Gipp also covered tuition and expenses for his friends. Although he didn't cite any specific name or time, years before his article came out Hunk Anderson told me the same thing. The football players had a partial scholarship, that previously mentioned "bed and table" type and only in the 1920 school year did Notre Dame begin to give athletes a full ride. They still had to work at campus jobs to earn it. Rockne convinced Father Burns that Notre Dame had to include tuition and fees to be in line with Big Ten conference rules and be competitive.

Gipp asked Hunk at the beginning of each school semester if Hunk had enough money for tuition and expenses and Hunk answered affirmatively. But Hunk did accept Gipp's off campus treats many times as did some of the other Larium friends of theirs. The only time Hunk had extra money in school was when he played baseball for teams in the outlying areas of South Bend each spring. Hunk's parents were sending his sister to a teachers' college and gave her fiscal priority because they felt it was still a man's world then, although women were beginning to make inroads into equality.

Hunk said if it wasn't for Gipp insisting on treating him, he wouldn't have had a social life while going to school at Notre Dame nor would he have met his wife-to-be, Marie Martin. Hunk tried to repay him during summer vacation when he had a job, but Gipp wouldn't take a penny.

I. I. Probst had been in contact with a 1922 Notre

Dame graduate who was honored as Notre Dame's oldest living alumnus at halftime of a home game a couple of years ago. He passed the hundred mark in age and then passed away in the new millennium. Romaine Reichert was his name. He told Probst that he borrowed a dollar from Gipp prior to Gipp's departure for the 1920 Northwestern game. Reichert said that he didn't see Gipp again to pay him back and this gnawed on his conscience for some 80 years. The truth of the matter is that Gipp never would expect to be paid back, and, even if Romaine tried to pay it back, Gipp would have refused to take it.

Jegier told about the time he and Gipp drove to the DeAmici Fraternal Club in nearby Mishawaka to check the place out for poker. There was no action and after a short beer they started back for downtown South Bend. It was twilight and John had his lights on. As they neared the bridge crossing the St. Joseph River, they saw a man near the rail seeming to want to lift himself onto it.

"Stop the car John, I think the guy wants to jump," Gipp said.

"Naw, it looks like he wants to take a leak," answered John as he applied the brakes.

The fellow was young; he was drunk and he said he was going to end it all because his girl friend dropped him and was going with another guy.

Gipp told him, "Hell, you can't kill yourself jumping from here. It's too shallow down there and you'll break your neck and end up in a wheel-chair the rest of your life. You don't want that do you?"

The guy just stared blankly while teetering unsteadily. Gipp then put his arm around him and advised him in a friendly tone. "Look, why don't you go home and get some sleep and tomorrow you'll forget about her. There are plenty fish in the ocean. Hop in the back seat...we'll drop you off downtown."

John said that Gipp figured that the guy had spent what money he had getting drunk, so Gipp suggested they drop him off at a coffee shop near Michigan and La Salle Streets. By the time they got there the guy had calmed down and Gipp gave him a buck and told him to drink some coffee before he went home. The young fellow meekly went into the coffee shop to do Gipp's bidding.

Gipp was also generous when it came to giving time to a friend or doing him a favor. Our country's servicemen were returning home from Europe after World War I and the Elks decided to give the vets a beer party with boxing for enter- tainment. Rockne, a former combatant at the Elks for five bucks a fight while a student, was asked to furnish the box- ers. Notre Dame had Inter Hall teams in all sports and Rockne found good fighters in all weight classes except the heavyweight. He couldn't find anyone willing to fight George Trafton because of his size. Trafton had some pugilistic ex- perience before coming to Notre Dame as well.

Rockne told Hunk he was to fight Dale Vosse, whom Rockne said was the champion of the Pacific Fleet in his weight class and also a local resident. Hunk wasn't sure if it was true or a Rockne creation. It was on the trolley to South Bend that Trafton sat down beside Hunk and told him glee- fully that he, not Vosse, was to be Hunk's opponent. Gipp, who had a date in town, got word that Trafton was fighting

Hunk and hurried to the Elks club where he met with Hunk and volunteered his services.

Trafton, who was to become a pro football hall of famer playing for the Chicago Bears, was 6' 3" and weighed about 215 pounds. Hunk stood in at 5'10" and weighed 168 pounds, a physical mismatch. Gipp, advising Hunk in his corner, told Hunk not to mix it up but to keep his distance until Gipp got a chance to see Trafton's style. So the first round was a typical feel-out round although Trafton tried some long haymakers.

When Hunk got back to his corner, Gipp had made astute observations and gave Hunk some good advice.

"Trafton drops his hands before he lashes out at you. I don't trust that kind of style because he might nail you unexpectedly. Best bet would be to stay away from him when he does that and then if there's an opening hit him with combinations...or when his hands go down, go inside and work his body over and then go to his chin."

As the second round opened, Trafton shuffled in with his hands high and then dropped them and Hunk, seeing his hands go downward, immediately crowded Trafton on the inside per Gipp's advice, as a long right hand lead and a looping left whistled past Anderson's ears. Hunk then, within a blink of an eye, stepped back and with his body behind it, unloaded a crushing left hook that sent big George over the second ring rope onto the ring apron and almost into the front row of seats. Trafton was unconscious and counted out. Thanks to Gipp's loyalty and acumen, "David slew Goliath."

Trafton retired from football and went into boxing as a pro. After a couple of easy wins, he fought Primo Carnera in March, 1930, and the Italian and future heavyweight champion knocked Trafton out in one round and George hung up his gloves alongside his cleats.

When Gipp obtained tickets to Notre Dame football games, he would give them to his friends in South Bend. My cousin, Gene Basker, said his father told him that Gipp would always remember to bring at least a couple of tickets downstairs to the Turkish baths at the Oliver Hotel and if his oldest brother Edward didn't want them, Frank, Gene's father, would then pass them on to his customers.

Gipp greedy? Not by a longshot.

# 15

## NORTHWESTERN, ST. JOSEPH'S AND THE END

Preparation for the Northwestern game was termed "light" by Rockne. It was devoid of scrimmages because the entire starting unit and the few subs who played were banged up from the tough Indiana game. Rockne had been negotiating with the big Eastern teams such as Colgate, Harvard, and Dartmouth for a game in the enlarged Cartier Field in 1921 but was being turned down. He was also hoping that Notre Dame would get a Rose Bowl bid and found out during that pre-Northwestern game week that the team representing the East would be either Ohio State or Princeton. Wanting to showcase his team out West in the warmer climate, Rockne contacted Lt. Commander J. Kaveney for a game with the Pacific Fleet team which lost only one game — and only by a field goal — to the University of California, the team that was representing the West in the Rose Bowl on

New Year's Day. (Ohio State ended up playing Cal in Pasadena and lost 28-0.) Rockne's contact with Lt. Commander Kaveney was made in spite of knowledge that a promoter of a post season game against Penn State in New York City had been turned down by the Notre Dame Faculty Athletics Board.

Gipp, upon his return Wednesday evening from Chicago, went to bed early that evening and stayed in bed all day Thursday. Hunk Anderson, who was in bad shape with sore muscles, knees and a sprained ankle, hobbled to class that day and after class he managed to look in on Gipp. Hunk had the kitchen help in the dining room fix George a plate of food and he brought it to Gipp's room.

George told Hunk that while the shoulder and neck area pain had lessened, his throat was a quite sore from the Indiana game and it had gotten worse since his Chicago visit. He thought the worsening was because of the cold winds off Lake Michigan that prevailed during his stay in a hotel only a few blocks from the lake. Gipp said that he now could raise his right arm and move it somewhat vigorously without causing the left side to smart. Gipp, with Hunk's help, removed the truss which, according to Hunk, was merely a pad in the armpit made up of wide tape set tightly over gauze. The tape ran from underneath the armpit, going upward front and back to the right side, with the tape ends crossing each other. A sling then immobilized the left arm. Aspirin was used by Gipp for pain as per the doctor's orders.

Separated shoulders and/or fractured collarbones suffered by today's players and treated with modern medical techniques still require about six weeks of recovery time before contact. Grant Irons, Notre Dame's two time defensive captain of the 2000 and 2001 squads, received a shoulder injury similar to Gipp's in the second game of the 2000 season and did not play for the rest of that year. When Rockne asked Gipp on Friday if he felt well enough to make the trip, Gipp told Rock that he "guessed" he was well enough and that he could make the trip. Both agreed that he would suit up to make the Chicago alumni and a large contingent of South Bend fans making the trip, happy, by merely being there and sitting on the bench. They were wrong. While Rockne knew for some time that the Chicago Notre Dame Alumni Association designated that November 20th Saturday as George Gipp Day, Gipp learned of it from Chicago's prominent Notre Dame alumnus James Hayden, who visited George during his stay at the Chicagoan Hotel to await tests and treatment on his shoulder. Hayden, with another alumnus, took Gipp out to dinner and told him about George Gipp Day. Gipp also received a wad of complimentary tickets to the game from Hayden.

A sellout crowd of 20,000 sat in Dyche Stadium to see Notre Dame and its star, George Gipp. Gipp was sitting on the bench with Rockne nearby in what was a first half of discomforting icy wind and drizzles that were penetrating to the bone. Most of the first string started except Gipp. Hunk started at left guard with his ankle taped and Rockne had Ed Degree ready to replace Hunk when needed.

The crowd began yelling for Gipp. The fans wanted Gipp to play and kept shouting "We want Gipp" throughout the entire game. Only when the game had a few minutes left to play did Rockne succumb to the crowd's desire, and only after Gipp finally joined the chorus and said, "Put me in Rock, we can't disappoint them."

Rockne answered Gipp, "Alright George, but remember, you don't run with the ball!"

The game's first touchdown was scored by Eddie Anderson on a pass from Brandy in the second quarter after the Irish recovered a fumbled punt by Northwestern's Penfield, deep in Purple territory. The second score was made on a sustained drive with Barry going over and the half ended with the Irish in front 14-0. It was Northwestern's turn as the third quarter began when the Purple quarterback, Grousnick, bootlegged the ball around right end for a 50-yard touchdown run. The kick was good and it was 14 to 7. After Danny Coughlin intercepted a Northwestern pass thrown by Patterson on the Purple 35-yard-line, he then gained 10 around end. On the next play, Norm Barry ran to the one and Eddie Anderson on an end around toss back from Barry, scored. Degree, in the game for a limping Hunk, kicked the extra point. The score was now 21 to 7 and the incessant chant of "We want Gipp" became deafening.

It was bedlam in the stands as Gipp entered the game after Northwestern relinquished the ball. On the first play from Northwestern's 35, Gipp threw a pass that Eddie Anderson easily cradled in his arms and went in for his third touchdown of the game. A banged up Kiley played but he shared half of the time with George Prokop. The Scholastic, in its game story, gave Kiley one of the touchdowns which was credited to Eddie Anderson by other game reports. After the score, Captain Frank Coughlin, who played a brilliant defensive game, was replaced by Hec Garvey. Degree missed the try for extra point and it was 27 to 7.

A fourth touchdown, credited to Eddie Anderson in some of the game reports, is listed as a 70-yard pass play from Gipp to Norm Barry in Notre Dame's Media Guide. There is an explanation for the confusion. With an isolated exception, players of Gipp's era did not wear numbers and just about every game report had flaws in it. One historian credits Bob Zuppke of Illinois as the first to use numbers on players' jerseys in 1915, because he could only see from the bench the players of the team who were on offense near the goal line. Bob couldn't see what the defensive players were doing and thought numbers would help. There were no public address systems on the field and the stadiums of that era generally had crude press boxes where the vantage point was terrible for any scribe trying to report a game for his paper. Notre Dame's Cartier Field, before its remodeling in 1920, had a press box that resembled a farmer's fruit stand on the highway. It had a belt-high base or counter about 15 feet long, and was open-aired to a roof which was supported by 2x4s — hardly an adequate press box for trying to report a game with exactness. Dyche Stadium was a bit better but very inadequate even for a high-school game by today's standards.

This is what happened on that Gipp pass play according to Hunk, who was out of the game and sitting on the bench. The pass was about a 55-yarder to Eddie Anderson, who hugged the sideline for 15 yards after the catch for what was thought to be his fourth TD. The linesman officiating, however, said that Ed's foot hit the sideline stripe on the one-yard-line. So it was a 69-yard play overall. A conference between the officials at the goal line resulted in a negated touchdown, and Norm Barry on the next play then scored. Gipp tried to kick the extra point but missed as his ailing side failed to synchronize with the right side and the ball dropped flat instead of point down.

In line with the Notre Dame Media Guide, some newspapers also credited Barry instead of Anderson with a pass reception touchdown on that pass from Gipp but had 55 yards as the distance covered. This was the first game that Arch Ward did not report for the Tribune that year and so the Tribune published a wire service game report without a byline. This Tribune account credited Ed Anderson for the TD in question. The reason Arch Ward did not report on the game for the Tribune was that his involvement in a disciplinary problem caused him to either be suspended or to quit school.

Desperate Northwestern failed to move the ball and had to kick. Gipp, the showman, decided to give the crowd a chance to see him run, so he told Brandy he would field the punt. Hunk, sitting next to Rockne said that Rockne upon seeing Gipp go back in safety position, became furious. This was the first time Hunk ever had seen Rockne get seriously angry with Gipp over his countermanding an order from him or changing a play.

The punt to Gipp was very high and Northwestern ends Penfield and Palmer were there to cover the kick before the ball came down. Some reports state that the ball hit the ground and bounced high. In any case, as Gipp caught the ball, they both grabbed Gipp, one waist high and the other at the ankles and gently sat him down on the turf. If sportsmanship awards were given, Penfield and Palmer would surely have had one that day. Northwestern players saw that

Gipp was visibly ill. They admired his gameness in coming out on the field to play in order to satisfy the chanting crowd, when he had no business being there. They, too, heard the crowd yelling for Gipp to enter the game and knew he would have been in the fray long before his surprisingly productive token appearance if he had been healthy enough to do so. Moments later the game was over with Notre Dame winning 33 to 7 — the Evanston crowd winning, too, because they saw Gipp perform. The loser? Gipp, because the whole Evanston episode — from sitting on the bench in a cold drizzle to making an appearance on the field weakened his body's resistance to fight invasive bacteria.

On the Tuesday after the Northwestern game the South Bend Rotary Club held its annual Awards Banquet at the Oliver Hotel with the Notre Dame team being the honored guest. As dinner was being served, the George Miller Orchestra played soft dinner music in the background. Gipp's favorite orchestra, led by Jules Stein, couldn't make an appearance because Stein was attending medical school at the University of Chicago during early week days. As the music played softly, the guests ate their meal but Gipp, sitting next to Hunk Anderson, did not touch his food.

"What's the matter George?" asked Hunk as he looked at the undisturbed food on Gipp's plate.

"I feel lousy, Hunk. I'm burning up with fever and my throat is so sore I can't even drink water."

Hunk knew it was serious because Gipp usually would bear his aches in silence. He put his hand on Gipp's forehead.

"Crissake, George, you're on fire! You better tell Rock. Hell, you belong in the hospital."

It didn't take much persuasion for Gipp to agree with Hunk and at an opportune moment, he beckoned to Rockne who then left the VIP speakers' table to see what George wanted. After Gipp told Rockne of his illness, Rockne, after delivering a short speech, made arrangements at St. Joseph's Hospital for diagnosis and treatment. In the early hours of Wednesday morning on November 24, Gipp was admitted to the hospital. His temperature was taken and it was 104 degrees.

Gipp was placed in a private room. He requested that his personal belongings be given to Hunk, who had left with Rockne but would return after classes. Dr. James McMeel was called. After an examination, Dr. McMeel diagnosed Gipp's illness to be tonsillitis. The swelling of the tonsils and the lymph glands with a severe sore throat was a sure sign for the diagnosis, but Dr. McMeel also called in Dr. Thomas Olney, not necessarily to confirm it, but to check Gipp in case Dr. McMeel overlooked something else.

Because tonsillitis can be caused by a variety of bacteria which can also cause other types of illnesses such as diphtheria, Dr. McMeel wanted a second opinion from Dr. Olney. Although Gipp's throat was very sore, both doctors ruled out streptococcus at that time.

Dr. McMeel had an illustrious and self-satisfying career in his short 63 years of life. Besides practicing medicine in downtown South Bend and at the hospital, Dr. McMeel became the head of St. Joseph's Hospital, having served on the board of directors and later as chairman of the board. He was the president of the St. Joseph County Medical Association; the president of the Indiana State Medical Association and also gained national renown by being elected to serve as president of the American Medical Association.

Dr. McMeel's love for Notre Dame and his residing on the East side of South Bend — 315 E. Corby Avenue, which was within minutes of Notre Dame campus — made him accept the position of Notre Dame physician. He was not only required to serve as doctor to the students, but was required to be present at every Notre Dame athletic event. This part of the job Dr. McMeel loved. He was appointed to the position in 1932 and served 15 years after which he retired from practicing medicine.

McMeel's treatment to bring the fever down and lessen the soreness in Gipp's throat began immediately after the examination by the two doctors. The country read about the Notre Dame hero being hospitalized but the gravity of his illness was not stressed because it was still a case of tonsillitis. With Gipp admitted to the hospital on November 24, the Notre Dame team had one more game to play and to win for another undefeated season. It was against Michigan A&M, now known as Michigan State. The game, even without Gipp, was an easy victory for Notre Dame over Coach Potsy Clark's Aggies. Rockne started his "shock troops" and they saw most of the action in both halves of the game. The game's highlight was Danny Coughlin's 80-yard touchdown run in the first half. Notre Dame won by a score of 25 to 0.

Earlier in the week of the Michigan Aggies game Rockne contacted Purdue trying to schedule a game for the Notre Dame freshmen to reward them for being cannon fodder for the varsity. For certain games, the freshmen would learn the plays of the opponents and then the varsity would scrimmage them on Tuesday or Wednesday. After Purdue officials told Rockne that the season was over for all their football teams, Rock then asked Hunk if he would check with his South Bend Arrows team for a game with the freshmen on the Sunday after the Thanksgiving Michigan Aggies game. Hunk said he would check, but he was sure that Manager Benko had signed a contract to play Gas City in Marion, Indiana, for the Indiana State Championship. When Hunk checked with the Arrows, he was assured that the contract with Marion city's businessmen who were financing the championship game, was iron clad because of an advance payment.

Then a short while after Hunk left Benko's office, Benko got a call from Charlie Pask of the Fort Wayne Friars looking for a game. He was told that the Arrows had a game but that Rockne was looking for one for his freshmen and that Pask ought to call Rockne, which he did. Rockne agreed to send the freshman team to Fort Wayne to play the Friars on the coming Saturday, November 27.

The game was played on a muddy field with assistant coach Walter Halas handling the team. There were plenty of fumbles on both sides and the pro team led the Irish freshmen 6-0 at the end of the third quarter. In the fourth quarter the last member of the Notre Dame Bergman family to play, freshman Joe, intercepted a Friar pass and ran 70 yards for a touchdown to tie the score. After that, Coach Halas decided to "open up." As the Fort Wayne Journal-Gazette described it, "Notre Dame cut loose with a bewildering array of passes, trick plays, shift formations and massed interference that spelled defeat for the locals." The Irish freshmen won 18-6.

While all this was going on, Gipp was undergoing treatment that brought down his fever and Dr. McMeel was cautiously optimistic. Then on November 29, Gipp's problem widened into pneumonia and the situation, as announced by the hospital on the 30th, had become critical. Gipp's mother, brother Matthew and his sister Dorothy arrived that day and were at his bedside almost immediately upon arrival in South Bend. Rockne made arrangements with his friend George Hull for Gipp's mother Isabella to stay at Hull's house, and he had Gipp's brother Matthew and sister Dorothy stay at his house. George Hull, and on the days George had to work at Hullie and Mike's, his son Stanley, drove the Gipp family to the hospital. The Hulls had to go to Rockne's house to pick up Gipp's brother and sister because Rockne's schedule was uncertain and he could make the hospital visit only in the late evening hours.

The same day that the hospital issued its "critical" bulletin on Gipp, two specialists were brought in from Chicago for consultation and help. Gipp's fever was high again and the specialists, Dr. Thomas O'Connor and Dr. C. H. Johnson along with Dr. McMeel, worked on reducing the fever with every method in their medical expertise.

Apparently George's childhood bout with rheumatic fever might have surfaced. His heart began to fail, causing his pulse rate to be dangerously low. Digitalis, a drug extracted from the leaves of the foxglove plant, was given to stimulate the heart.

Hunk Anderson, whose blood was tested earlier and found to be compatible with Gipp's, gave George some of his blood in a person-to-person transfusion. This was in an era

228

when the method of storing blood in plasma form had not yet been discovered. Direct transfusions from donor to recipient was the method employed.

Transfusions were used sparingly prior to World War II. They required a person with the correct type blood to be on standby, available to give blood when needed. Another reason for the reluctance of doctors to use transfusions was that the donor's blood might be carrying a disease. There weren't many tests available to screen the blood thoroughly. Transfusions, when used, were generally used during operations and childbirth to replenish the loss of blood. In Gipp's case, McMeel and the specialists apparently felt that new blood would introduce more leukocytes, the bacteria-destroying cells. Penicillin was yet to be discovered.

On Sunday, November 28, Hunk Anderson's team beat undefeated Gas City 6-0 for the Indiana State Championship for Independents, as the pros were called in those days. There were fights between the players and later the fans became involved. The game was cut short by two minutes to avoid a riot. Hunk could have earned some extra money if he accompanied the team, but chose to be with his pal in the hospital.

On December 2, Gipp regained consciousness and felt better. After observing Gipp for a few hours, the team of doctors felt that the pneumonia had been beaten and Gipp had improved. With guarded optimism they said Gipp would recover but also cautioned that Gipp was still in the critical stage. The specialists returned to Chicago. The bulletin regarding Gipp's improvement cheered not only Notre Dame students and South Benders, but the entire nation which had been following Gipp's fight for life in the newspapers.

Gipp's recovery seemed to be progressing satisfactorily. His father, Matthew Gipp Sr., arrived on December 4. He was quite elderly and in poor health and upon seeing that George was now feeling better, returned home. Apparently that was what happened because Hunk says he did not see Matthew Sr. after that first visit. Gipp began receiving visitors. On the staff were nuns and lay nurses working the various shifts. Sister Austina Ryan, C.S.C., was in charge of the nurses who were polite, efficient and accommodating to the extent that the doctors' orders permitted.

Hunk mentioned that Gipp's mother suggested to George that he be moved to Epworth Hospital because the nuns at the hospital and the priests visiting Gipp "made her nervous." One of the lay nurses told Hunk that she came into Gipp's room at the end of the mother's conversation, and heard Gipp tell his mother that he was getting the best of care and that was all that mattered and said, in effect, for the mother to mind her own business. Apparently Gipp's mother, Isabella Taylor Gipp, a Scotch-Irish daughter of immigrants from Northern Ireland, had her parents' prejudices imbued in her. The nurses, including Sister Austina, kept Hunk informed as to the goings-on in Gipp's room during Hunk's absence. Being uncomfortable with nuns and priests present, it is reasonable to assume that his mother could have requested clergy of her faith to attend Gipp, except that she knew George would not allow her to do that. Hullie could have brought in his own Methodist minister if Gipp's mother asked except she sensed that Gipp would not okay such a move, either. The frequency of Father Pat Haggerty's visits and the rapport between her son and the priest probably sent her a "message."

During the time leading to Gipp's apparent victory over pneumonia, he was named first team All-America on several mythical teams including Walter Camp's prestigious team. On December 2, Bill Veeck, president of the Chicago Cubs, hired a new manager, Johnny Evers of the famous Tinker to Evers to Chance double play combination, and sent Evers on December 3 to Gipp's hospital bed to sign him to play for the Cubs in the coming season. In the meantime, Rockne received an answer from Lt. Commander Kaveney that the Pacific Fleet team has been disbanded and therefore could not play a post-season game.

During the entire first week of December newspaper reports said that Gipp was stable and there was optimism that he would soon be over the critical stage. Hunk said that Gipp got out of bed and was able to walk on his own and, in fact, would walk down the hall to the bathroom unassisted. As a precaution, the nurse followed him to the door and back. Members of his family were breathing easier and spent a little more time away from the hospital, taking time to enjoy their meals, be it at Hullie's house or a nearby restaurant. Father Haggerty, from day one, was a daily visitor and an eagerly awaited one by Gipp.

Gipp told Hunk on one of his more cheerful days that week that he was making inquiries of Father Haggerty about becoming a Catholic. That surprised Hunk, who knew Gipp was at best ambivalent when it came to religion. When Hunk, a Protestant, volunteered to help carry the canopy that covered the priests overhead during a procession, or one of the

231

church flags, Gipp would make fun of him. Hunk never became a Catholic, but he felt grateful and obligated for the scholarship and education he received. He once told me that all religions are roads leading to the same place and it didn't make any difference which road you took, you'd still get there if you followed the rules of the road. Apparently, Gipp felt he found a short cut.

"So you're thinking of becoming a Catholic, eh? What the hell you want to do that for?"

"Look Hunk, my problems aren't over and I don't think I'll make it. I don't want to take chances going to the wrong place. The odds are better if I hold the right cards." (He may have known that the Catholic Church taught at that time that there was no salvation outside the Catholic Church.) Although Gipp was feeling better, his ever-recurring premonition of an early death seemed to have kicked in.

Rockne, who had met Iris Trippeer and had once invited Gipp to bring her to the house before they went out on a date to savor some of Bonnie Rockne's delicious coffee cake, did not know they had broken up. According to some writers, there was a telegram from Rockne to Iris Trippeer saying, "George improved. Wishes to see you." Iris did come to see Gipp on the weekend. She had the benefit of her father's or husband's free-travel railroad pass that white collar and blue collar employees of the railroad companies used to get when passenger and cargo delivery trains ruled the country in the field of transportation.

When a nurse told Hunk that George had a visit from a girlfriend, he assumed that it was the girl whom he had seen on several occasions sitting in the lobby and waiting for an opportune moment to inquire about Gipp and/or perhaps to see him. It was a few days later that Hunk discovered it was Iris.

During recovery from his bout with pneumonia, Gipp, unaccustomed to confinement, inquired of Hunk about what was going on at the Oliver Hotel and in the movies and Hunk told him. Hunk couldn't remember when I asked what was playing but in checking back in the Tribune on that first week in December, research shows that a new orchestra, Harry Denny's, was now playing in the Tapestry Room on the Oliver's mezzanine floor. At the movies, the Auditorium featured Buck Jones, with a mid-week start of "High and Dizzy" starring Harold Lloyd and "Two Fisted Lover" starring Hoot Gibson. The Oliver Opera House/Theater featured Richard Barthelmess and Lillian Gish in "Way Down East" on screen and live on stage was Billie Burke. Hunk didn't remember these but did remember that Gipp indicated he would have loved to see the cowboy movies.

According to the Tribune, Gipp now had a strep throat but was in no danger and Dr. Johnson returned to Chicago. The Tribune did not mention the parasitic bacteria but used the word "toxins" in the blood stream that come from the bacteria. The strep throat was no more bothersome than the sore throat he had been nursing all along. On December 6 Gipp was suffering only mild discomfort. Later, the paper indicated that Gipp was still in danger and would probably need a transfusion. Gipp's recovery had regressed on December 7 and a call for blood donors was made. Hunk again volunteered but was rejected because he had given blood the previous week. The Tribune reported on December 9 that 150

Notre Dame students had volunteered to give blood. Of those whose blood was tested, 10 were chosen as suitable but placed on standby. On campus, prayers were being said for Gipp's recovery.

On December 11, the Tribune indicated that Dr. C. H. Johnson had returned from Chicago. Transfusion was set aside as Gipp rallied and showed some improvement. On Sunday, December 12, Hunk visited Gipp and the Gipp family was there, but left to get something to eat. Gipp told Hunk that he still felt lousy and said, "I don't think I'll make it, Hunk. Thanks for everything, Hunk." The words, the pallor and the look on Gipp's face made Hunk speechless.

"A thousand words couldn't describe what I saw in his face," said Hunk. "For the first time since his illness began, I, too, didn't think he'd make it."

After Hunk left, Gipp's serious downturn began. Early Monday morning of the 13th, at 4 a.m., Dr. McMeel worked on Gipp and he himself administered a shot of heparin, with the nurse standing by. This is what the nurse told Hunk when they bumped into each other in the lobby that Monday morning. Hunk had one class in the morning which he cut to be in the hospital.

Heparin is a drug that prevents blood clotting and was the best available at that time. It does not dissolve clots as recently discovered drugs do. Whether heparin, a relatively new drug then and first used by Dr. William Howell in 1918 in cardiac cases, was used by Dr. McMeel in desperation "to try something" or whether there was something he detected in Gipp's vascular system that required the drug, is not known.

Gipp again rallied but the rally was of slight duration

and there wasn't optimism. There was only hope that Gipp again might proceed onward to recovery. Gipp's immune system had been challenged and overtaxed on a continuing basis without respite, from the Indiana game, on through to what was his current ordeal. Dr. McMeel called Rockne to fill him in on the past 12 hours. Hunk, feeling that the end was near for Gipp, decided to stay in the hospital and forget his afternoon classwork, even though Dr. McMeel told him he could only look in on Gipp but not converse, because he thought the only thing left in treating Gipp was rest, hope and prayer.

Gipp fell in and out of a coma at intervals. Father Haggerty and Hunk were silent onlookers with Gipp's family as the evening approached. Hunk left the hospital, feeling that his presence now was of no value to Gipp. Stanley Hull drove Gipp's mother to eat a quick supper at Hull's house and brought her back in less than an hour after receiving a phone call from the hospital to come at once. Father Haggerty stayed with Gipp. The family had been enduring sleepless nights, and would often nod off into a nap of short duration at bedside.

Dr. McMeel and a nurse were attending to Gipp as Gipp's mother entered the room and sat down. Minutes later Rockne came into the room and so as not to disturb the silence permeating the room, merely nodded his head in greeting everyone. Stanley Hull was standing near the back of the room and when the nurse on her way out spotted him, she told Stanley to go outside the room because he was not a family member.

Gipp said something to Dr. McMeel and the doctor, stepping aside, motioned to Rockne that George wanted him.

This is what George Hull said about that moment in an interview on a radio broadcast aired by WSBT-South Bend which I heard more than two decades later. The scene, in paraphrase, as told by Hullie and as I remember it: The door was open and Stanley Hull could see everything that was transpiring in the room. Father John O'Hara arrived but upon looking into the crowded room, did not enter. He told Stanley that if anyone should ask for him, he would be in the hospital chapel, praying. Stanley observed that Gipp was talking to Rockne, whose head was bent to hear Gipp's feeble voice. After Gipp finished, Rockne moved away and the mother came forward. Stanley saw her stroking Gipp's forehead as Father Haggerty, after conversation outside the room with Stanley Hull, reentered the room. He told Stanley that he was surprised to see George awake at this time because during the day when he visited, George was in a coma.

On the air, George Hull said that when Rockne left the room, he stopped to talk to Hull's son, Stanley, and Stanley asked Rock what was said by Gipp to him. Rockne answered that Gipp told him he wasn't going to make it. Then Gipp asked Rockne that if someday a Notre Dame team was in a spot and needed a victory, to ask the team to win that game for the "Gipper and that he'd know about it and he'd be happy." (An elaboration to follow in the next chapter.)

Monday slipped into Tuesday. Gipp was hanging on but losing the fight. It is possible and probable that Dr. McMeel had earlier stimulated Gipp with digitalis or some other medication to keep him conscious as long as he had been that last evening of his life. His fighting spirit might also have had something to do with it. As the minutes ticked on into the early morning hours, Gipp again lapsed into a coma for the last time. Pat Chelland wrote that Father Pat Haggerty gave Gipp conditional baptism and conditional absolution as Gipp's drowsy mother, his sister and brother observed the ritual. After that, Father John O'Hara administered the last rites of the Catholic Church. Both priests then stepped back and prayed in silence as Dr. McMeel came to Gipp's bedside and the nurse followed.

As the Gipp family, physically and mentally exhausted, was trying hard to stay awake, Dr. McMeel saw a slight movement by Gipp and immediately checked his pulse and Gipp's chest with a stethoscope. The doctor turned to the family shaking his head negatively, indicating that George was dead. This was 3:30 a.m., Wednesday, December 14, 1920. The lobby was deserted and the pool table area closed at the Oliver Hotel, but by prearrangement the night clerk got a call from a nurse at the hospital and pulled the master switch on and off three times indicating to the night staff and cleaning crew, that their friend George Gipp was dead.

Because the death occurred so early in the morning, the Tribune was able to publish the story for the evening paper that very same day, furnishing details regarding arrangements.

The body was sent to the McGann Funeral Parlor at 333 N. Michigan Street and the undertaker had it ready for viewing at precisely noon, where it laid in state until 9:55 the next morning, when the march to South Bend's New York Central Station began.

When Gipp died, Notre Dame lowered the flag to half staff and messages of sympathy poured into South Bend for

Notre Dame and for the Gipp family. The next day, Thursday, an early Requiem Mass was offered for the repose of Gipp's soul at the Sacred Heart Church on campus. Father Burns, Notre Dame's president, was the celebrant.

The procession of students and townsmen from McGann's to the railroad station was led by six of Gipp's teammates who would accompany the body to Calumet and serve as pall bearers. The six teammates were team captain Frank Coughlin, Joe Brandy, Norm Barry and Gipp's Laurium pals, Hunk Anderson, Ojay Larson and Perce Wilcox.

On December 17 the South Bend Tribune reported: "Funeral services will be held in the Gipp residence at 1 p.m. tomorrow. The body will be moved to the armory where it will lay in state for two hours."

The article went on to say that more than 200 people met the train and high school cadets formed an escort and marched with the body to the Gipp residence.

On Saturday, December 17, the Reverend F. A. O'Connor, a Baptist minister, and the Reverend J. P. Robertson of the Congregational Church, officiated at services which were held at the armory in order to accommodate the crowd of mourners that was expected and which did turn up to pay last respects to their local hero.

The interment was challenging. With four days of heavy snowfall clogging the impassible streets, the body had to be placed on a sled drawn by two horses in order to reach Lakeview Cemetery. The South Bend Tribune published a wire service report about the funeral which in part stated: "Floundering through eight feet of snow, the Gipp family and close friends took his body to a bleak hillside overlooking

Lake Superior and paid final honors at the grave. The body was carried five miles to the cemetery on a horse-drawn sled, because the snow made automobiles impossible.

"Gipp's aged father and mother, although worn out with grief and the strain of three weeks' worry while he fought throat trouble in the hospital at South Bend, Indiana, went to the cemetery despite admonitions of physicians."

Gipp's body was interred but he lives on in spirit, in legend and in sports history.

# 16

## GIPP'S LAST REQUESTS

The upheaval that started in the mid-1960s — caused by the inequities in law, social standards and denial of civil rights to citizens of color — challenged and defied authority to the extent that many changes were made for the better. Still, tagging along supporting good causes were people who were also bent on expunging God from our lives, minimizing patriotism, promoting immorality and revising history to their liking.

There have been attempts in some recent books to revise Notre Dame's history and to scuttle its traditions. There is nothing wrong with "setting the record straight" if it is substantiated by proof. However, inferences, hearsay and speculative scenarios are not proof.

Several books and articles have cast doubt that Rockne asked the 1928 Notre Dame team playing Army, its foremost rival at that time, to win the game for Gipp. When people who were in the locker room at the time — people like Frank Leahy, Ed Healy and Francis Wallace along with a resurrected headline from the New York News, "Gipp's Ghost Beats Army," — came forward to state that they heard Rockne say it, then another target was selected by the "hit men." The revisionists now say it is very unlikely that Gipp was capable of making such a dying man's request — his request of Rockne to ask a Notre Dame team in trouble to "win one for the Gipper." It was said that a fellow with a poolroom and taxi cab background didn't possess such sentiment and that Rockne made it up. Well, that is a lame reason to say Gipp did not make the "win one" request. Gipp was an intelligent young man who structured his language and actions according to one of his favorite mottos, which he expounded on more than one occasion, i.e, "When in Rome, do as the Romans do." As far as Gipp not being able to harbor or express such sentiment, the critics should read Gipp's love letters to Iris Trippeer published in John Bacon's story on Gipp in the Detroit News in 1997.

There are other unsubstantiated inferences that Gipp did not make the request of Rockne because he was in a coma. It would be valid if he had stayed in a coma, but newspaper reports as well as statements by those present in his room, indicate otherwise.

The first published report of the "Win one for the Gipper" request goes back to an article Rockne wrote for Collier's Magazine in November, 1930. It was then detailed in Rockne's autobiography, which was published in 1931 after his death, in the chapter titled "Gipp the Great." It soon joined the sports lexicon after becoming one of the most memorable scenes in the 1940 Warner Brothers film, "Knute Rockne — All American," with Ronald Reagan as Gipp and Pat O'Brien as Rockne.

Despite the fact that it is acknowledged that Rockne told his 1928 team about the request during the game in New York City vs. Army, there is some evidence that he used the Gipp request more than once prior to that time. Wells Twombly, who wrote "Shake Down the Thunder," the biography of Frank Leahy, mentioned one of those probable occasions in his book. He tried to corroborate it but couldn't. Possibly the reason that he couldn't was that Frank Leahy (who told him about it) had the wrong team involved — Indiana — but he did have the right year. Leahy heard it from some players who were on Notre Dame's 1921 team. There was no reason for Rockne to use the "win one for the Gipper" request as an inspirational ploy in 1921 for the Indiana game because Indiana had a poor team that year.

However, it seems to be true that an earlier request to "Win one for the Gipper" was made in 1921 by Rockne, but not for the Indiana game but rather for the game with Iowa. It wasn't as emotional as it was in the 1928 Army game because only two Notre Dame substitutes remembered it, and as far as is known, none of the first stringers did. Of course, if Notre Dame had been facing a possible losing season as it was in 1928 the Gipp request might have been appropriate and remembered...or it might have been remembered had Notre Dame won as it did in 1928. Notre Dame was riding the crest of a 21-game winning streak and was behind 10-7 at halftime in the Iowa game. Chet Grant, who quarterbacked that 1921 team, said that neither the team nor Rockne thought they would lose, even at halftime with a score of 10-7 against them. To Rockne, the Gipp request was an after-thought and obviously lacked conviction and intensity. That was Chet's opinion as to why he didn't recall hearing it. It seems that only the subs were glued to Rockne's rhetoric while the regulars were rehashing their problems.

Hunk Anderson had a rough time in that first half against Iowa. Neither he nor Rockne ever experienced or had seen a "mouse trap" play and Coach Howard Jones, who later coached successfully at Notre Dame's traditional rival, the University of Southern California, had a very mobile tackle named Duke Slater who executed it expertly on Hunk. Anderson was allowed to penetrate the Iowa defense only to get sideswiped with a body block by Slater, hence the "mouse trap" nomenclature for the play.

Early in the game Notre Dame marched down the field and into scoring position, but a reverse hand-off was fumbled by Dan Coughlin and Iowa recovered. Then Iowa took over. The trapping by the Hawkeyes wasn't only used on Hunk. Depending on what plays were called, the other side of the Notre Dame line got trapped as well. Aggressive Buck Shaw was vulnerable and got blindsided by the other Iowa guard in the unbalanced line. Iowa led 10-0 at the end of the first quarter with their star Aubrey Devine making good gains outside and inside the traps. Before the half ended, Notre Dame managed to score on a pass from Mohardt to Kiley to make it 10-7.

So the buzz at halftime among the first stringers was about coping with Iowa's trap plays and their tandem blocking used to make a hole. Rockne, by going to individual players and talking with them near the end of the intermission, probably made his speech before his tour began. He was talking to Chet Grant when the official call was made for the team to reenter the playing field. All Chet remembered regarding that conversation was Rockne had asked him about his knee which was operated on that summer at the Mayo Clinic.

Harvey Brown, who was a sub that year, told Chet about Rockne's Gipper speech that Chet didn't remember. Also Fod Cotton, another sub, told Chet he heard Rockne mention that Gipp, on his death bed, had asked his teammates "to win one for him." Many on the 1921 squad were Gipp's teammates.

Earlier during halftime, Hunk suggested to Rockne that he overshift a bit on defense when Iowa used the balanced line, so he could play Duke Slater almost head on. Rockne told Hunk to stay in position and let Slater make the first move before Hunk tried to penetrate or pursue through his position. Hunk said that when Rockne was talking to the team, he, Ojay Larson and Garvey had their own strategy session and weren't paying attention to Rockne until Rockne came around to talk to them.

Rockne also told each lineman individually to hesitate and not penetrate until the Hawkeye players moved first and then react and that did the trick in the second half. Iowa's offense couldn't move for as much yardage as it did the first half due to the now flexible Irish defense, but neither did Notre Dame do too well on the ground. The passing game moved them down the field but was thwarted by Iowa's Belding who made three crucial interceptions when Notre Dame got deep into Hawkeye territory. The game ended 10-7, Notre Dame's unbeaten streak was broken and Howard Jones' Iowa team was undefeated that year although it was ignored by and not invited to play in the Rose Bowl game on New Year's Day. Both Anderson and Grant said that Iowa was the best of the eleven teams played that year by the Irish. Rockne's first attempt at rallying a team with Gipp's request was unsuccessful probably because it was not the right time for it.

George Hull, a partner in the very successful South Bend cigar store known as Hullie and Mike's, as reported earlier in this book, made a radio statement some years ago concerning the death bed request of Rockne by Gipp but an attempt to try to get someone to check South Bend radio station WSBT's archives regarding information on the broadcast was unsuccessful. In fact, my letter was ignored.

Hull was a Notre Dame man, heart and soul, without actually being an alumnus. From about 1901, he had a referral business relationship with Mike Calnon and then in 1905, Hull and Calnon became partners in the cigar store business.

Both Hullie and Mike, with a group of Irish fans, would follow Notre Dame to West Point and in later years, New York City, for every Army game. The annual trek lasted a little past Elmer Layden's head coaching tenure at Notre Dame which ran from 1934 to 1940.

Hull was very popular in South Bend. In 1921, while still in partnership with Calnon, he ran for the position of South Bend City Commissioner and won. He kept getting reelected and served the city in that position continuously for 26 years. Hull died in late 1947 while still in office. The commissioner's job was not a full time position, so it did not interfere with his business; besides, Hull and Calnon sold Hullie and Mike's in 1923 to John Pulschen and Ray Buckles who kept the Hullie and Mike's name for a few years after the purchase. Hull then became an automobile salesman, selling Studebaker cars.

It was Hull's love of music that made him promote free band concerts in the park and in the auditorium of the First Methodist Church, to which he belonged. While promoting one of these concerts during a radio interview in the 1940s, Hull's remarks shifted from music to football. My recollection is that the interviewer was a fellow named Charley Egenroad who also, prior to Jim Britt's taking over sports at the local South Bend station, did the play-by-play of Notre Dame home football games.

As reported in the previous chapter, Hull mentioned that his son Stanley was in the hospital outside Gipp's room when Gipp made the request of Rockne to win one for him.

That the final hours of Gipp's hospital stay would bring doubt regarding Gipp's "Win one for the Gipper" request is understandable, except there is evidence that it was really made. My feeling about that night when Stanley was there is that the feeble whisper carried a reminder by Gipp to Rockne about what he had said earlier during the previous week when Gipp was strong and lucid. On the other hand, there's no question that Gipp was a remarkable young man, especially under pressure, and he could have, in his last moments of consciousness, said it the way Rockne had it in his autobiography and as Rockne had used it. Hunk Anderson believed that Gipp made the request exactly as quoted by

Rockne "because that's just like something George would say and the way he'd say it." When Gipp finished talking to Rock, he fell into his final coma.

This is the accepted version of Gipp's request that Rockne used in the locker room of that 1928 Army game: "I've got to go, Rock. It's all right. I'm not afraid. Sometime Rock, when the team is up against it, when things are wrong and the breaks are beating the boys, tell them to go in there with all they've got and win one for the Gipper. I don't know where I'll be then, Rock, but I'll know about it and I'll be happy."

Hull, in that WSBT radio interview, wasn't quoting but merely paraphrasing his son Stanley, who paraphrased Rockne who — if the quotation in the above paragraph is accepted as the true one — paraphrased Gipp. Stanley said that Gipp told Rockne he wasn't going to make it and that if someday a Notre Dame team was in a spot and needed a victory, for Rock to ask the team to win that game for the Gipper and that he'd know about it and he'd be happy.

Frank Leahy's version of Rockne's "win one speech" which he heard in the locker room was identical to the accepted version except there was a short preface about who Gipp was.

In 1986, Tony DiMarco had written an article for the Football News about Gipp in which he wondered too, whether the "Win one for the Gipper" speech was authentic or if Rockne made it up to spur his team to victory. DiMarco sent the article to President Reagan and heard from him shortly thereafter. Reagan wrote that when he was making the Rockne movie he asked Bonnie Rockne, Knute's wife, about it and Bonnie told him it was in Rockne's diary, word for word.

Here's exactly what President Reagan wrote:

"Thank you for sending me your article on the Gipper. Some of the things you told were familiar to me and many of them I hadn't known. One question you asked and couldn't answer had to do with Gipp's dying request of Rockne to ask a Notre Dame team to win a game for him. I believe I have the answer. Rock's widow, Bonny *(sic)* Rockne, spent some time on the set while we were making the picture. She was asked that question and her answer was, 'Yes, it was true and, word for word, was in Rock's diary.' Incidentally, I didn't have to learn those particular lines. As a sports announcer for WHO radio station in Des Moines, Iowa in the 1930's, I told that part of the Gipp story on one of my broadcasts. When I was put under contract at Warner Brothers in 1937 I almost immediately started talking to everyone who would listen about doing the life story of Rockne. Of course, I had one thought in mind — I would play George Gipp."

That's pretty good corroborating evidence as offered by President Reagan.

Famed sportswriter Grantland Rice, the man who wrote probably the most famous lead in the history of sports reporting in which he tagged Notre Dame's 1925 backfield as "The Four Horsemen," mentioned the Gipp request in his 1954 autobiography, "The Tumult and the Shouting." Rice wrote that the night before the 1928 Army game Rockne called him at his flat at 1158 Fifth Avenue in New York and said, "How about coming down and sitting around with Hunk and me here at the hotel?"

Instead, Rice says, he suggested Rockne come to his apartment, an invitation that Rockne accepted. It was during this meeting, the night before the Army-Notre Dame game, that Rice says Rockne told him about the Gipp deathbed request. Rice adds that Rockne told him, "Grant, I've never asked the boys to pull one out for Gipp. Tomorrow I might have to."

Pretty strong evidence that Rockne made Gipp's request of the 1928 team. But Murray Sperber, in his book "Shake Down the Thunder," claims that not only did Rockne not tell the story to Rice, but Rice wasn't even in town the night before the Army game! Why a writer of Rice's repute would fabricate several pages in his autobiography to tell the "Win one for the Gipper" story makes one wonder which writer had his facts straight. Sperber says that Rice filed a story on the Georgia Tech-Vanderbilt game in Atlanta and that "newspapers in that city noted his presence in the press box," which means, if Sperber is correct, there appears to be no way Rice could have been in New York on Friday night and in Atlanta the following day, since travel in those days was by train and not air. Furman Bisher, the veteran sports columnist of the Atlanta Journal, wrote me that he could not confirm Rice's presence at the Georgia Tech-Vanderbilt game. But, he added, "I can hardly believe, that with Army playing Notre Dame, he would not have been covering that game."

Because sometimes writers have an "agenda" and also for the sake of accuracy, I asked my granddaughter, Julie Charba, a very busy account supervisor for a New York public relations firm, to spare some time and do some checking for me. The New York Herald-Tribune no longer exists, but Julie, being only three years out of college, still knows how to find things and do research. I also asked my daughter Denise, living in Atlanta, who is an expert in sign language and its dialects and equally busy, if she too could spare some of her time to check the Atlanta Journal of November 11, 1928. Both responded with success.

Yes, there was a first-hand story written by Grantland Rice in the New York paper about the Vanderbilt-Georgia Tech game. On top of that, the Atlanta Journal's O. B. Keeler, in his article about the Tech-Vandy game, mentions Rice — whom he calls "America's greatest sportswriter" — not only as sitting in the press box with him, but he also intersperses Rice's opinion of the game throughout his game story.

Rice has been caught in a major fib by writer Sperber. However, the Friday night meeting of Rice and Rockne in which Rock revealed he would ask the team to win for the Gipper, sounds authentic. The advance tip by Rockne is something friends Rockne and Rice would do for each other, knowing how each man held the other in high esteem. I, too, felt as Furman Bisher did, that with Notre Dame playing Army, there was no way Rice would miss that game. In giving Rice the benefit of the doubt, I'll venture that perhaps that's why he stayed in New York City until he met with Rockne before departing for Atlanta.

But wait! There was no air travel as we know it today and he would not have made the Tech-Vandy game in time going by train. But then I reminded myself that in the plane crash which killed Rockne near Bazaar, Kansas in 1931, U. S. mail that was not burned was found at the wreckage. So a bit of research of the U.S air mail system was in order. It turns out that a bit of local area mail was sent by plane between two New York cities in 1911, which was the first air mail. By

1918, the U.S. Post Office had started the transportation of postal matter by air from New York to Washington, D.C. and transcontinental service by air to San Francisco began three years later, in 1921. Night flying of postal matter was inaugurated in 1924. In 1927, the Post Office Department withdrew from direct operation of air mail service and contracted with private carriers for the service. By 1928 there were many companies involved in transporting mail as new routes were established.

The year 1928 saw the continuing of an almost decade long economic boom and New York City had a plethora of corporate offices, financial institutions and the stock exchange. Rapid delivery of contracts, orders, sealed bids, title transfers and other business paper was essential. Many routes were established along the Atlantic seaboard and Atlanta was a postal base for relay flights in the South.

The transport companies moved not only mail but also *passengers*. Most companies used the three-engine Fokker that could carry a load with great speed. The plane, built by Anthony Fokker, a Dutch aircraft designer who established his first factory in Germany and then became a U. S. citizen after World War I, was ideal for flying both cargo and passengers. It is conceivable, therefore, that with the many mail flights emanating in the daytime and at night from New York, Grantland Rice could have arranged to be on one to Atlanta in order to also have been with his friend Knute Rockne on Friday, and at the Georgia Tech-Vanderbilt game at 2 p.m. on Saturday. Why the Tech-Vandy game? Tech was unbeaten and Vandy was Nashville-native Grantland Rice's alma mater. I have been told by airline experts that even in those

251

days Rice could have left New York as late as 7 a.m. Saturday and arrived in Atlanta, about 800 air miles away, in time for the 2 p.m. kickoff.

So, while there seems to be no question as to Rice's being in Atlanta on the Saturday of the Army-Notre Dame game in New York, it is not beyond the realm of possibility that he was in New York, where he wrote in his autobiography that he met with Rockne, on the night before. Grantland Rice used a direct quote from Rockne which asked Rice to come visit with him and Hunk at the hotel. Although Hunk was always with Rockne the night before an Army game, in 1928 he wasn't because Hunk coached St. Louis University that year. One explantion can be Rice's own — that he dictated his autobiography with "sometimes fading memories." In spite of Rice's fib about being at the Army-Notre Dame game, I'd like to believe he was in New York with Rockne the night before the game.

Hunk Anderson told me that Rockne kept a black appointment book on him. Besides his appointments and schedule he also included his impressions of the people he met, which were jotted in margins and in note sheets in back of the book. Then he would enter the information in his diary when he got home, combining his impressions with the events of his day's routine. It is quite likely that it was in this book that Rockne first wrote about Gipp's request.

But when authors Michael Bonifer and L. G. Weaver tried to locate the appointment book, diary and letters for excerpting purposes for their book about Notre Dame entitled "Out of Bounds," they found out from Rockne's daughter, Jean, that upon her mother's death most of Rockne's personal effects were burned. Too bad. It is true that Rockne, in jotting down impressions about people he had met, had uncomplimentary opinions about some, including businessmen, alumni and coaches. Perhaps Bonnie Rockne thought those things were best left unsaid. Hunk told me he once peeked in Rock's appointment book laying on the desk in Rock's office. One descriptive item Hunk remembered seeing was: "Big windbag who likes to hear himself talk." About a priest who shall remain unnamed, and who apparently would not allow Rockne to spend money on something for the football team: "Parsimonious Father _____ would make Scrooge look like a spendthrift." It is fascinating to imagine what other comments Rockne may have written and what, if anything, he had to say about that night before the Army game, the "win one" request and even the meeting with Grantland Rice, as Rice reported it. We'll never know.

After Gipp had beaten pneumonia and seemed to be on his way to recovery, he apparently contradicted that favorable situation by being resigned to the fact that it was his time to go. When he told Hunk about wanting to accept the Catholic faith because he didn't think he'd "make it," it is this writer's feeling that Gipp was getting things in order while he was still able to do so. This included activating a latent desire to be remembered in Notre Dame's future. It could have been in that week of recovery that he made the now famous "win one" request. He told Hunk, "I don't think I'll make it." He told Rockne, "I've got to go, Rock, I'm not afraid," and he told Father Haggerty, "Don't let me go, Father, without getting me 'fixed' up." I believe it was then, too, that George Gipp received his conditional baptism.

The required instruction in the Catholic faith could have been given discretely at that time, because with the emergency status in abatement, Gipp's family lingered away from the hospital for longer periods of time. Father Haggerty's visits of three or four times a day offered him plenty opportunity to fulfill the Catholic Church's requirements and he could have gotten help from Sister Austina by her not allowing anyone to go into the room until Father Haggerty was finished. The consensus of Notre Dame historians is that Father Haggerty gave Gipp conditional baptism and absolution after George lapsed into his final coma, about an hour before he died, with the Gipp family looking on. No one reported that Father Haggerty used holy water and the required candle at that time. Perhaps the situation exempted such formality. Gipp's mother denied that the conversion took place and was supported in that denial by Gipp's brother and sister, Matthew and Dorothy.

The family denial of the conversion and the controversy over a huge doctor and hospital bill of which the Gipps refused to pay any part created ill will between Notre Dame (which paid the bill) and the Gipps. As for the conversion, Father Haggerty offered an olive branch by saying that the conversion was one of interpreted intent as opposed to one of concrete expression. Hunk and I discussed that over a Reuben sandwich and a Schlitz beer at a West Palm Beach deli. Said Hunk, a non-Catholic: "I knew George better than most people and we talked about it when he mentioned that he wanted to become a Catholic before he 'went.' It was concrete with him because that's what he wanted to do and, hopefully, without hurting his mother's feelings by her not knowing about it."

Supporting Hunk's statement was something researcher Vince Gratzer told me. Herb Juliano informed Vince that Chet Grant had a letter from Father Haggerty which answered Chet's query regarding the Gipp conversion. Quite likely, with the passage of time, Father Haggerty felt it reasonable to be candid. The letter told Chet that Gipp's conversion was indeed valid. Chet's interest was perhaps his desire for information for one of his proposed books or maybe because Chet himself was a convert to Catholicism, and just anxious to know if Gipp made it.

I believe the conversion happened during Father Haggerty's earlier visits because Gipp expressed his desire to become a Catholic and it was the ideal time for both, Gipp and Father Pat, to go through with it. I tried to compare Gipp's conversion with Rockne's to see if there was any difference between the two besides the death bed. According to Father John Cavanaugh in his postscript to Rockne's autobiography, Rockne received conditional baptism because all conversions from another faith are conditional. This applied to both Gipp and Rockne. Rockne surely "expressed concretely" his desire to be Catholic and to be baptized in that faith and yet his baptism was conditional nonetheless, according to Father John. Father Haggerty gave Gipp conditional baptism and later said the conversion was conditional based on "interpreted intention" and not "concrete expression."

Father Cavanaugh explained Rockne's conversion as conditional because "it was a requirement for security's sake." He did not use the words concrete expression or interpreted intention as having any part in making it conditional. Neither did Father John define what the word "security" meant in conversions, but it might refer to a situation whereby someone might not have been sure or sincere in accepting the Catholic faith and that would make the baptism invalid. Perhaps a theologian would have a better answer, but I believe, in Gipp's case, Father Haggerty fulfilled the requirements of the Church. If concrete expression is indeed required, how about Gipp asking Father Haggerty: "Don't let me go, Father, without getting me fixed up." Yes, Gipp died a Catholic. Father Haggerty said so in his letter to Grant when he used the word valid.

Both of Gipp's last requests were fulfilled — one by Rockne in the Army game of 1928 when the coach asked the team to "Win one for the Gipper" and the other by Father Haggerty at St. Joseph's Hospital.

# 17

# WHY NOT A
# GIPP MOVIE?

Gipp's life story is a fascinating one, yet the appearance of Ronald Reagan portraying George Gipp in the 1940 Warner Brothers film "Knute Rockne — All American" is the only time Gipp has been portrayed on the big screen and at that it was nothing more than a vignette that barely touched on the details of his multi-faceted life story. But the conspicuous absence of a full-fledged Gipp movie is not because there has been a lack of trying.

Writers/producers David Ketchum and Tony DiMarco have had a movie script based on Patrick Chelland's excellent biography, "One for The Gipper," available in Hollywood since the early 1980s. In 1986 the script was approved by Notre Dame's executive vice-president, Father Edmund Joyce, during the Father Hesburgh regime, a rare accomplishment considering how difficult it is to get Notre Dame to approve film projects involving the university. Ketchum and DiMarco have tried to interest movie companies that had cash and clout as well as the big TV and cable-TV networks in the project but have been turned down usually without much more than a cursory meeting. Their agent has had the same problem.

The late Jason Miller, a Pulitzer Prize winning play-write for "That Championship Season," as well as an Academy Award nominee for his role as a priest in "The Exorcist," had been working on a Gipp project of his own for almost the same length of time as Ketchum/DiMarco. Miller told the Scranton Sunday Times in 1989 that he did not have a script but that Columbia Pictures was interested in a Gipp movie. Miller added that he would not pursue the project without Notre Dame's support but the interest at Columbia apparently was temporary because there was a change in management of the company and, as is typical in Hollywood, when top executives are replaced at a movie company their projects generally fall by the wayside also. It is quite likely that Miller would not have gained Notre Dame's approval of his project anyway because in a newspaper article mentioning the film at the time it was stated that, "This time the Notre Dame great won't be the squeaky clean guy portrayed by Ronald Reagan in the 1940 film. Instead, this film will center on George Gipp's little known 'dark side.'"

Actor Jason Patric (Jason Miller's son) has had a desire to play Gipp on the screen that is as strong as Reagan's desire was, which the President mentioned in his letter to Di-Marco. While the Columbia project, in which it was announced that Patric would portray Gipp, never came to fruition, Patric did spend a small bundle of his own money to produce a 15-minute promo/preview film, in which he played Gipp in three separate scenes — an actual football scrimmage, a tender love scene and an emotional conversation with an actor portraying Rockne. According to researcher Vince Gratzer, who helped in the production of the promo, Patric's portrayal of Gipp in all the scenes was excellent. But Gratzer points out that Patric's solicitation of movie studios and producers, fortified with the tape of his portrayal of Gipp, was unsuccessful. Whether Patric was still intent on portraying Gipp's so-called "dark side" in his version of the story is not known but in either case the project is still aborning.

Perhaps the closest a Gipp story came to reaching the screen was in 1983 when The Mirisch Corporation, a longtime and highly reputable Hollywood production firm, interested CBS Television in doing a TV movie-of-the-week based on The Gipper. CBS funded development money, reportedly $50,000, for the project and writer-director Mike Robe was dispatched to South Bend to research material for the screenplay in the Sports and Games Section of the Notre Dame Library, where Herb Juliano was the curator.

Robe was given the Patrick Chelland book, "One for the Gipper," the only completely definitive book ever written about Gipp, as his main source of material. Robe subsequently wrote a script for Mirisch-CBS. Soon thereafter, Juliano inquired of Robe as to the progress of the project and was told that it had been dropped because CBS felt that such a movie would have low ratings. That seems strange because one would assume that the determination of potential ratings would have been the first item for CBS to entertain before starting on any phase of the project. Later, I found out that CBS discovered that the rights to Chelland's book were in the possession of someone else (Ketchum/DiMarco) and rather than take a chance of being accused of infringing upon already-owned material, CBS dropped the project. Interestingly, a mistake in a statistic in the Chelland book had been used in the Robe script, pretty much validating where he got his material.

Along the way, more specifically in 1988, an article in USA Today announced that a highly accredited British film company, Goldcrest, which had produced such films as "Gandhi" and "Chariots of Fire," was going to make a film based on Gipp's life entitled "Golden Glory." The material for their project had been provided them by a young man who based his outline on the unauthorized use of the Ketchum-DiMarco screenplay. In addition, this same young man had had a previous run-in with Notre Dame when he advertised a non-existent book in the Notre Dame football programs. The incident embarrassed the University and it's obvious the fellow was going to have a hard time getting the school to cooperate on a Gipp film, knowing his somewhat shaky background. In an article in the South Bend Tribune in November, 1988, Notre Dame officials flat out stated they would not give the movie the University's blessings. The article went on to say that Goldcrest nevertheless would continue with the project and even announced John Quested, its managing director, as the film's producer. However, with so many roadblocks in its path, it's easy to understand why this proposed Gipp movie was doomed from the beginning and never progressed beyond its initial publicity.

But what is bewildering is that a British movie production company was interested in making a film about an American football legend and yet there has not been one feature film maker in the United States willing to explore that possibility. The question is, why?

I am told there are a million reasons why a movie does not get made. The fact of the matter is not so much why a particular movie does *not* get made but why it *does* get made. So many factors enter into movie making that it is a totally daunting endeavor to say the least. But, that being said, the fact remains that film and television projects are launched practically every day, many of them with far less gripping stories than the life of George Gipp. And films about sports personalities, from Lou Gehrig to Jack Dempsey to Jim Thorpe have been staples in the industry practically from the beginning of the movie business. With the advent of television, there seems to be an even greater desire to do sports biographies, witness the fact that not one but two films were made about University of Oregon track star Steve Prefontaine almost simultaneously and that the highly-acclaimed "Brian's Song," about Chicago Bears football players Brian Piccolo and Gale Sayers, was remade only a few years after the original version was aired. Films have been made about sports personalities while they were still alive and about those who were long gone, so it's a given that the movie industry is not averse to doing sports films providing there is at least a scintilla of a story to tell.

The Gipp story is more than just the saga of a great football player who died young at the height of his career. It has more than its share of plot necessities — action, romance, intrigue, humor, pathos, relationships and a death-bed scene that is a guaranteed tear jerker. Plus, in this age of the film industry's acknowledged catering to the youth market, it is a story entirely dominated by young people. At 25, Gipp was the "old man" among his peers who were all college-aged men and women in their late teens and early 20s. Even Rockne was only 30 when he first coached "The Gipper."

So why has the Gipp story never been told on the screen? It is an intriguing question with, in this writer's opinion, an even more intriguing answer — or, at least, a partial answer. It is the Reagan connection.

It is a well-known fact that former president Ronald Reagan has been called "The Gipper" because of his excellent portrayal of Gipp in the 1940 Rockne film-biography. Once Reagan got into the political arena, it was a bonanza for cartoonists and comedians as well as serious writers to refer to Reagan as "The Gipper," a nickname whose use Reagan unabashedly encouraged. He made no secret of the fact that portraying Gipp was one of his favorite movie roles. Friends called Reagan "Gipper" with admiration; his enemies did call him "Gipper," too, but with derision. In either case, "Gipper" became synonymous with Reagan to the point that many people to this day have no idea that George Gipp — "The Gipper" — was a real person and not just a sobriquet of the former actor who became this nation's 40th president.

And therein lies the problem. According to neutral observers, it is no secret that the political leanings of most people in Hollywood, especially those in higher echelon decision-making positions, are strictly to the left. They bristled when Reagan, despite being one of their own as an actor, became a successful Republican politician. It was bad enough for them to have to tolerate Reagan becoming governor of California, but when he won the highest political office in the land and became president, it rankled them no end — and it still does to this day. To them, mention "Gipper" and they immediately think Reagan. And even though a motion picture or television movie about Gipp would have absolutely nothing to do with the former president, there is still that name association that is inescapable.

There is, of course, no way to prove this theory. It's too easy to dismiss a movie project with a myriad of other oftentimes quite legitimate reasons. But in the case of a Gipp movie, there is always that nagging caveat over the Gipper-Reagan connection. I have first-hand information that was given to me by a prominent Hollywood insider to back up my theory. Some years ago, while discussing a Gipp project with the head of one of Hollywood's major studios, an agent was told by the studio chief, "I wouldn't touch a Gipp movie project with a ten-foot pole because of the political implications." This seems to still be the prevailing attitude in the industry despite the fact that former President Reagan has been out of office since 1989. Apparently liberal-leaning Hollywood has never forgiven Ronald Reagan — more famous as "The Gipper" than George Gipp himself — for becoming president.

So will the Gipp story ever come to fruition as a motion picture and/or television feature? The old adage, "never say never," probably is the key here. Someday, some studio or television executive will possibly realize that the time has come to do the Gipp epic. It will have been a long wait but, hopefully, if the picture is done right, it will have been worth it.

# 18

# COMPENDIUM OF
# SIDELIGHTS

When Gipp signed a baseball contract with the Chicago Cubs before his death, while in St. Joseph's Hospital, that was the second time he had received a contract from the Cubs. Actually, he received a contract from both the Cubs and the Chicago White Sox with an identical offer of $4000 per season during a 1920 pre-spring practice just before his first expulsion from school.

The sun was shining but the day was a cold one, so the players warmed up quite gingerly to keep warm and to avoid muscle injury. Gus Dorais, the Notre Dame team manager, knew that both the White Sox and Cubs had scouts at Cartier Field primarily to watch Gipp, so Gus made sure that word got back to Gipp about the scouts being in attendance.

Hunk Anderson was going to catch the batting practice before an abbreviated intra-squad game began. Gipp, wanting the odds to be in his favor, asked Hunk to let him know what the pitch was going to be and Hunk agreed.

After giving the pitcher a signal for a pitch and the pitcher nodded his head in agreement, Hunk would raise his mitt to hide his mouth and would pound his fist into it at that level while whispering loud enough for Gipp to hear what kind of pitch to expect. Gipp slammed one pitch after another over the Cartier Field fence in left field and if he hit it to the opposite field, where two gridirons began, it would be over the right fielder's head and certainly an easy inside the park home run. The pitcher soon caught on and fooled Hunk and Gipp by throwing something other than the signaled pitch. Gipp still managed to park the ball over the fence at least three more times, according to Hunk, and then Gipp gave way to Norm Barry who had been shouting, "Come on George, let someone else get a turn at bat."

Gipp failed to sign any of those two contracts given to him that day because they were typical league contracts that included minor league stipulations and not a special-provisioned clause like the one he later signed in the hospital. George, a law student, didn't like some of the clauses in the contracts according to Hunk and he certainly didn't want to play in the minors.

◆

Two paragraphs in the report in the South Bend Tribune of the 1920 Thanksgiving Day game with Michigan Aggies, revealed that Jack Dempsey's manager, Jack Kearns, was in discussions with Princeton's Keene Fitzpatrick trying to arrange a Princeton-Notre Dame post season game to be played in Chicago. He was negotiating on behalf of Gene Kessler, a South Bend Tribune sports columnist and promoter, and Floyd Fitzpatrick of Benton Harbor, Michigan. The deal was eventually turned down by Princeton.

◆

On the Saturday after the Thanksgiving game, Notre Dame had the 1920 championship season team photo taken and in the back row middle, a spot was left open for Gipp, who was in the hospital. South Bend's Bagby Studios later cleverly inserted a photo of Gipp that was taken the previous season in that open slot. This was the official team photo with Gipp in it. One writer used that photo in his book, noting in his caption that "Gipp got out of his hospital bed to pose with the team," which, of course, was not true.

◆

While Notre Dame's Faculty Athletics Board denied Notre Dame participation in a post season game against Ohio State in 1920, the Big Ten also forbade Ohio State to play Notre Dame. However, a week later it allowed the Buckeyes to accept an invitation to play in the Rose Bowl. In that game, unbeaten California whipped the Buckeyes 28-0 and the Golden Bears were named National Champions by the Helms Foundation, which since 1900 was considered the official selector of that coveted collegiate prize. A lesser known selector, retired coach Parke Davis for the "The Official Football

Guide," named Notre Dame and Princeton the 1920 Co-National Champions. Davis had also named Notre Dame and Illinois Co-National Champions in 1919.

◆

Concerning the Gipp reinstatement exam, I asked Chet Grant why would an end of April exam be considered a final in a subject when all other Notre Dame departments had their finals in the first week of June? Chet had a logical answer. From his observations, he surmised that the month of May was used for practical class work "in the field."

Chet did not enroll at Notre Dame for the 1919-20 school term but worked for the South Bend Tribune that year. As a city-beat reporter, he'd notice some Notre Dame law students entering and leaving the courthouse. He even waved to Norm Barry (who later was to become a judge in Chicago) who carried a bundle of papers as he entered the courthouse and deduced that in the month of May, the dean made arrangements for law students to get on-the-job experience.

Chet guessed that some students worked in lawyers' offices; some with the courthouse personnel and some merely observed trials and then, after a certain amount of days, they'd switch jobs among themselves. It was commendable that South Bend's and the County's legal systems cooperated, if, indeed, that was field work with which the students were involved as Chet thought it to be. Chet never bothered to ask anyone about it.

◆

When Gipp received his injuries in the 1920 Indiana game he got under a hot shower and later the next day sat in a hot tub with his shoulder soaking in the hot water. Heat was the immediate remedy then and doctors now say it was the wrong one to use. Today's methods are to put ice packs on the injury or wrap it up in ice because there is hemorrhaging involved and that must be stopped as quickly as possible in order for healing to begin.

◆

Hullie and Mike's was almost declared off-limits by Father Burns a few months after he assumed the Notre Dame presidency. It seems some students wanted to get some quick and easy money by betting on a sure thing, the Chicago White Sox in the 1919 World Series against Cincinnati. When the students lost everything at Hullie and Mike's and wrote home for money, the parents found out about the bets and complained to Father Burns. Rockne intervened and persuaded Father Burns to hold off and give Hullie and Mike's another chance. He cited many favorable things that the entrepreneurs did for the students and the university, such as offering reasonably priced food, sponsoring the annual football banquet and advertising in the student yearbook, The Dome.

◆

During Gipp's work as a house player and his stay as guest at South Bend's Oliver Hotel, he became very friendly with Jules Stein, the young orchestra leader whose orchestra played the Oliver on weekends. Gipp loved to listen and dance to Stein's music. Stein was a unique person. During the week he not only attended classes at the University of Chicago Medical School during the day, but at night he played backup violin to a young stage performer from Brooklyn named Mary Jane West. She changed her name to Mae West and became a major star in the movies by the 1930s. Jules Stein eventually became one of the most powerful moguls in Hollywood through his company, Music Corporation of America (MCA).

◆

William Frye, a producer at Universal Pictures for 17 years whose credits include the big hits "Airport '75" and "Airport '77," among others, told Tony DiMarco an interesting story about Jules Stein whom Frye knew quite well after Stein's MCA purchased Universal. Stein and Frye were frequent dinner guests at each other's homes and Stein knew that Frye was a good friend of Greta Garbo because Garbo was Frye's neighbor when she visited Los Angeles. Stein was a big fan of Greta Garbo but never had the opportunity to meet her, primarily because of her reclusiveness.

When Stein became seriously ill, Stein's wife called Frye and asked if he could arrange for Stein to meet Garbo. Frye did make the arrangements and Garbo, despite her reclusiveness, went to Stein's home where Stein got up from his sickbed to meet with her. A few days after the meeting, Stein died, but one of his lifetime dreams was fulfilled, thanks to Bill Frye.

Frye, who was a friend of writers Ketchum and Di-Marco, gave then President Ronald Reagan a copy of the Ketchum-DiMarco script, "One for the Gipper." (Frye was good friends with Reagan, having produced "GE Theater" which Reagan hosted from 1954-1962.) The President read the script while on a weekend at the western White House in Santa Barbara and thought it was an excellent even-handed grasp and portrayal of the Gipp character. The President also offered a couple of suggestions which Frye relayed to the writers. According to DiMarco, these suggestions were good and were incorporated into the script. In a note to DiMarco, President Reagan, with his keen sense of humor, said, "I'm glad to hear of progress on the "Gipper" project, and yet I say this with mixed emotions. One side of me hates to think of anyone else being the "Gipper." Can there be any doubt as to Ronald Reagan's favorite acting role?

◆

Old time Studebaker auto workers claimed that the United Auto Workers Union had an organizational meeting in a South Bend tavern shortly after Franklin D. Roosevelt was elected president. Auto worker Walter Reuther, UAW's first president, is supposed to have hitch-hiked from Detroit to organize the union. From that meeting the UAW was formed and then finalized with legalities in Detroit.

The tavern, situated on Main Street near the Studebaker auto plant, was renamed the Union Tavern. It was formerly known as Goldie Mann's, the place where Gipp won his biggest pots in poker and his biggest bets playing pool. A check was made with the UAW in Detroit regarding the meeting but it could not be confirmed because the spokesman said that the UAW library had no historian.

◆

Gene Kessler's column, "Serving the Punch," mentioned that George Gipp and Arthur "Dutch" Bergman signed contracts to play pro ball in 1921 with the Aksar-Ben Club of Omaha, Nebraska. It was a brief notice that didn't include the information that Bergman had finished his eligibility at Notre Dame in 1919, but was remembered for his stellar play in the game against Nebraska that year. The signing was done prior to the 1920 Indiana game but not made public until it appeared in Kessler's column.

◆

Players returning from the armed forces in 1919 after World War I helped Rockne gain his first undefeated season. Rockne thought that it would be better for the team if the lockers were assigned to have the linemen together and the backs together so they could discuss their particular problems regarding running plays and blocking assignments. While back Pete Bahan saw the towel incident causing a rift between Gipp and Grover Malone, lineman Hunk Anderson was unaware of the feud.

◆

After Pete Bahan was dropped by Notre Dame for scholastic reasons, he played for Detroit University in 1920. In 1921, Pete enrolled at St. Mary's University in Moraga, California, where his Notre Dame buddy, Edward "Slip" Madigan, coached. When asked about eligibility at St. Mary's, he said he had one more year coming because of the war.

Bahan was elected Galloping Gael's captain, so Pete not only captained Notre Dame twice, but also St. Mary's in 1921 and was selected All Coast quarterback that year. He tried the pros after that season, playing with the Cleveland Indians, who became the Rams, a team that has migrated in its existence to several different cities and now calls St. Louis home. Bahan, who played just that one year for Cleveland, was given the opportunity to buy the team for $5000 and after mulling it over, turned the offer down.

◆

Bahan and Gipp had a business partnership while at Notre Dame during World War I. They had some campus calendars, small gold and blue pennants and Notre Dame buttons made and sold them on campus. They took orders between classes and then delivered the merchandise the next day. Bahan said that the profit was good and only material shortages put them out of business.

◆

Although the South Bend of Gipp's era was emerging from the horse and buggy days that were being supplanted by the automobile, law enforcement was almost completely in the hands of the cop on the beat, who walked his designated area or neighborhood. Radio, in its infancy, wasn't yet available for squad car patrolling and the cop on the beat usually handled minor law infractions on the spot, using common sense and discretion. If he needed assistance or a paddy wagon, he'd have telephone call boxes which were located on telephone poles and wired directly to the police station. These call boxes were situated perhaps a block or two apart. There were two motorcycle policemen who covered South Bend up to the city limits. The first automatic traffic signals in South Bend were installed at major intersections in 1922.

◆

When Rockne was killed in 1931 in the Kansas plane crash, Hunk Anderson replaced him as Notre Dame's coach. Immediately he was told by the new athletic director, Jess Harper, that he had to decide after spring practice what 22 players he wanted on scholarships, because football scholarships were being cut in half. Notre Dame's president, Father Hugh O'Donnell, cited the Depression along with unpaid mortgages on the newly constructed stadium and buildings as the reason for the cuts. Hunk told Father O'Donnell that "If you don't feed the goose, it will stop laying the golden eggs," to which Father O'Donnell replied, "The goose has been overfed and while it is digesting its feed, it will continue to lay the golden eggs." Father O'Donnell thought that because of Notre Dame's football reputation, good athletes would want to play for Notre Dame even if they had to pay tuition and other expenses themselves.

Thus, in 1931, Hunk became a victim of Notre Dame's first de-emphasis of football. In 1933, Hunk also became the first Notre Dame coach in its history to suffer a losing season, going 3-5-1. In Hunk's last game as coach his Notre Dame team stunned the football world with a 13-12 victory over undefeated Army. Unknown to Anderson, the decision to replace him with former Irish fullback and member of the famed "Four Horsemen," Elmer Layden, had already been made. To follow Rockne with a .630 winning percentage plus a losing season wasn't good enough.

This is what Francis Wallace told me on the condition that I keep it off the record while Hunk was still alive. He said he was responsible for Hunk getting fired. Said Frank: "After the Army victory, Father John O'Hara wanted to give Hunk a reprieve. I talked him out of it, saying that Elmer Layden had already agreed to take the job after his season at Duquesne was over and after he had attended to some unfinished duties."

Shortly after the Army game, Hunk was asked to resign, which he did and when he asked if Notre Dame had someone in mind to take over, he was told that Layden had already been hired. The reason Hunk asked was that he was going to recommend Gus Dorais or "Slip" Madigan. Francis Wallace said that at that time, when he and Father O'Hara's unofficial advisory committee (which Wallace organized) were trying to decide on Hunk's replacement, neither he nor any member of the committee was aware of Notre Dame fielding a team with only 22 scholarships. Frank wasn't sure if that would have made a difference if they had known about the cuts. Father John O'Hara had replaced an ailing Father Hugh O'Donnell, who was responsible for that scholarship policy and supposedly wasn't aware that the existing scholarships were cut down from a larger number.

When Layden met with Hunk Anderson to get orientation and information on what to expect, Hunk told Elmer that he only had 22 scholarships per year to offer prospects providing they were available through graduation and dropouts. Layden was quite surprised and asked Hunk to accompany him when he met with Father O'Hara. Father O'Hara was reluctant to make concessions, saying that you could only play eleven men in a game at one time anyhow, but relented grudgingly when Layden told O'Hara that he had more scholarships at Duquesne than he would have at Notre Dame. The mention of Duquesne, a lesser known Catholic college, did the trick and concessions were made by Father O'Hara but not without conditions. "If football players are going to get scholarships, by God, they better be scholars," proclaimed O'Hara.

That's when the requirement of football players scoring higher passing grades than the rest of the student body at Notre Dame was instituted. It was 75 for the players to pass; 70 for others.

◆

In the summer of 1920, when Gipp and Bahan were working at the General Motors Buick plant in Flint, Michigan and playing baseball in the factory league, they relaxed at night by attending dances. One evening a dance contest was held in Flint and Gipp asked an unescorted young lady to participate and she accepted. Gipp was as adept on the dance floor as he was on the athletic field and he and his partner won the dance contest as he was to do in South Bend at the Oliver a few months later.

◆

A movie about a women's professional baseball league entitled "A League of Their Own" came out in 1992 and is now seen occasionally on TV. One team in that league was the South Bend Blue Sox and it was managed by Chet Grant in 1946 and 1947. Chet lamented the fact that after he left the team, the Blue Sox won the league championship. Chet spent one year managing the Kenosha Comets in 1948 and after that season ended, Chet decided to quit. He didn't care for the travel involved.

◆

Hunk Anderson was so highly regarded by George Halas that Halas, on several occasions, when Anderson's name came up, would say, "Hunk Anderson is the greatest line coach who ever lived." Rockne's praise of Hunk ran in a similar vein. "There isn't anyone who knows more about line play or can teach it better than Hunk Anderson." Few people, however, know that Anderson was also a great innovator. He introduced "blitzing" to football in 1939 when he was a line coach in charge of defense for the Detroit Lions.

It was called "red dog" by Hunk before the scribes and

radio announcers renamed it "blitzing." Fred Vanzo and Alex Wojciecowicz were the first to blitz. Hunk tried the maneuver earlier at Notre Dame against USC in 1933 with Steve Banas blitzing, but the timing was off and it required a lot of practice time, so Hunk abandoned it and resurrected it when he joined the Lions. When the Chicago Bears played the Lions in 1939, Hunk's defense and "red dogs" held the Bears to a paltry total of 50 yards and, in 1940, Halas hired Anderson away from Detroit to coach the line and set the defenses for the Bears.

◆

Hunk also fathered the "safety blitz" in 1940 when he blitzed George McAfee against the Green Bay Packers. The Packers tried to score from the four yard line with fullback Clark Hinkle carrying the ball on all four downs. McAfee blitzed each time, stopping Hinkle short of the goal line on every attempt.

◆

The January, 2002 issue of "Coffin Corner" rated the Chicago Bears defense of 1942 as the best defense in the history of the NFL. This publication is the official magazine/newsletter of the Pro Football Researchers Association and the statistical research was done by T. J. Troup. The 1942 Bears, in 11 games, yielded only 519 yards rushing (47 yards per game) and 1179 passing (107 per game) and allowed only nine touchdowns in 11 games. The Bears defense of the 1940's also was the best defense in any decade in NFL history. The architect of those record holding defenses was Hunk Anderson, who had sole charge of coaching and setting up the defense for the Bears, while Halas and Luke Johnsos took care of the offense.

◆

After Gipp's sister, Dorothy (Dolly) Gipp Taylor, had retired from teaching, Jim Beach managed to locate her and interview her. She had many interesting stories to tell and Jim made a note of some. One was about the house in Laurium, Michigan, in which the Gipp family resided. Their paternal grandfather, Antoine Gipp, immigrated from Germany with his wife Agnes. He was a stone mason by trade but also did carpentry work. Dolly told Jim that the house in which the Gipp's lived on Hecla Street was built by the grandfather. Gipp's father, Matthew Sr., as a young man, helped to build it. Matthew later worked as a carpenter for the C&H Mining Company.

◆

There were eight children in Matthew Sr. and Isabella Gipp's family. Alexander was the oldest child and George was the second youngest with Dorothy being the youngest.

◆

Although George was a bright young man, he was not one to hit the books. He hated homework and his grades showed a lack of preparation and interest in his school subjects. He carried this negative trait  on into college. At Calumet High, his pranks often got George into trouble and according to Ojay Larson, his friend and schoolmate, Gipp suffered many suspensions. George was an excellent athlete, but managed to play only basketball at Calumet High and was by far the best player on the team during the short period he was eligible, scoring 52 points in one game. This was a monumental feat because the rules of those days did not accommodate the fast break after a basket was made and required a center jump after every basket.

◆

When it came for Gipp to rise early in the morning to play baseball or attend to other personal obligations, he preferred to sleep-in late and had to be awakened by his teammates or family members. But upon finishing high school, Gipp managed to get to work on time for the jobs he had. He was a good, hard worker in every paying job he held. He would climb telephone poles while stringing wire for the telephone company in the summer. He worked for a construction company, driving its dump truck; he drove a taxi and he waited on tables in Calumet as he was to do later in his freshman year at Notre Dame and everyone said he was a good waiter in both venues. When he changed jobs, it wasn't for more money but to change the scenery or because of the completion of the job, such as the stringing of telephone wires for the phone company.

◆

Most historians agree that the evolution of rules and the shape of the ball played an important part in establishing the modern game of football. They also agree that after the 73-0 rout of the Washington Redskins by the Chicago Bears in 1940, featuring a revamped T-formation, the modernization was finalized. Pro and college coaches, including Frank Leahy, began adopting the T-formation. In 1939, after the University of Chicago abandoned football, Clark Shaughnessy joined the staff of the Chicago Bears under George Halas. Because of Clark's presence and because college football was still dominant and was considered to have the coaching masters of the game, much credit was given to Shaughnessy for the modernization and success of the revamped T-formation. Actually, Shaughnessy's part in the updating of the T-formation was minor and George Halas has said that the modernization of the "T" was a staff operation that began in 1929 and was completed in 1940 when Hunk Anderson came aboard as an assistant coach.

Halas wrote the history of the Chicago Bears in 14 chapters for the Chicago Tribune in 1967. In it he said that upon his first retirement in 1929, he and partner Dutch Sternaman hired the college coach who was with Bob Zuppke at Illinois, to coach the Bears. It was Ralph Jones who started to make the old "T" more effective by spreading the ends almost to the sidelines. Then he added a man in motion who ended up as a flanker, thus spreading the defense.

The next innovation came in 1939, when team quarterback and part time assistant coach Carl Brumbaugh came up with a new method of the snap from center which was actually having the quarterback positioned on the heels of the center and receiving a quick handback from him. The pressure of the quarterback's hand up against the crotch gave the center a spot to quick snap the ball without looking back under his legs for the quarterback's hands.

According to Chet Grant, who played quarterback at Notre Dame, in the Notre Dame "T" from which plays would be run without a shift, his hands to receive the ball were about a half yard away from the center and near the center's ankles, like an infielder about to catch a grounder. The center had to look back to see where to snap the ball, whereas in the Brumbaugh method, the center knew by pressure applied where the ball was to go and that helped his other job of blocking.

Halas gave Shaughnessy credit for the signal calling system and the counter play. But with all that in place in 1939, Green Bay won the division title and played the New York Giants for the championship. The Bears lost three games, one to the mediocre Detroit Lions when Hunk's blitzing defense held the Bears to 50 total yards.

Hunk knew the Bear's problem and, fortunately for the Bears, George Halas was smart enough to hire Anderson away from Detroit. The problem Hunk saw was that the new T-formation was a quick striking offense and the Bears had three quick running backs in George McAfee, Scooter Mc-Clean and Bill Osmanski, but they still had the old blocking system that slowed those backs down because the holes were not opened quickly enough. What Hunk did was to have linemen strike from a sprinter's stance and he eliminated the coil spring block (lunge and drive from a squatting position) and the body block to open holes. The body block was still used downfield and for containment in the line away from the hole to eliminate pursuit, but not to open holes. Hunk also introduced the standing obstruction block sometimes used on quick openers. The result of these changes by Hunk was the catalyst that brought about modern football.

◆

When Gipp was chosen All America by Walter Camp, Camp's Eastern-bent bias was evident in his selecting process. Gipp, undoubtedly the best left halfback in America, was placed in the fullback position and preference was given to C. A. Way, from Penn State, for the left halfback spot. The Helms Athletic Foundation, having been in the selecting business since 1900, saw fit not only to put Gipp in his normal left halfback spot, but gave Gipp the added honor of "College Football Player of the Year." This Helm's Foundation award was equivalent to what the Heisman Trophy given by the New York Athletic Club is today. The Helms award began in 1900 and lasted until 1951. Its first recipient was Truxton Hare, a guard from Pennsylvania U. and the last recipient was end Bill McColl of Stanford in 1951.

◆

Jay Berwanger of University of Chicago received both the Helms Award and the Heisman Trophy in 1935. Berwanger was the first ever Heisman award winner. After

Gipp, the other Notre Dame players to receive the Helms Foundation honor were Jack Cannon, in 1929, Frank Carideo in 1930, Angelo Bertelli (also the Heisman) in 1943 and Leon Hart (also the Heisman) in 1949.

◆

I first heard of the Helm's award to Gipp from Jim Beach. He wasn't sure if it was a scroll or a plaque and noted that Gipp's sister didn't know about it. Jim thought that Notre Dame had it. He never did tell me about other Gipp artifacts that Gipp's sister mentioned she had. It was Vince Gratzer, a collector of Notre Dame memorabilia, who said that there was a Gipp wallet, with contents including a poem supposedly written by Iris Trippeer. Gratzer would also like to know what happened to Gipp's major league contracts besides the Cubs contract which is buried with Gipp. Also telegrams from U.S. Military Academy Superintendent Douglas MacArthur and Army coach Charles Daly and a letter from Glenn "Pop" Warner from Pittsburgh.

◆

The great Jim Thorpe is the player from that era to whom Gipp is mostly compared. Thorpe's great performance against Harvard in 1912 brought him instant recognition. The Helms Foundation named him College Player of the Year that season as it did Gipp eight years later. (It is interesting to note that Glen "Pop" Warner, who coached Thorpe at Carlisle and Ernie Nevers at Stanford, stated in 1930 that the best football player he ever coached during his career was Nevers.) Gipp's national recognition, like Thorpe's, also came from playing an Eastern powerhouse, Army. Bo McMillen of Centre College beat Harvard with a 95 yard touchdown in 1919 and led Centre to an undefeated nine-game season that year to win the same Helms award, showing how Eastern-oriented football was in those early days.

◆

Knute Rockne and Frank Leahy still have the best winning percentage record in college football with .897 for Rockne and .891 for Leahy, which includes his Boston College years. These percentages were published in the Orlando Sentinel. Notre Dame has Rockne and Leahy's average a few points lower. The differences might be in method of factoring tie games.

◆

George Hull, of Hullie and Mike's, a Mason, was a close friend of Rockne's. This association brought on rumors that Rockne, who became a Catholic on November 20, 1925, was also a Mason. Hull was a 32nd degree Freemason, belonging to the South Bend Consistory and the Shrine Club, both Masonic orders. The Catholic Church did not agree with some of the Masonic religious proclamations and forbade Catholics to join that fraternal and charitable organization.

◆

When Rockne gave up medical school at St. Louis University in 1914 because he was not permitted by the university to coach a local high school team, the "just married" groom accepted a teaching job at Notre Dame. He and his bride moved into a rooming house on St. Louis Blvd. in South Bend. One version has it that the room Rock and Bonnie rented was the same one Walter O'Keefe once had. Walter became a well known figure in the entertainment field on Broadway and had his own radio show in the 1930's. O'Keefe's version was that Rockne rented the house and he subleased a room from Rockne.

◆

In a previous chapter, it had been noted that Gipp, after playing cards all night, would come downstairs to my Uncle Frank's Turkish baths at the Oliver to get refreshed and also get his bothersome leg rubbed-down before he went on to play in that Saturday afternoon's game. Although Gipp had been drinking during the course of the evening and early morning, Frank said that Gipp was a bit more talkative but *never* drunk. One author quotes Walter O'Keefe, a student then working for the South Bend Tribune, as having seen Gipp "stumble" from the elevator on the morning of the 1920 Purdue game while appearing to be "soggy." The meaning of soggy in context with the stumbling would indicate that soggy meant drunk and not perspiring.

In view of what my Uncle said about Gipp's condition as having reached "contentment before capacity" on the occasions (including that Purdue game) he came downstairs to be refreshed and rubbed-down, a closer look has to be taken at the contents of what O'Keefe was supposed to have said for the book, and let the reader decide.

Unlike modern elevators, which are run electronically and automatically adjust to the floor level before the doors open, pre-1948 elevators were run by an operator who, depending on the load, had to jockey up and down to get it even with the floor. Stumbling out of these elevators was not unusual by people who weren't inebriated — in fact, I had such an experience coming down with my bride Sheila, from an upper floor in the Building and Loan Tower on Washington Street near the courthouse in South Bend. The elevator was a fraction low when the operator opened the outside door and my heel caught the floor edge sending me sprawling. I abraised my knee and tore my trousers. It seems that a very tired Gipp fared better stumbling, if he did indeed stumble, than I did.

Gipp was on the go from early Friday morning. He ate breakfast on campus, attended one class, practiced at Cartier Field and was available for homecoming old timers to meet him. This was an unusual stint and smacked of Rockne's involvement. Gipp's schedule was full, including the parade, pep rally and judging, with Hunk, 15 four-round fights and three wrestling matches. Also, Anderson said that Gipp met on campus his buddy Wilbur "Dolly" Gray, who got him the Notre Dame scholarship, talked a while with him and promised to get together with Dolly at the Oliver after his commitments were over.

On Homecoming Friday, the curfew hour was ex-

tended to midnight and at about 11:30 p.m., the campus fes-
tivities ended. Gipp asked Hunk if he wanted to go with him
to see Dolly Gray at the hotel but Hunk said he preferred
going to bed. Gipp spent the rest of the night with his buddy,
Gray. So by Saturday morning he was a "wreck," as anyone
would be who did as much as Gipp had done.

What is incredible about O'Keefe's story is that he
supposedly lectured Gipp, "giving him hell for staying up all
night, playing cards...etc." I can't visualize Gipp taking "hell"
from a student or anyone for that matter. What makes this
story incongruous is the O'Keefe inference of a drunken Gipp
with words such as "stumbled" and "soggy." Yet after the
O'Keefe lecture, Gipp's reply was lucid and apparently not
slurred or O'Keefe would have mentioned that it was.

Walter's motive? Well, he goes on to say that Gipp had
a tremendous afternoon on the gridiron against Purdue in
spite of his condition that morning. Perhaps Walter wanted to
showcase Gipp's durability to perform at his best regardless
of the personal obstacles involved. O'Keefe didn't say outright
that Gipp was drunk when he saw him, but he created that
very vivid impression.

◆

My boyhood, hometown friend, Chicago stock broker
Eddie Chrobot, put me in communication in 1995 with a
client of his. It was Ojay Larson's daughter, Linda Larson. In
my helping Jim Beach gather information for his proposed
Gipp book, I contacted her hoping to get new material on
Gipp. What she knew wasn't new, but she did send me a pho-

tocopy page that she said appeared in a 1979 Sports Illustrated edition. It had a photo of Notre Dame's 1918 football squad.

The story running with the photo was a short, three paragraph biography of George Gipp. One new point of interest in it was that Ojay Larson was the first center to snap the ball with one hand like most modern-day centers do. George Gipp was such a fast starter that Larson found it better to snap the ball with one hand to get the ball to Gipp than to try to synchronize both hands on the fat football of that era for the snapback.

◆

Gipp had to be in South Bend in the summer of 1916 to take a Notre Dame entrance exam in lieu of having a high school diploma. Jim Beach mentioned that Wilbur "Dolly" Gray made arrangements for Gipp to stay in Mishawaka in August and to play baseball for a Mishawaka factory team while waiting to take the test. Gipp did take the exam and, according to Beach and Hunk Anderson, he passed quite easily. Some authors (without a given source) claim that Gipp barely made a passing grade.

◆

Those who knew George Gipp well, while describing him, would usually mention his pleasant speaking voice. Gipp's sister, Dolly, said that brother George had a "mellifluous" voice. Rockne mentioned it in his autobiography, saying, "Gipp's voice was a warm, vibrant baritone, full of life." And sister Dolly stated that he could also sing exceptionally well, but sang only at the Gipp family Christmas gathering in the Gipp residence when Dolly played Christmas carols on the parlor piano. She said that one could hear George descant the carols, adding a special touch to the songs.

◆

Hunk Anderson said that when the "Knute Rockne - All American" movie was being prepared in 1939, he was visited by Lloyd Bacon who was to direct the movie. J. Arthur Haley, who was a business manager for athletics, served as a liaison with the movie people for Notre Dame and accompanied Bacon. Bacon wanted to get a "handle" on Gipp and Rockne by interviewing people who knew both men, but Bacon dwelled mostly on Gipp. He wanted to learn more about Gipp than Rockne because there was little information on Gipp's personality and he wanted Ronald Reagan to capture the real Gipp in a story in which the Gipp scenes were only a small part of the overall picture.

"We'll, how was Reagan as Gipp in the movie?" I asked Hunk.

"Pretty darn close to being Gipp...in fact, very close in my book," replied Hunk. "Reagan did a good job."

Will there be another actor who can capture Gipp effectively in an expanded role in a movie solely about Gipp? In fact, will there ever be a movie made about Gipp?

# ACKNOWLEDGEMENTS
# & BIBLIOGRAPHY

Posthumous though it may be, my gratitude goes to Gipp's friends and teammates who through the years have given me material on Gipp which has made this book possible. While working with Hunk Anderson on his autobiography, it seemed that he would delight in interrupting my interview or his narration to interject something about his close friend Gipp which at that moment had come to mind. Much of the Gipp material in this book came from Hunk's vast storehouse of memories.

Leonard "Pete" Bahan was quite helpful. I met Pete when I lived in Long Beach, California. It was few years later, after I had moved to Florida, that I began to receive many of his phone calls from Los Angeles, where he lived, and Fort Worth, where he went to care for his sister who was ill. Pete would call because he said he wanted to help us with Hunk's book and wanted to talk about Notre Dame, past and present, and also his old teammates, among them, George Gipp. Gipp was Pete's friend, his teammate and his partner in campus business ventures.

Although a teammate of Gipp's, Chet Grant did not get to know Gipp too well during his playing days. He learned a bit about George when they would bump into each other during 1919. Chet did not return to Notre Dame that year, which was immediately after the war, but went to work for the South Bend Tribune instead. Chet also learned more about Gipp from other teammates such as Ojay Larson, Dutch Bergman and Hunk Anderson when they'd drop in on Chet during his coaching days under Elmer Layden, and later when he became curator of the International Sports and Games Research Collection in the basement of the Notre Dame Library.

Francis Wallace, with whom I was in regular contact when he moved to Florida, had some unsolicited insights on Gipp while I was trying to get information from him for Anderson's book.

Another view of Gipp, Rockne and Notre Dame came from South Bend old timers who played "pro" football in the Gipp era, and who received coaching from Notre Dame players. They were my father, John "Curley" Klosinski, George Greenberg, Steve Sobieralski, Joe "Bush" Prokop, Ila Shafer and John Jegier. Arthur "Dutch" Bergman was also helpful. My cousin Gene Basker had a goldmine full of stories about Gipp from Gene's dad, Frank Koszewski, who managed the Turkish steam baths at the Oliver Hotel in South Bend during Gipp's time. My posthumous gratitude to all of the above named.

Son-in-law Jim Stansberry expended a lot of his valuable time researching via computer and telephone. Son Marc also helped in similar fashion. Daughter Sheril Stansberry,

MD, MS, checked and interpreted the reports of Gipp's injuries and his critical illness for me. Other members of the Klosinski family involved in the project as helpers and encouragers were my dear wife Sheila, daughter Denise Klosinski, Lucie Klosinski and grandchildren David Charba and Julie Charba. Last but not least familywise, Natalie Klosinski, my granddaughter, who was two-years-old when this project began, deserves a mention and a hug and kiss for being a pleasant diversion with her intrusions and quizzing interruptions while work was in progress.

Also my gratitude and appreciation to individuals who gave their valuable time and information, namely: I. I. Probst, Notre Dame class of 1926, who still manages to write two quarterly columns for the Notre Dame Magazine; Martha Beach, Carrboro, N.C., Jim Beach's daughter; Bob Dorais, Malvern, Pennsylvania and Vince Gratzer, Los Angeles, California.

Most of those old timers mentioned above who had a story to tell about Gipp said that was the way it happened. As one put it, using a catch phrase common about two or three decades ago: "I'm telling it like it is." Well, telling it like it is...or was, is an approach that is presumptuous. At best it can be told as the teller thinks it was — a point of view qualified by our endless fallibility and the obscuring done by the passage of time. A verification of correctness of statements, dates and events therefore had to be undertaken to the best of our resources available. In that respect, I received assistance from some wonderful people and my sincere and profound gratitude goes to them, the researchers and corroborators.

Listed in no particular order because they were all equally important to this project, are researcher John Kovach, South Bend, (a Rockne historian); John Bucholtz, Indianapolis; Don Hanyzewski, Michael Klosinski, South Bend; Irvin Morse, St. Joseph County (Indiana) Public Library; John Palmer, St. Joseph County Public Library. I. I. Probst for checking Notre Dame's annual — The Dome — of various years for vital information as well as his abundant correspondence which included valuable data I asked him to check for me. Jim Platt, V.P. of Sports Immortals Showcase, also helped.

Peter Lysy, University of Notre Dame Archives, who excerpted information from Rev. Arthur Hope's "Notre Dame: One Hundred Years" and a portion of David Arthur's dissertation on the history of Notre Dame's fund raising up to the end of 1922; staffs of the Marion County (Indiana) Public Library and Marion County Microfilm Archives and to Dwight King, head researcher of the Kresge Library, Notre Dame Law School, for breaching the policy of not replying to letters, by sending me vital information. Also, Joel Platt, founder of Sports Immortals Museum in Boca Raton, Florida. To all the above, a debt of gratitude is owed.

Last but not least, is a special "thank you" to Donald J. Napoli, Director of the St. Joseph County Library, for making the library "author friendly" to queries and research requests, with diligent staffers, some of whom volunteer their time and energies and answer letters. That's an anomaly in these days of mandatory computer on-line communication and the telephones' "press one, press 4, press 10, etcetera"...a maze that oftentimes leads into a dead end and wasted time.

# BIBLIOGRAPHY

ONE FOR THE GIPPER - George Gipp, Knute Rockne and Notre Dame, by Patrick Chelland, Henry Regnery Company, 1973, Chicago; Updated Edition, Panoply Publicaions, 2008, N. Hollywood, CA.

NOTRE DAME FOOTBALL, by Jim Beach, McFadden-Bartell, 1962, New York, NY.

THE AUTOBIOGRAPHY OF KNUTE K. ROCKNE, edited by Mrs. Knute K. Rockne, Bobbs-Merrill Company, 1931, Indianapolis. IN.

NOTRE DAME -ITS PEOPLE AND ITS LEGENDS, by Francis Wallace, David McKay Company, Inc., 1969, New York, NY.

THE NOTRE DAME STORY, by Francis Wallace, Rinehart and Company, 1949, New York, Toronto.

The above sources were the first publications to contain biographical material about Gipp. Other authors "borrowed" from that basic material — especially Pat Chelland's — for their books or chapters about Gipp, and did give credit in their bibliographies for it, but certainly far from the deserved credit due for the amount used from Chelland's book.

Pat Chelland's book, "One for the Gipper," was the most frequently used resource because it was by far the most complete, the most in-depth researched as well as interviewed Gipp biography available.

We looked at books in search of pristine material on Gipp, but little was found. Moreso, we checked for discrepancies and the sources for those discrepancies if given in text or in footnotes. If not given, our assumption was that the author had taken liberties to enhance the "dark side" of Gipp; to ignore facts or to create new derogatory incidents and behavior on the part of George Gipp.

In the search of possible new material, biographical discrepancies, statistical and technical data the following books and articles were checked:

SHAKE DOWN THE THUNDER! - The Official Biography of Notre Dame's Frank Leahy, by Wells Twombly, Chilton Book Company, 1974, Radnor, PA.

OUT OF BOUNDS - The Anecdotal History of Notre Dame Football, by Michael Bonifer and L.G. Weaver, Piper, 1978, Blue Earth, MN.

THE BIG BOWL FOOTBALL GUIDE - Revised Edition, by Anthony DiMarco, G.P. Putnam's Sons, 1974, New York, NY.

BASEBALL - America's Diamond Mind, a University of Central Florida book, by (Professor) Richard C. Crepeau, 1980, University Presses of Florida, Orlando, FL.

THE LAST MOGUL, by Dennis McDougal, Crown Publishers, Inc., 2001, New York, NY.

SHAKE DOWN THE THUNDER - The Creation of Notre Dame Football, by (Professor) Murray Sperber, Henry Holt and Company, Inc., 1993, New York, NY.

ONWARD TO VICTORY - The Crisis That Shaped College Sports, by (Professor) Murray Sperber, Henry Holt and Company, Inc., 1998, New York, NY.

GIPPER - The Life & Times of George Gipp, by George Gekas, And Books Publisher, 1987, South Bend, IN.

ROCKNE OF NOTRE DAME - The Making of a Football Legend, by Ray Robinson, Oxford University Press, 1999, New York, NY.

WE REMEMBER ROCKNE, by John D McCallum & Paul Castner, Our Sunday Visitor Inc., 1975, Huntington, IN.

KNUTE ROCKNE, A BIO-BIBLIOGRAPHY, by Michael R. Steele, Greenwood Press, 1983, Westport, CT. 1983.

THE GOLDEN PEOPLE, by Paul Gallico, Doubleday & Co., Garden City, 1964, New York, NY.

ROCKNE: IDOL OF AMERICAN FOOTBALL, by Robert Harron, A. L. Burt, 1931, New York, NY.

KNUTE ROCKNE, by Francis Wallace, Doubleday & Co., Garden City, 1960, New York, NY.

KNUTE ROCKNE, MAN BUILDER, by Harry A. Stuhldreher, Grosset & Dunlap, 1931,New York, NY.

WAKE UP THE ECHOES, by Ken Rapporport, Strode Publishers, 1975, Huntsville, AL,

BEING CATHOLIC, BEING AMERICAN - The Notre Dame Story, 1842-1934, by Robert E. Burns, University of Notre Dame Press, 1999, Notre Dame, IN.

FOOTBALL: FACTS AND FIGURES by Dr. L.H. Baker, Farrar and Rinehart, Inc., 1945, New York, NY.

NOTRE DAME 2001 FOOTBALL (Media Guide), Notre Dame Sports Information, Ave Maria Press, 2001, Notre Dame, IN.

FUNK AND WAGNALLS ENCYCLOPEDIA - New York.

MERCK MANUAL - Merck and Company, Inc., 1982, Rahway, NJ.

RITES OF AUTUMN by Richard Whittingham, The

Free Press, 2001, New York, NY.


ARTICLES

GIPP of NOTRE DAME by Jim Beach, Saga Magazine, September, 1958.

THE REAL STORY of THE GIPPER by John U. Bacon, Detroit News, January 5, 1997.

GIPP DEATHBED: An Untold Story by Scott Ostler, Los Angeles Times, November 25, 1982.

TRUE STORY: Irish Won One For the Gypper (sic) by Ron Rappoport.

Between the Lines column, Chicago Sun Times, November 10, 1998.

NEWSPAPERS

South Bend Tribune, South Bend News-Times, South Bend News, Indianapolis Star, Rockford Register-Gazette, Fort Wayne Journal-Gazette, Atlanta Journal, Orlando Sentinel, New York Herald-Tribune and Sporting News.

•

Information was also used from the works of the author of this book. The books, entitled "Pro Football in the Days of Rockne" (Carlton Press Inc., New York, 1970) and a collaboration with Hunk Anderson on his memoirs entitled, "Notre Dame, Chicago Bears and Hunk," (Florida Sun-Gator Publishing Co., Orlando, 1976) were helpful as were the following articles:

"Knute Rockne's Pro Football Roots;"

"Inflation of 1920: A tale of Two Cities;"

"When Notre Dame Won The Rockford City Championship;"

297

"A Hunk of History;"
"Who Really Did It?;"
"Move Over Gipp, Thorpe, Make Room for Bowser"
and "A Place in the Hall for Hunk?"

PHOTOS: Author's collection.

# INDEX

## A

## B

168-174, 177, 180, 182-184, 186, 194-196, 199, 200, 204, 213-215. 217-224, 226, 229, 234, 236-238, 240-245, 248, 249, 252-254, 257, 258, 260, 264, 266, 267, 271, 272-275, 277, 279, 281, 283-285, 288, 289
Nowak, Paul "Giz" 175

O

O'Brien, Pat 242
O'Connor, Dr. Thomas 228
O'Connor, Rev. F. A. 238
O'Donnell, Theresa 126
O'Donnell, Father Hugh 273, 275
O'Donnell, Father Charles L. 161, 174, 188
O'Hara, Father John 236, 237, 274, 275
O'Keefe, Walter 285, 286, 287
Ohio State University 111, 174, 218, 219, 266
Oliver, J. D. 64, 145
Oliver, Don 69
Oliver Hotel 11, 12, 22, 50, 59, 63, 65, 67, 87, 90, 98, 104, 115, 116, 117, 118, 122, 124, 133, 140, 178, 191, 195, 197, 213, 217, 224, 233, 237, 268, 269, 276, 286
Olney, Dr. Thomas 225
Oorang Indians 9
Oregon, University of 261
Orlando Sentinel 29, 35, 284
Osmanski, Bill 281
Ostler, Scott 87, 88, 89, 90, 103

P

Pask, Charlie 227
Patric, Jason 258, 259
Pennsylvania, University of 282
Penn State 180, 219, 282
Phair, Victoria 89
Phelan, Bob 150
Philadelphia Phillies 152
Philbin, Regis 173
Piccolo, Brian 261
Pittsburgh, University of 283
Pittsburgh Pirates 22, 123
Plante, Joseph O. 122
Powell, Dick 83
Prefontaine, Steve 261
Princeton University 145, 218, 265-267
Probst, I. I. 83, 85, 100, 137, 187, 213, 214
Prokop, George 127, 221
Pulschen, John 246
Purdue University 21, 71, 111, 142, 147, 149, 161, 177-181, 226, 227, 286, 287

Q

Quested, John 260

R

Rappoport, Ken 39

Virginia Tech 35
Vosse, Dale 215
Vurpillat, Francis J. 119-127, 134

**W**

Wabash College 30
Waddell, "Rube" 23
Wade, Frank 175
Walde, Jim 69
Wallace, Francis 28, 39, 40, 42, 130, 131, 171, 173-176, 194, 195, 241, 274, 275
Walsh, Father Matthew 138, 170, 171, 174, 188
Ward, Arch 128, 168, 169, 178, 223
Warner, Glenn "Pop" 283, 284
Washington Redskins 35, 280
Way, C. A. 282
Weaver, Buck 70, 152
Weaver, L. G. 252
Weinke, Chris 11
Weisberg, Andy 117, 122
Welch, Jimmie 8
West, Mary Jane (Mae) 269
Western State Normal 25, 107, 139, 142
Whittingham, Richard 198
Wilcox, Percy "Perce" 33, 238
Willard, Jess 147
Williams, Claude 70, 152
Wisconsin, University of 112, 181, 184
Witucki, Frank 206
Wojciecowicz, Alex 277
Wukovits, Tommy 175
Wynne, Chet 147, 156, 157, 160, 180, 186

**Y**

Yale University 10, 122, 145
Yost, Fielding "Hurry Up" 21, 169
Young, Cy 23

**Z**

Zuppke, Bob 112, 113, 222, 280

# ABOUT THE AUTHOR

Emil Klosinski has been seeped in a football atmosphere all his life, since his birth in South Bend, Indiana, home of Notre Dame and its legendary football teams, players and coaches. Klosinski's father, John, was an old-time football player and in his youth the author heard many tales about the pioneers of the game, including Knute Rockne, George Gipp, "Hunk" Anderson and many others.

Klosinski attended Notre Dame and has been a football player and coach and later scouted and recruited football talent in the midwest.

He and his wife, Sheila, have three children, three grandchildren and two great-grandchildren and have resided in Florida for over 50 years.

*Emil passed away in 2017, at 96 years of age. This newly-printed edition is part of his legacy, and in honor of the sports pioneers he revered and wrote about in his books.*

Emil Klosinski and his wife, Sheila, while visiting the newly refurbished Notre Dame Stadium in 2002.

Made in the USA
Columbia, SC
20 March 2023

14063397R00172